Successful Approaches to RTI

Collaborative Practices for Improving K-12 Literacy

Marjorie Y. Lipson & Karen K. Wixson, Editors

INTERNATIONAL
Reading Association
800 BARKSDALE ROAD, PO BOX 8139
NEWARK, DE 19714-8139, USA
www.reading.org

The International Reading Association attempts, through its publications, to provide a forum for a wide spectrum of opinions on reading. This policy permits divergent viewpoints without implying the endorsement of the Association.

Executive Editor, Books   Corinne M. Mooney
Developmental Editor   Charlene M. Nichols
Developmental Editor   Tori Mello Bachman
Developmental Editor   Stacey L. Reid
Editorial Production Manager   Shannon T. Fortner
Design and Composition Manager   Anette Schuetz

Project Editors   Stacey L. Reid and Christina M. Terranova

Cover   Design, Lise Holliker Dykes; Photographs, © Shutterstock Images LLC (background, photo frames, and far left photo), © iStockphoto.com/track5 (all other photos)

Library of Congress Cataloging-in-Publication Data
Successful approaches to RTI : collaborative practices for improving K-12 literacy / edited by Marjorie Y. Lipson and Karen K. Wixson.
    p. cm.
  Includes bibliographical references and index.
  ISBN 978-0-87207-834-5
  1. Remedial teaching--United States. 2. Slow learning children--Education--United States.
  3. Learning disabled children--Education--United States. 4. Effective teaching--United States.
I. Lipson, Marjorie Y. II. Wixson, Karen K. III. International Reading Association.
  LB1029.R4S84 2010
  371.9'043--dc22

                                                                          2010005715

We dedicate this book to all of the professionals whose hard work and determined pursuit of excellence has led more students to achieve literacy success and who have, in the process, shown us what is possible.

CONTENTS

 **Marjorie Y. Lipson** is Professor Emerita of Education in the College of Education and Social Services at the University of Vermont, Burlington, USA, where she was named University Scholar for 2008–2009. Her scholarship focuses on reading difficulties, reading comprehension, and factors influencing literacy success. She is currently the principal investigator of the Vermont Reads Institute, a consortium of research and development projects focused on improving literacy achievement in grades K–12.

Her research related to successful schools and school change has been published in *The Elementary School Journal*, *Journal of Literacy Research*, and *The Reading Teacher*. She is coauthor, with Karen Wixson, of *Assessment & Instruction of Reading and Writing Difficulties: An Interactive Approach*, now in its fourth edition. She has recently published *Teaching Reading Beyond the Primary Grades*, a text that provides guidance to teachers in grades 3–6. She has served on the Board of Directors of the National Reading Conference and on numerous editorial boards of journals. She is cochair of the International Reading Association Commission on Response to Intervention (RTI).

Prior to receiving her doctorate from the University of Michigan, Ann Arbor, USA, Marge taught elementary school in a Spanish–English bilingual setting in the Midwest and for several years in Washington, DC. She continues to work in schools and closely with teachers to improve literacy development of all students.

Marge and her husband, Michael, have traveled widely and enjoy spending time with their family and friends. She has become an enthusiastic bicyclist in recent years and is a voracious reader of mystery novels, science fiction, and children's books.

 **Karen K. Wixson** is Professor of Education at the University of Michigan, Ann Arbor, USA, where she served as Dean from 1998 to 2005. Prior to receiving her doctorate in reading education from Syracuse University, New York, USA, she worked as both a remedial reading specialist and a learning disabilities teacher.

Karen has published widely in the areas of literacy curriculum, instruction, and assessment in books and journals such as *Reading Research Quarterly*, *The Reading Teacher*, *The Elementary School Journal*, *Review of Research in Education*, and the *Handbook of Reading Research* (Volumes 2 and 3). She is also an author on a basal reading program and coauthor, with Marjorie Lipson, of a popular text on the assessment and instruction of reading and writing difficulties. She codirected the federally funded Michigan English Language Arts Framework standards project and served as codirector and principal investigator of the U.S. Department of Education's Center for the Improvement of Early Reading Achievement.

She has been a longtime consultant for the National Assessment of Educational Progress reading tests and recently served as a member of the National Research Council (NRC) Committee on the Evaluation of Teacher Certification by the National Board for Professional Teaching Standards as well as the NRC Steering Committee for Workshops on Assessing the Role of K–12 Academic Standards in States. She served as a member of the Board of Directors of the National Reading Conference and the International Reading Association (IRA) and is currently cochair of the IRA Commission on RTI.

Karen lives in Ann Arbor with her husband, Wiley, youngest son, Alex, and parents, William and Sally Kring. Her two grown children, Ray and Stacy, live in Ypsilanti, Michigan, USA, and Denver, Colorado, USA, respectively. She enjoys listening to music in all its forms, reading historical fiction, and practicing Pilates.

CONTRIBUTORS

Kimberly L. Anderson
Research Associate
Child Research and Study Center
University at Albany, State University
   of New York
Albany, New York, USA

Karen A. Costello
Administrator for Program
   Improvement
East Lyme Public Schools
East Lyme, Connecticut, USA

Linda J. Dorn
Professor and Director,
   Center for Literacy
University of Arkansas at Little Rock
Little Rock, Arkansas, USA

Barbara J. Ehren
Professor and Director of the
   Doctoral Program
Department of Communication
   Sciences and Disorders
University of Central Florida
Orlando, Florida, USA

Lynn M. Gelzheiser
Associate Professor
Child Research and Study Center
University at Albany, State University
   of New York
Albany, New York, USA

Sandra K. Goetze
Associate Professor of Literacy
   Education
Oklahoma State University
Stillwater, Oklahoma, USA

Laura Hallgren-Flynn
Teacher Supervisor
Child Research and Study Center
University at Albany, State University
   of New York
Albany, New York, USA

Alysia Hayas
Fourth-Grade Teacher
Boulder Valley School District
Boulder, Colorado, USA

Shannon C. Henderson
Assistant Professor
University of Arkansas at Little Rock
Little Rock, Arkansas, USA

Peter H. Johnston
Professor and Chair, Reading
   Department
University at Albany, State University
   of New York
Albany, New York, USA

Janette K. Klingner
Professor
School of Education
University of Colorado at Boulder
Boulder, Colorado, USA

Barbara Laster
Professor
Department of Educational
    Technology and Literacy
Towson University
Towson, Maryland, USA

Nonie Lesaux
Marie and Max Kargman Associate
    Professor in Human Development
    and Urban Education
    Advancement
Harvard Graduate School of
    Education
Cambridge, Massachusetts, USA

Marjorie Y. Lipson
Professor Emerita of Education
College of Education and Social
    Services
University of Vermont
Burlington, Vermont, USA

Barbara Marinak
Assistant Professor and Graduate
    Program Coordinator for Literacy
    Education
Penn State Harrisburg
Middletown, Pennsylvania, USA

Kathryn E. Meyer
Literacy Coach
Washington School for
    Comprehensive Literacy
Sheboygan Area School District
Sheboygan, Wisconsin, USA

Brian L. Reindl
Literacy Coach
Washington School for
    Comprehensive Literacy
Sheboygan Area School District
Sheboygan, Wisconsin, USA

Donna M. Scanlon
Professor
Department of Teacher Education
Michigan State University
East Lansing, Michigan, USA

Lucinda Soltero-González
Assistant Professor
Division of Educational Equity and
    Cultural Diversity
School of Education
University of Colorado at Boulder
Boulder, Colorado, USA

Karen K. Wixson
Professor of Education
University of Michigan
Ann Arbor, Michigan, USA

Mary F. Zolman
Supervisor, English Language Arts
Arlington Public Schools
Arlington, Virginia, USA

For many of us, it seems as though discussions about RTI are everywhere. We agreed to cochair the IRA Commission on RTI because we have spent the better part of our professional lives working at the intersection of regular and special education—working with struggling readers and writers and helping teachers improve their expertise in this area. One of us was trained as a general educator and the other as a special educator, so when we began to collaborate on issues related to reading difficulties, we brought both perspectives to the problem. In our writing about this in the 1980s, we used the convention "(dis)ability" to denote our thinking that ability and disability are not distinct concepts. Instead, we argued, reading achievement and performance are the results of a complex set of factors that interact—sometimes resulting in capable reading and sometimes not. RTI appeared to be a perfect fit for our long-standing (and evolved) thinking in this area.

We also agreed to take on this task because we were very worried that the promise and potential of RTI might go unrealized. We noticed schools, districts, and states jumping quickly to take action. Some of these actions seemed unproductive, and some seemed likely to undo important work that had occurred in the field over the past two decades. We were especially concerned that one type of approach and one orientation to assessment and instruction was dominating the conversation and policymaking decisions surrounding RTI. We do not think that the prevalence of one model or approach to RTI is necessarily good for struggling readers. Instead, multiple models and approaches have been validated by research, and these need wider dissemination. Context matters: Different solutions may be needed in different settings, given diverse students and varied instructional resources and histories.

Reading teachers and specialists are uniquely poised to ensure success in RTI, but their involvement should be informed by a broad understanding of the issues and options. Over the past year, we heard from many literacy educators who are concerned about the extent to which one model or approach has been adopted in their schools and districts. As well, many administrators and school leaders report a lack of collaborative participation by general educators and reading specialists. Thoughtful and committed professionals across disciplines and roles want information about alternatives, and they want ideas about how to influence both policy and practice.

In preparing this book, we had three main goals. First, we wanted to remind teachers that there is a good deal of research to support and guide effective literacy instruction. Second, we wanted to assure reading professionals that there is very good evidence about the effectiveness of interventions that make instructional decision-making and teacher expertise the centerpiece of their approach. In this book, there are detailed descriptions of several approaches that have yielded excellent results, reducing the number of students identified as learning disabled and preventing language and literacy difficulties among highly diverse student populations. Third, we provide advice and tools for getting started in your own school or district.

The chapters in this book mirror the three goals just described. There is an introductory chapter that provides background on RTI and reviews relevant research. Then the central portion of the book describes approaches and provides examples of effective and successful RTI initiatives. Finally, there is a closing chapter that invites educators to take action in order to improve literacy achievement for all students. Taken together, these chapters provide research about effective practices and approaches in RTI from kindergarten to secondary grades. Topics that are especially important to RTI, such as progress monitoring and the nature of instruction and intervention, are addressed throughout.

In Chapter 1, we provide background information about RTI—what it is and why it is important. We briefly examine existing research on RTI and note how different perspectives may lead to different practices. We suggest that reading professionals adopt an instructional (versus measurement) perspective. Finally, we introduce IRA's position statement on RTI, which appears as a set of guiding principles. These principles can and should be used to assess the value and appropriateness of any RTI approach, including the approaches in this book.

In Chapters 2–9, evidence-based approaches are described and the evidence for practices related to a special topic is detailed. We then spotlight the approaches or practices by including case studies of specific schools or teachers as the approaches or techniques are used. For example, in Chapter 2, Donna Scanlon and Kimberly Anderson describe the rationale and practices associated with the Interactive Strategies Approach (ISA). This approach has been researched for more than a decade, and these authors bring the weight of this evidence to their description of interventions for kindergarten and first grade. They distinguish their approach from the standard protocol model and offer a framework for providing excellent instruction and intervention within RTI. In

Chapter 3, Kimberly Anderson takes a closer look at ISA in "Spotlight on the Interactive Strategies Approach: The Case of Roosevelt Elementary School."

In Chapter 4, Linda Dorn and Shannon Henderson take a systems approach to RTI, providing us with a description of the Comprehensive Intervention Model (CIM). They describe in detail the rationale and research base for this model and share specific practices and materials from their extensive experience working in schools. In Chapter 5, "Spotlight on the Comprehensive Intervention Model: The Case of Washington School for Comprehensive Literacy," Kathryn Meyer and Brian Reindl offer an insightful examination of one school's evolution and the specific practices they employ as part of an RTI approach.

Literacy professionals everywhere are increasingly concerned about their ability to work effectively with English-language learners (ELLs). In Chapter 6, Janette Klingner, Lucinda Soltero-González, and Nonie Lesaux focus on special concerns associated with RTI among linguistically and culturally diverse students. They highlight the difficulties of assessing the literacy abilities of ELLs and provide guidance about the types of good first instruction necessary for all students to succeed. In Chapter 7, "Spotlight on RTI for English-Language Learners: The Case of Mountain Creek Elementary," Alysia Hayas and Janette Klingner spotlight the challenges of improving literacy achievement for ELLs while implementing RTI in an urban school.

Despite the intensive focus on RTI for early prevention of reading disabilities, there are many adolescents who are struggling readers. In Chapter 8, Sandra Goetze, Barbara Laster, and Barbara Ehren discuss RTI from an adolescent literacy perspective and provide guidance on the types of practices that are essential for success in middle and high school. However, it is important to note that they also tackle the systemic and schoolwide issues that must be addressed in order for RTI to work for adolescents and their teachers. In Chapter 9, "Spotlight on RTI for Adolescents: An Example of Intensive Middle School Intervention Using the Interactive Strategies Approach-Extended," Lynn Gelzheiser, Donna Scanlon, and Laura Hallgren-Flynn spotlight an intensive, extended version of ISA for adolescents (ISA-X) as it was implemented in two middle schools.

In Chapter 10, Karen Costello, Marjorie Lipson, Barbara Marinak, and Mary Zolman offer information to guide RTI activities in schools and districts with the idea that professionals need and want to take action and that they will be in a good position to do that based on the models and ideas presented earlier in this book. These authors speak from the perspective of school-based professionals and address several of the challenges that face many RTI efforts. This chapter contains a number of practical materials and examples that profession-als can use immediately to guide their work. Throughout this book, there are also reproducible forms that you may use in your classroom.

We think that you will be impressed by the passion, commitment, and ex-traordinary quality of the efforts described in this book. Reading professionals and school leaders need the very best information they can get to help influence policy and practice. The distinguished authors and researchers represented in this book have done an excellent job of integrating research and practice. If RTI is to realize its promise, literacy educators must be responsibly involved at every level. As a group, we hope that you find guidance for both specific practices and more general decision making.

ACKNOWLEDGMENTS

First and foremost, we acknowledge the astonishing authors whose work is presented in this book. On a tight timeline and without hesitation, they agreed to share their experiences and write about their work because they believe in the promise and potential of response to intervention/instruction. We are grateful for their commitment to excellence and determination to help classroom teachers, reading specialists, allied professionals, and administrators realize that promise.

We also acknowledge the vision and drive that led IRA to focus attention on RTI. Past-president Barbara Walker deserves special acknowledgment for envisioning the IRA Commission on RTI and giving us the latitude to do our work. We would also like to thank the Committee members for their unflagging hard work. Many members contributed directly to the writing of this book, but every one contributed over the past year with ideas and discussion that have expanded our views of RTI and improved the quality of the work. In addition, Richard Long deserves our thanks for his tireless work behind the scenes—from convincing us to undertake the Commission task to supporting our dissemination efforts. Of course, we also thank the IRA Board of Directors for its ongoing support of this work and for its interest in providing the membership of IRA with a range of options about how to provide leadership to promote effective RTI projects.

CHAPTER 1

Making the Most of RTI

Karen K. Wixson
University of Michigan

Marjorie Y. Lipson
University of Vermont

Peter H. Johnston
University at Albany, State University of New York

R TI is the name given to a method of identifying students as learning disabled (LD) that provides an alternative to the traditional discrepancy model of identification. Because the overwhelming majority of students identified as LD have difficulties involving language and literacy, the International Reading Association (IRA) formed the Commission on RTI in 2008 to help provide guidance to its members and others as they develop and implement various approaches to RTI. Notable among the activities of the Commission is the creation of IRA's Guiding Principles, which were approved by IRA's Board of Directors in October of 2009 (see www.reading .org/Libraries/Resources/RTI_brochure_web.sflb.ashx). The perspectives presented in this book, which is also a product of the IRA Commission on RTI, reflect these Guiding Principles.

Language related to RTI was written into law with the 2004 reauthorization of the Individuals With Disabilities Education Act, now known as the Individuals With Disabilities Education Improvement Act. This law indicates that school districts are no longer required to take into consideration whether a student has a severe discrepancy between achievement and intellectual ability in determining eligibility for learning disability services. Rather, school districts may use an alternative approach that determines whether the student responds first to scientific, research-based classroom instruction and then to more intensive, targeted interventions. After receiving this more tailored and intensive instruction, students who do not demonstrate adequate progress are then considered for an evaluation for a specific learning disability.

The concept of RTI builds on a recommendation made by the President's Commission on Excellence in Special Education (U.S. Department of Education, 2002) that students with disabilities should first be considered general education students, embracing a model of prevention as opposed to a model of failure (National Association of State Directors of Special Education & Council of Administrators of Special Education, 2006). A preventative approach is intended to rectify a number of long-standing problems, including the disproportionate number of minorities and English-language learners (ELLs) identified as LD and the need to wait for documented failure before providing services. The RTI provision allows local school districts that meet certain criteria to allocate up to 15% of their funding for students with disabilities toward general education interventions designed to prevent language and literacy difficulties. This explains why RTI is often perceived as a special education initiative when most, including special educators, describe it as a general education initiative.

Both the IRA Guiding Principles and this volume embrace the concept of RTI and seek to clarify it with regard to issues related to language and literacy. Toward this end, it is helpful to think of RTI as a comprehensive, systemic approach to teaching and learning designed to address language and literacy problems for all students through increasingly differentiated and intensified language and literacy assessment and instruction. Equally important is the idea that qualified professionals with appropriate expertise should provide this instruction. From this perspective, RTI is a process that cuts across general, compensatory, and special education, and is not exclusively a general or special education initiative. Similarly, it is not simply a prereferral process that must be carried out before students are identified as LD. Carefully selected assessment, dedication to differentiated instruction, quality professional development, and genuine collaboration across teachers, specialists, administrators, and parents are among the factors that are important for the success of RTI.

What Does RTI Look Like?

RTI most frequently involves a multitiered approach to the implementation of instructional modifications. The number of tiers varies considerably, but the most widely described models involve either three or four tiers. In the three-tiered model, low-performing students are identified and monitored as they participate in their classroom, or Tier 1, instruction. Most models suggest that at least 80% of students are successful and make good progress in response to good first teaching. Those who do not make sufficient progress in Tier 1 instruction are provided with a second, more intensive tier of instruction intended to accelerate their progress (i.e., Tier 2). Intensification might be accomplished by providing more time in instruction, smaller instructional groupings, or alternative methods of instruction (Scanlon & Sweeney, 2008). Tier 2 instruction is intended as an addition to the Tier 1 instruction and might be provided by the classroom teacher or a specialist in a small-group context. Students' progress continues to be monitored and an additional 15% of students are expected to succeed with this supplemental instruction. Those who do not demonstrate accelerated progress with Tier 2 intervention(s) are considered for even more intensive and targeted intervention in Tier 3 instruction, possible learning disability evaluation/classification, or both (Fuchs, Stecker, & Fuchs, 2008).

Within a four-tiered model, proponents generally distinguish between good first (or core) instruction and differentiated instruction that supplements core instruction but is offered within the classroom, typically in small groups. In other words, teachers adapt or refine instruction to focus more on the needs of individual students within the overall literacy program.

The tiered model of RTI is frequently characterized in the literature as one of two types: standard protocol or problem solving. The standard protocol approach (Fuchs, Mock, Morgan, & Young, 2003) emphasizes standardized (often scripted) interventions used for a standard amount of time with teachers often monitored for treatment fidelity (Gresham, 2007). The problem-solving approach (Marston, Muyskens, Lau, & Canter, 2003) involves collaborative efforts on the part of several members of the school community to identify and implement optimal instructional interventions for each student who appears to be at risk for learning difficulties. Within this approach, a team of professionals assembles and develops an instructional plan designed to be responsive to the needs of the individual student. The student's response to such interventions determines future intervention plans in an iterative manner.

Although differences are often noted between standard protocol and problem-solving approaches, many researchers argue that these distinctions break down quickly and that "most RTI models described in the literature combine the two approaches...and probably function optimally when integrated into one three-tiered service delivery system" (Jimerson, Burns, & VanDerHeyden, 2007, p. 4). Indeed, writing from a problem-solving perspective, Burns and Coolong-Chaffin

(2006) observe that "most Tier 2 interventions have a standardized component" (p. 6), whether they are focused on the needs of individuals or groups of individuals.

There are important gradations within the standard protocol and problem-solving approaches that are often ignored in the literature. For example, both Reading Recovery (RR) and the Interactive Strategies Approach (ISA; Scanlon & Vellutino, 1996; Scanlon, Vellutino, Small, Fanuele, & Sweeney, 2005) have been referred to as standard protocol programs and described as "scripted" because there are consistent lesson segments (Fuchs & Fuchs, 2006; Gresham, 2007). However, these approaches are standard only to the extent that the teachers who provide these interventions have been trained to plan and deliver instruction that is responsive to students' needs by taking into account what they know and are able to do and considering the characteristics and expectations of the classroom curriculum. This is quite different from the highly prescriptive interventions typically used in most standard protocol approaches to RTI.

The point here is that there are a number of different approaches to RTI and the legislation does not specify any particular model or approach to RTI. In fact, the United States government purposely provides few details for the development and implementation of RTI procedures, stating specifically that states and districts should have the flexibility to establish approaches that reflect their communities' unique situations. This means that the most widely used models are neither mandated nor the only possible approaches to RTI. Similarly, the statute and regulations do not mandate screening assessments or any particular assessment per se, although they do require data-based documentation of repeated assessments of achievement at reasonable intervals.

Johnston (2010) has proposed a way of thinking about existing approaches to RTI that captures the most important distinctions among them. He describes approaches in terms of their primary emphasis on either measurement or instruction, arguing that the basis for this distinction comes from the legislation itself. More specifically, he notes that the legislation frames RTI as a measurement problem replacing the IQ discrepancy identification strategy and also as a strategy for reducing the number of students who end up with serious learning difficulties, part of guaranteeing appropriate instruction.

Framed as a strategy for accurately identifying students with disabilities, RTI becomes a measurement problem, emphasizing standardization in timing, interventions, and assessments. Most standard protocol and problem-solving models can be characterized as measurement approaches. Proponents of a measurement approach favor standard intervention packages, preferably scripted, to increase the standardization. This type of approach implies that an intervention effective on average in one setting will be effective with each new student in any new setting if implemented with fidelity and increasing intensity. If the intervention is not successful, the student is the likely source of the problem (e.g., LD, treatment resister, chronic nonresponder), because research has demonstrated that the instruction is effective. This is the perspective described by many special educators and school psychologists (e.g., Fuchs & Fuchs, 2006).

Framed as a strategy for preventing serious learning difficulties, RTI becomes an instructional problem, emphasizing optimal instruction for individual students and providing the means and context for improving teaching and teacher expertise. In this frame, assessment must be informative about the qualities of learning and teaching, giving direction to instruction. In other words, instruction is not evidence based unless assessment shows it is effective for the student in question. If intervention is not successful in such an approach, teachers would first look to the instruction as the source of difficulty before the student. This is the perspective embodied in the IRA Guiding Principles and illustrated in the chapters of this book.

Using Johnston's (2010) reasoning, RR and ISA are instructional approaches as opposed to standard protocol or measurement approaches. Neither program is scripted, and neither program would work if it were scripted (Clay, 2005; Vellutino & Scanlon, 2002). Suppose, for example, that during instruction a student reads a word incorrectly. A scripted program would prescribe the teacher's response. By contrast, in RR and ISA the teacher's response would depend on, among other things, the text difficulty, the instructional opportunity offered by the word, the context of the error, and the student's current processing strategies. Monitoring the teacher for treatment fidelity would miss the adaptive teacher expertise taking place and risk discouraging the teacher from adapting instruction as needed. To be clear, however, interventions such as RR and ISA are not "anything goes." They focus on developing teacher expertise rather than fidelity to programs that may or may not work for individual students.

In a measurement frame, the valued expertise is the design and selection of tests and packaged programs rather than the teacher's ability to adapt instruction. Expertise is minimized by the selection of instructional packages, particularly scripted ones, and testing instruments that can be used by people with limited expertise. Consistent with Johnston's (2010) classification scheme, scholars who promote measurement approaches describe RTI intervention as a test of whether the student is LD (Fuchs & Fuchs, 2006), whereas those who promote instructional approaches describe intervention as a test of the appropriateness of the instruction (Scanlon, in press).

In short, RTI is not a model to be imposed on schools but rather a framework to help schools identify and support students before the difficulties they encounter with language and literacy become more serious. According to the research, relatively few students who are having difficulty in language and literacy have specific learning disabilities (Vellutino, Scanlon, & Tanzman, 1998). Many other factors, including the nature of educational opportunities provided, affect students' academic and social growth. For example, teaching practices and assessment tools that are insensitive to cultural and linguistic differences can lead to ineffective instruction or misjudgments in evaluation. Both the IRA Guiding Principles and this volume assume that instruction/intervention can and will be effective for the overwhelming majority of students who are presently experiencing school/literacy difficulties. It is our responsibility to identify students' needs and help students succeed.

What Does Research Tell Us About RTI?

It is important for many reasons to consider what the research says about RTI. However, one of the issues for language and literacy professionals is knowing which research to consider—in other words, research by whom, for whom, and about what? Given the origin of RTI within special education, it is not surprising that a large proportion of the research in this area has been done by and for special educators and school psychologists. The research questions that have been pursued focus more heavily on issues associated with RTI and the identification of learning disabilities than on those associated with the prevention of learning disabilities, although there is some evidence that this trend may be changing (e.g., 2008 *Journal of Learning Disabilities* special issue, Volume 41, Issue 2).

To date, the types of research questions that have been addressed include those focusing on the validity and feasibility of using an RTI approach for identifying students with LD (Case, Speece, & Molloy, 2003; Speece & Case, 2001; Vaughn, Linan-Thompson, & Hickman, 2003; Vellutino, Scanlon, Small, & Fanuele, 2006), the impact of RTI on problems associated with the discrepancy model such as high levels of referrals and disproportionate numbers of poor and minority students being identified (Torgesen, 2009; VanDerHeyden, Witt,

& Gilbertson, 2007), and how refinements to the standard RTI models can and should be made (Jenkins, Graff, & Miglioretti, 2009).

In contrast, professionals working in the areas of language and literacy are interested in questions about the impact of RTI on student performance. They are interested in knowing more about issues such as how different types of instruction affect the performance of students struggling with language and literacy and how one can best know if students are progressing. Although RTI research is just starting to address these questions, professionals in the areas of language and literacy already have a knowledge base from which to draw. For example, we know that early intervention makes a difference (Clay, 1985; Lyons, Pinnell, Short, & Young, 1986; Pinnell, Lyons, DeFord, Bryk, & Seltzer, 1994; Santa & Høien, 1999; Vellutino et al., 1996). We also know that in some cases small-group intervention is just as effective as one-to-one instruction (Hiebert & Taylor, 2000; Santa & Høien, 1999). In addition, there is ample evidence that instruction in phonics improves the outcomes for many struggling readers and that these effects may not persist beyond second or third grade or generalize to comprehension (e.g., Iversen & Tunmer, 1993; Morris, Shaw, & Perney, 1990; Santa & Høien, 1999; White, 2005). Furthermore, we have evidence that teacher expertise matters (Lipson, Mosenthal, Mekkelsen, & Russ, 2004; Taylor, Pearson, Peterson, & Rodriguez, 2003).

Classroom teachers and specialists often feel pressured to adopt specialized programs for struggling students, and issues of program and approach are hotly debated in many schools, sometimes limiting collaborative efforts. Studies that shed light on "what instruction" and "which measures" suggest there is not one approach that is essential for accelerating students' reading achievement. Indeed, there is evidence that differing approaches can be equally successful as long as there is expert teaching and careful attention to student progress.

For example, a study by Torgesen et al. (2001) examined the effects of two types of interventions for students who are LD, each focused on phonics: a synthetic, free-standing auditory discrimination approach and embedded phonics. Although there were dramatic differences in the content of instruction, the materials enacted, and the activities employed to teach students to read, the long-term outcomes were essentially the same for both groups of students. Both groups experienced significant growth during the instruction and both maintained that advantage after two years. It is also important to note, however, that only half of the students attained average-level reading skills during these intensive one-to-one (50 minutes per day) interventions.

In a more-or-less direct test of differences between the standard protocol and the problem-solving models, Mathes et al. (2005) have found that students benefited from either approach. Small-group instruction of either sort was more effective than classroom instruction only. These authors conclude have

> Perhaps the most important finding of this research is that supplemental intervention approaches derived from different theoretical perspectives were both effective. These findings suggest to us that there is likely not "one best approach" and not one right philosophy or theory for how to best meet the needs of struggling readers. (p. 179)

Despite the apparent success of these interventions, it is still the case that many students were not performing as well as their classmates after intervention and that neither Torgesen et al. (2001) nor Mathes et al. (2005) examined their data more closely so that we might gain insight into what works for which students.

As research on RTI has progressed, we are learning more about the nuances of instructional interventions. For example, a study by Wanzek and Vaughn (2008) calls into question assumptions that approaches that are effective on average within an experimental group will be effective for every student within a new context and that increasing intensity, or dosage, will increase effectiveness. These researchers used a standard protocol intervention focused primarily on word knowledge and reading speed and accuracy. To examine the effectiveness of increased instructional intensity, some students received intervention 30 minutes per day, and a double-dose group received it 60 minutes per day.

Interestingly, the students who received the double dose did no better in word attack and less well in oral reading speed than the single intervention students and marginally worse on these measures than a control group focused on comprehension. Wanzek and Vaughn (2008) indicate that the lack of academic progress from increased intensity was at least partly because "tutors reported difficulties throughout the 13-week intervention with student fatigue, group management, and increased problem behavior during the second 30-minute session" (p. 139). This research suggests that when an intervention is not working for a student, simply increasing its intensity might not be the best course of action.

Wanzek and Vaughn (2008) also report what other researchers often neglect, that although the intervention had some positive effect on average, many students did not improve. For example, the performance of 24% of the single-intervention students and 35% of the double-dose students deteriorated by at least half of a standard deviation in word attack, a primary focus of the intervention. We cannot take an intervention that worked on average with some students in one setting and expect it to work with each student in every setting even if it is implemented with fidelity. This research implies that it might be better for teachers to adapt their instruction to the student rather than continuing to teach a program that is not working to ensure the fidelity of instruction. Indeed, professional development can be as effective at reducing the number of students at risk as intervention provided by trained interventionists (Scanlon, Gelzheiser, Vellutino, Schatschneider, & Sweeney, 2008).

Research also raises questions about assessment practices associated with RTI. Two major concerns are the quality of the information obtained given the tools in use and the recommendations about the frequency of assessment. Many districts have opted to use what are referred to as curriculum-based measures (CBMs) focused on the number of words students read correctly per minute (WCPM) using assessments such as DIBELS (Good, Kaminski, Smith, Laimon, & Dill, 2001) or AIMSweb (www.AIMSweb.com). Although such measures were once related to specific curricula, this is no longer the case, which means that the label *CBM* is an inaccurate descriptor for these assessments. Most of the available research has focused on the use of these measures to screen students and the extent to which these tools correctly identify students who are at risk for reading difficulties (Fuchs, Fuchs, McMaster, & Al Otaiba, 2003; Hintze & Silberglitt, 2005).

Although there are strong correlations between students' performance on these tests and their performance on other measures, there is virtually no evidence that students' reading is improved by using these assessments to plan instruction and monitor progress. Indeed, even the strongest advocates and authors of these assessments have expressed concerns about the uses and abuses of these measures:

> [U]se of any single indicator of competence to make important decisions, such as teacher evaluation or funding, violates professional standards of measurement (AERA, 1999). The importance of using other relevant information, including multiple forms of assessment, and viewing assessment results within the context of the school cannot be overstated. It is our concern that the use of DIBELS data for high stakes decisions will lead to misuse of DIBELS data and will compromise instructional practices. Some practices we have seen and find alarming, for example, include "teaching the test" in ways that raise test scores but do not focus on needs of students and promote broader learning of critical skills. (Kaminski et al., 2006, p. 2)

Concerns about the frequency of assessment arise from recommendations that progress monitoring should occur "at least monthly and, ideally weekly or biweekly," according to Fuchs and Fuchs (as cited in Hughes & Dexter, n.d.).

However, a study conducted by Jenkins et al. (2009) suggests that this is neither necessary nor desirable. The progress of students in this study was assessed on widely used CBM passages and procedures, testing the adequacy of the information about students' growth using different schedules for monitoring progress. The researchers conclude that it is possible to obtain valid assessments of students' progress from assessments given every three weeks and even as infrequently as every nine weeks. At the same time, they argue that somewhat more information is needed if teachers are going to move to less frequent assessments. As we gain more insight into the complexities of RTI initiatives, we need to be sure that we are using our scarce resources of time and expertise effectively.

In addition to concerns about the frequency of assessment, research raises questions about the types of assessment information collected. Valencia et al. (2006) administered a battery of assessments to students in grades 2, 4, and 6 to examine the relations between reading proficiency and its components, defined as accuracy, rate, expression, and comprehension. The first finding relevant for our purposes is that WCPM assessments are largely measures of rate as opposed to accuracy, expression, or comprehension. Not surprisingly, when separate indicators of rate, accuracy, expression, and comprehension were used in assessment, the results provided a finer grained understanding of students' strengths and weaknesses. This implies that RTI approaches relying almost exclusively on WCPM measures are essentially screening, planning intervention, and monitoring progress based on information about students' reading rate and without information about students' accuracy, expression, and comprehension that is necessary to appropriately address their reading needs.

Valencia et al. (2006) also found a substantial number of false negatives, or students whose WCPM scores indicated they were low risk but who scored below grade-level expectations on a standardized measure of comprehension. Although there was some variation across grade levels and in relation to the criteria used for determining proficiency based on WCPM performance in general, approximately 20% of students could be classified as false negatives. Further analyses revealed that 69% of the students in grade 6 identified as low risk using WCPM measures demonstrated below-grade-level performance on a standardized measure of comprehension. In the context of an RTI approach that relies heavily on WCPM data for screening, these students would not have been identified for intervention, though they were likely to be at risk based on their comprehension scores.

The fact that WCPM measures miss a number of students who are likely to need intervention illustrates the difficulties of relying on a single screening measure, especially one that does not evaluate the full range of reading components. This is particularly true beyond grade 2 as factors other than word recognition play an increasingly important role in reading proficiency (see Paris, 2005). This point is also supported by evidence from the Valencia et al. (2006) study about false positives—students who appeared to be at risk on the basis of their WCPM scores but were at or above grade level on a standardized measure of comprehension. Specifically, the number of false positives was substantially greater in grades 4 and 6 than in grade 2, indicating that WCPM is more highly related to comprehension at grade 2 than at grades 4 and 6.

An additional finding from Valencia et al. (2006) of importance for our purposes is that at-risk students have different patterns of difficulty in the component areas of reading that would require different instructional emphases. In general, word recognition accuracy was not a primary area of difficulty with 14% of the students in grade 2 demonstrating problems in this area and 5% of the students in grades 4 and 6 demonstrating similar problems. Although the proportion of students demonstrating difficulty with word recognition accuracy is greatest at grade 2, it is still far from the majority of students deemed at risk. Using separate measures of accuracy, rate, expression, and comprehension, the proportion of at-risk students in grade 2 demonstrating problems in each of these areas was 14% for accuracy, 62% for rate, 100% for expression, and 67% for comprehension. More important, perhaps, is that individual students demonstrate varying degrees of difficulty across these component areas of reading that require differentiated instructional approaches.

It is also the case that the word-level assessments commonly used to evaluate progress do not generalize to the more complex requirements of state and national assessments, particularly for poor and minority students. In a review of intensive, standardized interventions, Al Otaiba and Torgesen (2007) conclude the following:

> Given that [state tests] require a much broader range of knowledge and skill than the word-level tests used to estimate success rates in this review, it is likely that poor and minority students, in particular, will not achieve the same success rates on them as for the simpler tests that assess only word reading accuracy. (p. 220)

They also note that the available research is limited in that "we still know little about how best to support the development of vocabulary, conceptual knowledge, reading comprehension, and thinking skills or how to address motivational or behavior management issues" (p. 220).

Collectively, research on RTI and language and literacy instruction suggests that there are serious reasons to step back from the measurement-oriented perspective currently framing many approaches to RTI and move toward an instructional perspective that will help us improve instruction for every struggling learner. The Guiding Principles developed by the IRA Commission on RTI are designed to help us move in this direction.

IRA's Guiding Principles

The IRA Guiding Principles are intended for language and literacy professionals and others as they work toward the goals of preventing language and literacy difficulties among youth in the United States and improving instruction in these areas for all students. The principles are organized according to six headings that reflect key topics in developing and implementing approaches to RTI. Although these topics overlap considerably, they help organize the Guilding Principles. The six topics and their descriptions follow:

I. *Instruction*—RTI is first and foremost intended to prevent problems by optimizing initial language and literacy instruction.

II. *Responsive Teaching and Differentiation*—The RTI process emphasizes increasingly differentiated and intensified instruction/intervention in language and literacy.

III. *Assessment*—An RTI approach demands assessment that can inform language and literacy instruction meaningfully.

IV. *Collaboration*—RTI requires a dynamic, positive, and productive collaboration among professionals with relevant expertise in language and literacy. Success also depends on strong and respectful partnerships among professionals, parents, and students.

V. *Systemic and Comprehensive*—RTI must be part of a comprehensive, systemic approach to language and literacy assessment and instruction that supports all preK–12 students and teachers.

VI. *Expertise*—All students have the right to receive instruction from well-prepared teachers who keep up to date and supplemental instruction from professionals specifically prepared to teach language and literacy. (IRA, 2000)

The first principle, Instruction, focuses primarily on the core instruction provided by the classroom teacher to all students. It states clearly that instruction and assessment conducted by the classroom teacher are central to the success of RTI and must address the needs of all students, including those from different cultural and linguistic backgrounds. Specifically, increasingly differentiated and customized assessment and instruction should prevent serious language and literacy problems and reduce the disproportionate number of minorities and ELLs identified as LD.

This principle also stresses that a successful RTI process begins with the highest quality classroom core instruction, that is, instruction that encompasses all areas of language and literacy as part of a coherent curriculum that is developmentally appropriate for pre-K–12 students and does not underestimate their potential for language and literacy learning. This core instruction may or may not involve commercial programs and, in all cases, must be provided by an informed, competent classroom teacher.

The Instruction principle notes further that the success of RTI depends on classroom teachers' use of research-based practices that have a record of success. Teachers have a responsibility to use techniques, approaches, and materials that can demonstrate with reliable, trustworthy, and valid evidence that students can be expected to make adequate gains in reading achievement (see IRA, 2002). However, it also makes clear that research on instructional practices must provide information not only about what works but also about what works with whom, by whom, in what contexts, and on which outcomes. The effectiveness of a particular practice needs to have been demonstrated with the types of students who will receive this instruction, notably students from rural and urban areas as well as from diverse cultural and linguistic backgrounds.

The second principle, Responsive Teaching and Differentiation, focuses on the differentiated instruction provided to students struggling with language and literacy. This principle builds on evidence that small-group instruction and individualized instruction are effective in reducing the number of students who become classified as LD. At the same time, the principle recognizes that not all students can be expected to respond similarly to instructional interventions, even when research-based practices are used. It makes clear that differentiated instruction must be flexible enough to respond to evidence from student performance and teaching interactions and not be constrained by packaged programs. Special note is made of attention to the needs of students from different cultural and linguistic backgrounds.

The third principle, Assessment, focuses on the importance of assessment practices that can inform language and literacy instruction meaningfully. This principle makes the point that assessment needs to reflect the multidimensional nature of language and literacy and the diversity among students being assessed.

Consistent with the principles on instruction, the Assessment principle makes clear that the quality of assessment information should not be sacrificed for the efficiency of an assessment procedure. It further notes that not all available assessments are appropriate for all purposes or students and that care should be taken in selecting assessments especially for ELLs and students whose dialects may differ from mainstream English dialects.

The Assessment principle also supports the need for an assessment system involving a layered approach in which screening techniques are used both to identify which students require further (diagnostic) assessment and to provide aggregate data about the nature of student achievement overall. It indicates that initial (screening) assessments should not be used as the sole mechanism for determining the appropriateness of targeted interventions and that ongoing progress monitoring must include an evaluation of the instruction itself and requires observation of the student in the classroom. This view makes clear that classroom teachers and reading/literacy specialists should play a central role in conducting language and literacy assessments and in using assessment results to plan instruction and monitor student performance.

The fourth principle, Collaboration, focuses on the need for a dynamic, positive, and productive collaboration among professionals with relevant expertise in language and literacy, as well as strong and respectful partnerships among professionals, parents, and students. This principle indicates that decision-making teams (e.g., intervention teams, problem-solving teams, RTI teams) at school, district, and state levels need to include members with relevant expertise in language and literacy, including second-language learning. Specifically, reading specialists/literacy coaches should provide leadership in every aspect of an RTI process: planning, assessment, provision of more intensified instruction and support, and making decisions about next steps.

In addition, this principle notes that collaboration should increase the congruence between core language/literacy instruction and interventions. As described in this principle, this requires a shared vision and common goals for language and literacy instruction and assessment, adequate time for communication and coordinated planning among general educators and specialist teachers, and integrated professional development. The importance of home, school, and community connections is also emphasized.

The fifth principle, Systemic and Comprehensive, emphasizes that RTI must be part of a comprehensive, systemic approach to language and literacy assessment and instruction that supports all pre-K–12 students and teachers.

This principle makes clear that specific approaches to RTI need to be appropriate for the particular school/district culture and take into account leadership, expertise, the diversity of the student population, and the available resources. Further, it notes that schools and districts should adopt an approach that best matches their needs and resources while accomplishing the overall goals of RTI.

The Systemic and Comprehensive principle also points out that approaches to RTI must be sensitive to developmental differences in language and literacy among students at different ages and grades, including middle and secondary school levels. In addition, systemic and comprehensive approaches to RTI require that administrators provide adequate resources and support for appropriate scheduling, ample time for all professionals to collaborate, and ongoing and embedded professional development for all educators involved in the RTI process.

The sixth and final principle, Expertise, highlights the rights of all students to receive instruction from well-prepared teachers who keep up-to-date and supplemental instruction from professionals specifically prepared to teach language and literacy (IRA, 2000). This principle emphasizes the importance of teacher expertise in addressing the needs of students struggling with language and literacy. As described within this principle, this expertise includes knowledge and understanding of language and literacy development, the ability to use powerful assessment tools and techniques, and the ability to translate information about student performance into instructionally relevant techniques.

The Expertise principle also makes clear that classroom teachers and specialists alike must have a high level of expertise in all aspects of language and literacy instruction and assessment and be capable of promoting language and literacy learning. This includes knowledge and skill in teaching culturally and linguistically diverse students in a variety of settings, as deep knowledge of cultural and linguistic differences is especially critical for the prevention of language and literacy problems in diverse student populations. Such knowledge and skill requires a comprehensive approach to professional preparation that involves preservice, induction, and inservice education. It also requires opportunities for extended practice under the guidance of knowledgeable and experienced mentors.

Concluding Thoughts

The IRA Guiding Principles provide a perspective on RTI that is more reflective of an instructional framework than a measurement framework. This perspective provides the basis for approaches to RTI described in the remaining chapters in this book. Until very recently, most of the books published about RTI have focused on special education and the implications for the identification of learning disabilities. This situation has created a vacuum of information, direction, and guidance for general educators and, especially, for those who are concerned about teaching literacy. Without a good reservoir of information about what the law actually requires and a clear understanding of good research-based options, many reading professionals are frustrated. It is also the case that classroom teachers, charged with providing excellent first instruction, and literacy specialists, charged with supporting teachers and providing excellent next "tier" intervention, are often excluded from genuine participation in decision making. This book is intended to remedy these problems in several ways by doing the following:

- Providing reading teachers and specialists with accurate, up-to-date information about what is (and is not) required by RTI legislation

- Describing at least three research-based RTI approaches that focus on reducing the numbers of struggling readers and students identified as LD based on poor reading performance

- Addressing systemic challenges and proposing an action-planning framework for professionals to use in their school settings

This book is particularly timely because the interest in RTI has risen sharply as schools, districts, and states take on the challenge. At the same time, many states and districts still have not adopted a specific model or approach, and well-informed literacy professionals may have an opportunity in these contexts to inform decisions.

REFERENCES

Al Otaiba, S., & Torgesen, J. (2007). Effects from intensive standardized kindergarten and first-grade interventions for the prevention of reading difficulties. In S.R. Jimerson, M.K. Burns, & A.M. VanDerHeyden (Eds.), *Handbook of Response to Intervention: The* *science and practice of assessment and intervention* (pp. 212–222). New York: Springer.

Burns, M.K., & Coolong-Chaffin, M. (2006). Response to Intervention: The role of and effect on school psychology. *School Psychology Forum: Research and Practice, 1*(1), 3–15.

Case, L.P., Speece, D.L., & Molloy, D.E. (2003). The validity of a response-to-instruction paradigm to identify reading disabilities: A longitudinal analysis of individual differences and contextual factors. *School Psychology Review, 32*(4), 557–582.

Clay, M.M. (1985). *The early detection of reading difficulties: A diagnostic survey with recovery procedures* (3rd ed.). Portsmouth, NH: Heinemann.

Clay, M.M. (2005). *Literacy lessons: Designed for individuals, part two: Teaching procedures.* Portsmouth, NH: Heinemann.

Fuchs, D., & Fuchs, L.S. (2006). Introduction to Response to Intervention: What, why, and how valid is it? *Reading Research Quarterly, 41*(1), 93–99. doi:10.1598/RRQ.41.1.4

Fuchs, D., Fuchs, L.S., McMaster, K.N., & Al Otaiba, S. (2003). Identifying children at risk for reading failure: Curriculum-based measurement and dual-discrepancy approach. In H.L. Swanson, K.R. Harris, & S. Graham (Eds.), *Handbook of learning disabilities* (pp. 431–449). New York: Guilford.

Fuchs, D., Mock, D., Morgan, P.L., & Young, C.L. (2003). Responsiveness-to-intervention: Definitions, evidence, and implications for the learning disabilities construct. *Learning Disabilities Research & Practice, 18*(3), 157–171. doi:10.1111/1540-5826.00072

Fuchs, D., Stecker, P.M., & Fuchs, L.S. (2008). Tier 3: Why special education must be the most intensive tier in a standards-driven, No Child Left Behind world. In D. Fuchs, L.S. Fuchs, & S. Vaughn (Eds.), *Response to Intervention: A framework for reading educators* (pp. 71–104). Newark, DE: International Reading Association.

Gresham, F.M. (2007). Evolution of the Response-to-Intervention concept: Empirical foundations and recent developments. In S.R. Jimerson, M.K. Burns, & A.M. VanDerHeyden (Eds.), *Handbook of Response to Intervention: The science and practice of assessment and intervention* (pp. 10–24). New York: Springer.

Hiebert, E.H., & Taylor, B.M. (2000). Beginning reading instruction: Research on early interventions. In M.L. Kamil, P.B. Mosenthal, P.D. Pearson, & R. Barr (Eds.), *Handbook of reading research* (Vol. 3, pp. 455–482). Mahwah, NJ: Erlbaum.

Hintze, J.M., & Silberglitt, B. (2005). A longitudinal examination of the diagnostic accuracy and predictive validity of R-CBM and high-stakes testing. *School Psychology Review, 34*(3), 372–386.

Hughes, C., & Dexter, D.D. (n.d.). *Response to Intervention: A research review.* Retrieved January 10, 2009, from www.rtinetwork.org/Learn/Research/ar/ResearchReview

International Reading Association. (2000). *Making a difference means making it different: Honoring children's rights to excellent reading instruction* (Position statement). Newark, DE: Author.

International Reading Association. (2002). *What is evidence-based reading instruction?* (Position statement). Newark, DE: Author.

Iversen, S.J., & Tunmer, W.E. (1993). Phonological processing skills and the Reading Recovery Program. *Journal of Educational Psychology, 85*(1), 112–125.

Jenkins, J.R., Graff, J.J., & Miglioretti, D.L. (2009). Estimating reading growth using intermittent CBM progress monitoring. *Exceptional Children, 75*(2), 151–163.

Jimerson, S.R., Burns, M.K., & VanDerHeyden, A.M. (Eds.). (2007). Response to Intervention at school: The science and practice of assessment and intervention. In S.R. Jimerson, M.K. Burns, & A.M. VanDerHeyden (Eds.), *Handbook of Response to Intervention: The science and practice of assessment and intervention* (pp. 3–9). New York: Springer.

Johnston, P.H. (2010). An instructional frame for RTI. *The Reading Teacher, 63*(7), 602–604.

Kaminski, R.A., Good, R.H., III, Baker, D., Cummings, K., Dufour-Martel, C., Fleming, K., et al. (2006). *Position paper on use of DIBELS for system-wide accountability decisions.* Eugene, OR: Dynamic Measurement Group. Retrieved March 15, 2010, from www.cde.state.co.us/coloradoliteracy/cbla/download/Accountability_2006-11-16.pdf

Lipson, M.Y., Mosenthal, J.H., Mekkelsen, J., & Russ, B. (2004). Building knowledge and fashioning success one school at a time. *The Reading Teacher, 57*(6), 534–542. doi:10.1598/RT.57.6.3

Lyons, C.A., Pinnell, G., Short, K., & Young, P. (1986). *The Ohio Reading Recovery project: Volume IV, pilot year, 1985–1986* (Tech. Rep.). Columbus: The Ohio State University.

Marston, D., Muyskens, P., Lau, M., & Canter, A. (2003). Problem-solving model for decision making with high-incidence disabilities: The Minneapolis experience. *Learning Disabilities Research & Practice, 18*(3), 187–200. doi:10.1111/1540-5826.00074

Mathes, P.G., Denton, C.A., Fletcher, J.M., Anthony, J.L., Francis, D.J., & Schatschneider, C. (2005). The effects of theoretically different instruction and student characteristics on the skills of struggling readers. *Reading Research Quarterly, 40*(2), 148–182. doi:10.1598/RRQ.40.2.2

Morris, D., Shaw, B., & Perney, J. (1990). Helping low readers in grades 2 and 3: An after-school volunteer tutoring program. *The Elementary School Journal, 91*(2), 132–150. doi:10.1086/461642

National Association of State Directors of Special Education & Council of Administrators of Special Education. (2006, May). *Response to Intervention: NASDSE and CASE white paper on RTI.* Retrieved January 7, 2010, from www.nasdse.org/Portals/0/Documents/Download%20Publications/RtIAnAdministratorsPerspective1-06.pdf

Paris, S.G. (2005). Reinterpreting the development of reading skills. *Reading Research Quarterly, 40*(2), 184–202. doi:10.1598/RRQ.40.2.3

Pinnell, G.S., Lyons, C.A., DeFord, D.E., Bryk, A.S., & Seltzer, M. (1994). Comparing instructional models for the literacy education of high-risk first graders. *Reading Research Quarterly, 29*(1), 9–39. doi:10.2307/747736

Santa, C.M., & Høien, T. (1999). An assessment of early steps: A program for early intervention of reading problems. *Reading Research Quarterly, 34*(1), 54–79. doi:10.1598/RRQ.34.1.4

Scanlon, D.M. (in press). Response to Intervention as an assessment: The role of assessment and instruction in the prevention and identification of reading disabilities. In R. Allington & A. McGill-Franzen (Eds.), *Handbook of reading disabilities research.*

Scanlon, D.M., Gelzheiser, L.M., Vellutino, F.R., Schatschneider, C., & Sweeney, J.M. (2008). Reducing the incidence of early reading difficulties: Professional development for classroom teachers versus direct interventions for children. *Learning and Individual Differences, 18*(3), 346–359. doi:10.1016/j.lindif.2008.05.002

Scanlon, D.M., & Sweeney, J.M. (2008). Response to Intervention: An overview: New hope for struggling learners. *Educator's Voice, 1,* 16–29.

Scanlon, D.M., & Vellutino, F.R. (1996). Prerequisite skills, early instruction, and success in first-grade reading: Selected results from a longitudinal study. *Mental Retardation and Developmental Disabilities Research Reviews, 2*(1), 54–63. doi:10.1002/(SICI)1098-2779(1996)2:1<54::AID-MRDD9>3.0.CO;2-X

Scanlon, D.M., Vellutino, F.R., Small, S.G., Fanuele, D.P., & Sweeney, J.M. (2005). Severe reading difficulties—can they be prevented? A comparison of prevention and intervention approaches. *Exceptionality, 13*(4), 209–227. doi:10.1207/s15327035ex1304_3

Speece, D.L., & Case, L.P. (2001). Classification in context: An alternative approach to identifying early reading disability. *Journal of Educational Psychology, 93*(4), 735–749. doi:10.1037/0022-0663.93.4.735

Taylor, B.M., Pearson, P.D., Peterson, D.S., & Rodriguez, M.C. (2003). Reading growth in high-poverty classrooms: The influence of teacher practices that encourage cognitive engagement in literacy learning. *The Elementary School Journal, 104*(1), 3–28. doi:10.1086/499740

Torgesen, J.K. (2009). The Response to Intervention instructional model: Some outcomes from a large-scale implementation in Reading First schools. *Child Development Perspectives*, *3*(1), 38–40. doi:10.1111/j.1750-8606.2009.00073.x

Torgesen, J.K., Alexander, A.W., Wagner, R.K., Rashotte, C.A., Voeller, K.K.S., & Conway, T. (2001). Intensive remedial instruction for children with severe reading disabilities: Immediate and long-term outcomes from two instructional approaches. *Journal of Learning Disabilities*, *34*(1), 33–58. doi:10.1177/002221940103400104

U.S. Department of Education. (2002, July). *A new era: Revitalizing special education for children and their families. A report of the President's Commission on Excellence in Special Education.* Retrieved January 7, 2010, from www.ed.gov/inits/commissionsboards/whspecialeducation/reports/index.html

Valencia, S.W., Smith, A., Reece, A., Newman, H., Li, M., & Wixson, K.K. (2006, April). *The rush for oral reading fluency assessment.* Paper presented at the annual conference of the American Educational Research Association, San Francisco, CA.

VanDerHeyden, A.M., Witt, J.C., & Gilbertson, D. (2007). A multi-year evaluation of the effects of a Response to Intervention (RTI) model on identification of children for special education. *Journal of School Psychology*, *45*(2), 225–256. doi:10.1016/j.jsp.2006.11.004

Vaughn, S., Linan-Thompson, S., & Hickman, P. (2003). Response to instruction as a means of identifying students with reading/learning disabilities. *Exceptional Children*, *69*(4), 391–409.

Vellutino, F.R., & Scanlon, D.M. (2002). The Interactive Strategies approach to reading intervention. *Contemporary Educational Psychology*, *27*(4), 573–635. doi:10.1016/S0361-476X(02)00002-4

Vellutino, F.R., Scanlon, D.M., Sipay, E.R., Small, S.G., Pratt, A., Chen, R.S., et al. (1996). Cognitive profiles of difficult-to-remediate and readily remediated poor readers: Early intervention as a vehicle for distinguishing between cognitive and experiential deficits as basic causes of specific reading disability. *Journal of Educational Psychology*, *88*(4), 601–638. doi:10.1037/0022-0663.88.4.601

Vellutino, F.R., Scanlon, D.M., Small, S., & Fanuele, D.P. (2006). Response to Intervention as a vehicle for distinguishing between children with and without reading disabilities. *Journal of Learning Disabilities*, *39*(2), 157–169. doi:10.1177/00222194060390020401

Vellutino, F.R., Scanlon, D.M., & Tanzman, M.S. (1998). The case for early intervention in diagnosing specific reading disability. *Journal of School Psychology*, *36*(4), 367–397. doi:10.1016/S0022-4405(98)00019-3

Wanzek, J., & Vaughn, S. (2008). Response to varying amounts of time in reading intervention for students with low response to intervention. *Journal of Learning Disabilities*, *41*(2), 126–142. doi:10.1177/0022219407313426

White, T.G. (2005). Effects of systematic and strategic analogy-based phonics on grade 2 students' word reading and reading comprehension. *Reading Research Quarterly*, *40*(2), 234–255. doi:10.1598/RRQ.40.2.5

Using the Interactive Strategies Approach to Prevent Reading Difficulties in an RTI Context

Donna M. Scanlon

Michigan State University

Kimberly L. Anderson

University at Albany, State University of New York

People vary tremendously in the ease with which they acquire academic and other skills. Teachers vary tremendously in their effectiveness in teaching various content areas and in their ability to effectively respond to various student characteristics (e.g., age, temperament, gender). The complex interactions between and among the student and teacher characteristics, as well as school, family, and community characteristics, combine to determine the student's academic success. Until recently, students for whom these forces had produced substantially less than optimal academic skill but who were judged to be at least average in their intellectual ability were often identified as learning disabled (LD), which locates the problem within the student and, potentially, signals to those responsible for that student's education (including the student's teachers and parents, and the student) that there may not be much hope for that student.

Indeed, until the last few decades, no serious consideration has been given to the possibility that, for a student with a discrepant profile between achievement and intelligence, the student's experience and instruction might be the locus of the "disability." We now know, however, that instructional experiences have a powerful influence on students' learning trajectories. Particularly with regard to early literacy development, there is a wealth of evidence indicating that, for most students, serious reading difficulties can be prevented by improving the quality, quantity, or intensity of the instruction that is provided.

The Emergence of RTI

Based on mounting evidence indicating that many students were being inappropriately identified as LD, the United States government passed legislation (Individuals With Disabilities Education Improvement Act [IDEIA]; 2004) that provides schools with the option to do away with the once-required IQ-achievement discrepancy criterion for LD classification and instead use a process in which struggling learners are provided with enhanced and, if need be, intensified instruction for the purpose of preventing long-term learning difficulties and avoiding inappropriate LD classifications. This process has come to be known as the RTI approach. Its basic premise is that a student should not be considered for learning disability designation until it can be documented that the student has received appropriately targeted and intensified instruction and that instruction has failed to accelerate the student's learning to the point where he or she can meet grade-level expectations.

In the years since the IDEIA was passed, a good deal has been written about the RTI process. However, most of the material written for educational practitioners has focused on issues related to documentation of interventions and progress monitoring and on decision making related to that progress. Remarkably little attention has been given to what, in our opinion, is the most important component of RTI: the nature and qualities of the instruction that is offered. Rather, schools are often advised to implement high-quality instructional programs with fidelity. Such recommendations suggest that there is a menu of programs available which, when implemented as intended, will yield demonstrably better outcomes for students. However, this is not the case. There are remarkably few instructional programs that, even when delivered with fidelity, yield achievement outcomes that are better than the outcomes that occur when students are provided with the type of instruction that was already available to them, and in fact, the implementation of some programs has been found to have a negative impact on student learning (see the What Works Clearinghouse website provided by the United States Department of Education's Institute of Education Sciences, which reviews the evidence on program effectiveness: ies .ed.gov/ncee/wwc).

Further, the practitioner literature on RTI does not reflect the fact that, regardless of efforts to standardize instruction, teachers using the same instructional program or approach deliver instruction that is variably effective. For example, in a study conducted by Tivnan and Hemphill (2005) in which four distinct instructional programs were implemented in different schools, the researchers found that the student outcomes were approximately the same across programs. However, within each program they found that the students in some classrooms made much more progress than did students in other classrooms. In other words, there was substantially more variation caused by teacher differences than there was by the instructional program adopted.

Based on this and other studies that have identified what teachers do, rather than which program they use, as the most critical factor in enhancing student learning, we are very concerned about the advice to adopt (commercial) programs and implement them with fidelity. There is simply no research to support this recommendation. Many educators understand the requirement to implement programs with fidelity to mean that instruction should be delivered exactly as prescribed in the program manual. Such an approach to instruction will clearly limit teachers' ability to be responsive to their students' instructional needs and thereby potentially limit the students' learning.

Of even greater concern is the widespread belief that if a student makes inadequate progress in a given instructional program, the student should be placed in a different program. We are aware of at least one local school district where students are ineligible for consideration for LD designation until they have been given a trial in at least three distinct programs. For students who find learning to read confusing and challenging, this program switching has the potential to exacerbate rather than alleviate their difficulties. Thus, although RTI has emerged as a viable means of preventing long-term reading difficulties and reducing the number of students who are inaccurately classified as LD, there is reason to be concerned about the potential long-term impacts of such a process if implemented in such disruptive ways. Indeed, we are concerned that some of the instructional recommendations being made in the name of RTI may ultimately serve to increase the number of students who experience prolonged reading difficulties.

RTI and the Interactive Strategies Approach

Our main purpose in this chapter is to describe an approach to preventing reading difficulties, the Interactive Strategies Approach (ISA; Scanlon, Anderson, & Sweeney, 2010; Vellutino & Scanlon, 2002). The ISA has been developed and tested over the course of several large-scale studies that focused on exploring ways to prevent long-term reading difficulties. The approach has been found to be effective in reducing the number of at-risk students who experience reading difficulties in the early primary grades. We have found that it is effective when provided by intervention teachers in both one-to-one and small-group contexts (Scanlon, Gelzheiser, Vellutino, Schatschneider, & Sweeney, 2008; Scanlon, Vellutino, Small, Fanuele, & Sweeney, 2005; Vellutino et al., 1996) and by classroom teachers (Scanlon et al., 2008; Scanlon, Anderson, Gelzheiser, & Vellutino, 2010).

It is important to note that research on the ISA, to a great extent, predates the move to RTI as a vehicle for preventing long-term reading difficulties and determining LD classifications. In fact, the research on the approach is a bit backward relative to the logic of RTI in that our earliest research focused on one-to-one intervention for first-grade struggling readers (Vellutino et al., 1996), which, from an RTI perspective, might be considered to be Tier 3 intervention. Realizing that one-to-one intervention is costly and probably unsustainable on a large scale and that most students probably do not need that level of intensity, our next major study focused on reducing the number of students who struggle with reading in first grade by providing small-group interventions for at-risk kindergartners (Scanlon et al., 2005), similar to a Tier 2 intervention from an RTI perspective. That study revealed that small-group intervention for kindergartners who were at risk of experiencing reading difficulties could substantially reduce the number of students who qualified as struggling readers in first grade. Further, small-group intervention in kindergarten reduced the number of students who demonstrated severe reading difficulties at the end of first grade regardless of the type of intervention they received in first grade.

In our most recent intervention study (Scanlon et al., 2008), we found that teaching classroom teachers about the ISA and supporting their implementation of it was also effective in reducing the number of students who qualified as struggling readers. Thus, although we have not explicitly researched the use of the ISA in an RTI context, we have researched its use in all of the contexts that are involved in RTI implementations (e.g., classroom, small-group, one-to-one intervention).

The ISA is an approach, not a program. In preparing teachers to implement the ISA, we provide them with in-depth information about many aspects of early reading development and guidance and with suggestions for how this information might influence and be incorporated into instruction at the classroom, small-group, and individual levels. We offer a way of thinking about early literacy instruction that can potentially help teachers more effectively promote literacy development regardless of the curriculum they are using. The

ISA does not delineate particular materials or provide instructional scripts. Rather, we offer suggestions for instructional materials and for how teachers might evaluate and use the materials they have on hand to more effectively meet the needs of their students, particularly those who find learning to read more challenging.

The ISA takes account of the fact that reading is a complex process that draws on a number of abilities, knowledge sources, and dispositions, including the ability to read words, general language skills, knowledge related to the content of the text, and the intention of making sense of what is read. These abilities and knowledge sources interact to enable comprehension of written text. We take the position that early and long-term reading difficulties can be prevented if literacy instruction is comprehensive, responsive to individual students' needs, and fosters student independence.

Because learning to read the words is the most common stumbling block for students who are identified as struggling learners at the early stages of literacy development as well as for some students who experience longer term difficulties with reading, a good deal of emphasis is placed on helping students develop and use word-learning strategies effectively. We emphasize the need to help students develop a self-teaching mechanism (Share, 1995) that enables them to use code-based and meaning-based strategies in interactive and confirmatory ways to solve unfamiliar words encountered in text. Unfamiliar words that are accurately identified on multiple occasions are ultimately learned so well that they become part of the students' sight vocabulary (i.e., the body of words that can be identified accurately and effortlessly). This enlarged sight vocabulary, in turn, allows the students to devote more of their thinking to understanding and interpreting the things they read, because they do not need to devote as much cognitive energy to figuring out the words.

To be effective word solvers, students need to have a firm grasp of the workings of the alphabetic code and must approach reading as a meaning-making enterprise. Only then will students be able to use both code-based and meaning-based strategies to direct and check their word-solving attempts. Therefore, in working with struggling readers as well as with students who learn to read with relative ease, teachers are encouraged to address all aspects of literacy development and to shift the emphasis of instruction based on the students' performance levels.

In what follows, we describe the ISA in greater detail and illustrate how the approach can be embedded in the larger context of RTI. We briefly describe a generalized model of RTI that we advocate and then describe the premises and structure of the ISA and the professional development and guidance that teachers involved in the research received.

A Model of RTI

Efforts to intervene on behalf of students who are considered to be at risk for literacy learning difficulties should begin as early as the students can be identified (see Scanlon, in press) and should be coordinated across the settings in which literacy instruction is provided so as to avoid presenting the students with conflicting and confusing views of the reading process. To this end, RTI should be implemented in the early primary grades, and classroom and specialist teachers should be encouraged to agree on and adopt common expectations, strategies, resources, and terminology for early literacy instruction. Further, when teachers share responsibility for instructing students, there should be ongoing communication between and among the teachers regarding the students' progress and areas of difficulty.

Ideally, all teachers would monitor the progress of the students they teach by documenting their observations of the students' skills and abilities during routine instructional interactions. Although more formal progress-monitoring tools such as DIBELS (Good et al., 2001) and AIMSweb Progress Monitoring and RTI System (www.AIMSweb.com) are often considered to be integral to an RTI process, we have not used such tools in our intervention efforts. These tools provide virtually no information that would guide instructional planning. Also, there is the risk that using such tools will lead to an emphasis on some aspects of the reading process (e.g., speedy word reading) and a deemphasis on the most important target of literacy instruction, comprehension (see Scanlon, in press, for a detailed discussion).

We realize, of course, that the use of assessments such as DIBELS and AIMSweb has the advantage of simplifying the decision making regarding whether students should receive more or less intensive forms of intervention. Further, performance on these measures tends to correlate with more comprehensive measures of reading ability. However, we are concerned that the frequent use of such measures consumes valuable instructional time and that, to date, there is little evidence that instructional decision making and student outcomes are enhanced by their use. In our research, we opted to use more comprehensive measures but to administer them less often—four times per year. We also provided teachers with observational progress-monitoring tools, which were used on an ongoing basis in small-group and one-to-one instruction. Examples of these tools are provided in a later section.

In the following sections, we describe the structure of an ISA-based RTI model that involves implementation at the kindergarten and first-grade levels. In later sections, we describe the professional development provided for teachers and how the instruction is implemented.

RTI in Kindergarten

There is a good deal of research (including our own) that indicates that students who are apt to experience difficulties at the early stages of learning to read can be identified at kindergarten entry (or before). Our research suggests that attempts to intervene should begin in kindergarten when the students' knowledge gaps, relative to their peers, are comparatively small and before the students who are at risk come to identify themselves as less able readers/learners.

In our studies, all students for whom we had parental consent were assessed using a measure of early literacy skill during the first few weeks of kindergarten. In our most recent study (Scanlon et al., 2008), we used the Phonological Awareness Literacy Screening (PALS; Invernizzi, Meier, & Juel, 2003–2007) to identify students who were at risk. The PALS provides a benchmark or cutoff for determining risk status, as do several other measures of early literacy skill. Generally, the cutoff is set at about the 25th or 30th percentile.

Such assessment is often referred to as "universal screening." Depending on the population served by a given school and on the instructional philosophies of the preschool settings students may have encountered before kindergarten entry, placing the cutoff at the 30th percentile might yield an at-risk group of anywhere from 10% to 60% (or more) of the entering kindergarten class. Although using the 30th percentile as a cutoff may seem overly inclusive, it is important to note that it is used primarily to help teachers identify those students whose progress needs to be closely monitored. Scoring below the 30th percentile does not mean that a student will have difficulty learning to read. It simply means that the student does not yet demonstrate the skills that are typical for an entering kindergartner. If a student continues to lag in acquiring those skills, significant reading difficulties are likely to emerge.

Lack of skill at kindergarten entry may be attributable to a variety of factors, including a lack of opportunity to acquire these skills (most often the case), a lack of interest in acquiring foundational literacy skills, and genuine difficulty with acquiring such skills. The student's response to high-quality and appropriately targeted instruction will help explain the initial lack of skill. In fact, the diagnostic value of a student's response to generally effective instruction/intervention is a central concept in RTI. However, in some RTI models, it is assumed that if a student does not profit from the type of instruction that is effective for most of his or her peers, which sometimes means whole-class and undifferentiated instruction, then that student may "suffer" from a learning disability. Although there can be no doubt that such a student suffers on some levels, this logic fails to take into account that young children differ tremendously in their understandings about how print and written language work. If instruction does not take account of these differences, it could be argued that the difficulties lie not with the student but with the instruction. We would argue that a student's response to instruction/intervention must be judged against the responsiveness and appropriateness of the intervention that is provided.

In commonly described RTI approaches, students who are identified as at risk would be monitored for a period of time as they participate in classroom language arts instruction, with an eye toward determining how readily they acquire the early literacy skills taught in the classroom language arts program. Because these students begin at a disadvantage, we would argue that, to close the gap between them and their peers, classroom language arts instruction needs to be modified to meet their needs. This can be accomplished most readily by providing small-group instruction for a portion of the time devoted to language arts instruction. Thus, language arts instruction in kindergarten would consist of a combination of whole-class and small-group instruction, with groups being formed on the basis of similarities in early literacy skills.

The focus of instruction in the small-group context should be geared to the students in the group. Sometimes when we make such a suggestion to teachers, they indicate that kindergartners are not ready for such focused instruction. To this we respond: Every student is ready to learn something. Our job is to figure out what he or she is ready to learn and teach it. When it appears that students are not ready for focused instruction, it is probably a sign that the focus of instruction is beyond their current point in literacy development. For example, students who know very little about the alphabet are ready to learn different things than are students who arrive in kindergarten already knowing the names of most of the letters and some of their associated sounds. There is no way that the needs of such a divergent class of students can be adequately met with whole-class instruction alone.

However, if the gap between the at-risk group and the remainder of the class is to be closed, the students at risk need to learn more in a given period of time than do their more knowledgeable peers. To accomplish this acceleration, small-group, differentiated instruction needs to be provided, and the least knowledgeable students should be provided with more small-group time than their higher performing peers. In the classroom, this can be accomplished by providing small-group instruction for the at-risk students four or five times a week while providing small-group instruction for the remainder of the students only three or four times per week, depending on the distribution of students in the class.

An alternative or addition to providing intensified instruction in the classroom would be to provide the at-risk students with instruction beyond the classroom as well. In an RTI framework, such instruction is typically referred to as Tier 2 instruction. In the most widely discussed RTI models (Fuchs & Fuchs, 2006; Mellard & Johnson, 2008), Tier 2 instruction occurs only after a period of classroom instruction alone, when it becomes evident that high-quality classroom instruction, by itself, is unsuccessful in accelerating the progress of the at-risk students. However, to our knowledge, there has been no systematic comparison of the relative advantages of providing students with a period of Tier 1 instruction only before deciding that too little growth is occurring and, therefore, adding a second tier of intervention. Such research needs to be done. In the interim, we are inclined to agree with the argument made by Dorn and Schubert (2008) that there should be a sense of urgency with regard to meeting the instructional needs of students who are at risk of experiencing reading difficulties. Therefore, we would argue that periods of Tier 1 instruction alone might best be relatively brief unless there is very clear evidence that a student is making strong progress that will allow him or her to meet grade-level expectations by the end of the school year.

In our studies, Tier 2–type intervention began in mid to late October (approximately four to six weeks into the school year) and continued through mid to late May. Students were seen in groups of three for 30 minutes twice each week. On average, the students received approximately 50 intervention sessions during their kindergarten year. Because we were conducting research, all students remained in intervention throughout their kindergarten year. However, for many of them, in a nonresearch, normal service delivery model, it would have been appropriate to discontinue their involvement earlier. We also found that as the school year progressed, classroom teachers, recognizing the progress that the students in intervention were making, would request that other students in their class who initially did not qualify for intervention be allowed to participate in the intervention instead of the students who no longer appeared to need it. The fact that these requests occurred makes it clear that in RTI implementations, there need to be multiple opportunities for teachers to determine, based on both observation and more formal assessment data, which students are in greatest need of more intensive intervention services and which can be appropriately supported with classroom instruction alone.

There were, of course, students who did not make the desired amount of progress with a combination of classroom instruction and Tier 2 intervention in kindergarten. In general, we did not provide intervention in kindergarten beyond Tier 2. However, there were a few instances in which kindergartners were provided with Tier 3 intervention. This occurred when a student's progress was so slow and divergent from the progress of the other students in the small-group settings that the student's continued inclusion in the small group impeded the progress of the other students in the group. Thus, the decision to provide one-to-one instruction for these students was determined to be in the best interests of the other students in the Tier 2 group as well as the individual student. In our research, the number of students who were provided with one-to-one instruction in kindergarten was very small—less than 1% of the students who participated in intervention.

RTI in First Grade

We advocate universal screening at the beginning of each school year and suggest that students who fall below the 25th or 30th percentile be given special attention. Exactly what sort of special attention they receive would depend on their instructional and achievement history. For example, students who were identified as at risk in kindergarten and demonstrated limited progress when provided with both Tier 1 and Tier 2 interventions would be provided with a combination of one-to-one intervention (Tier 3) and differentiated classroom instruction (Tier 1) at the beginning of first grade (see Scanlon et al., 2010). Students who were at risk in kindergarten and had made good progress with Tier 1 and Tier 2 interventions might be provided with a period of less intensive intervention (a combination of Tier 1 and Tier 2) at the beginning of first grade on the assumption that their performance levels at the beginning of first grade were the result of limited engagement with literacy over the summer months and that classroom and supplemental small-group instruction could compensate for these limitations.

For students who had never been identified as at risk in kindergarten, poor performance at the beginning of first grade might, once again, be due to limited literacy engagement over the summer months. For these students, a period of classroom instruction alone (Tier 1) might be the most appropriate first step. For students who are new to the school at the beginning of first grade and come with limited instructional histories, the most logical move might be to provide them with a combination of Tier 1 and Tier 2 interventions, if there are appropriate instructional groups available for them, as their limited skills might well be attributable to limitations in instruction. If their skills are extremely low, a combination of both Tier 3 and Tier 1 interventions is likely to be the most effective way to institute the degree of acceleration necessary to allow them to meet grade-level expectations. Thus, at grade 1, decisions about the level of intervention to offer students who qualify for the close-monitoring group hinge on the students' histories (or lack thereof) of responding to instructional interventions.

As the school year progresses, adjustments should be made in the intensity of intervention offered to the students receiving various tiers of intervention. Adjustments might include reducing or increasing the intensity of intervention. For students who make very limited progress despite highly intensive, comprehensive, and responsive intervention (i.e., daily one-to-one intervention provided over a protracted period of time by a teacher with expertise in supporting early literacy development), next steps might include referring the student for additional forms of evaluation to identify potential barriers to progress and identifying the student as being in need of special education services. Although there is little evidence that such a designation will enhance literacy development, it is often necessary for the purposes of providing the students with the level of ongoing support that they will need to cope with the demands of learning grade-level content related to literacy and other academic domains. However, once a student is identified as LD, it is important to continue to provide literacy instruction that is as comprehensive and intensive as possible (see Chapter 4). Our work with older students identified as LD suggests that intensive, responsive, and comprehensive literacy instruction can dramatically accelerate the progress of students identified as LD (see Chapter 9).

RTI in Second Grade and Beyond

Although we have yet to do formal intervention research in second and third grade, we have provided consultation and guidance for teachers who are providing intervention at these grade levels. In our experience, some schools have taken seriously the notion that, in an RTI model, students should progress through three successive tiers regardless of the grade level at which the process begins. We strongly advise against such a plan. Students who are performing far below their grade-level peers are unlikely to benefit from a period of Tier 1 intervention alone (see Chapters 3 and 4). More intensive interventions should be instituted as early in the school year as possible.

Professional Development Based on the ISA

Structure of the Professional Development Program

Implied but unaddressed in the earlier discussion of the RTI model is the importance of providing students identified as at risk with appropriately targeted and high-quality instruction. A basic tenet of RTI is that high-quality instruction is provided at each of the tiers of intervention and schools are expected to document the quality of instruction by demonstrating that most students make progress. One potential use of the periodic assessments is to identify instructional situations that are not working for students and take steps to strengthen that instruction. As noted earlier, we are impressed by the research indicating that what the teacher knows and does is more important to student achievement than the program that the teacher uses. In preparing teachers to more effectively promote students' reading development, our emphases are on developing teacher knowledge and skills and encouraging schools to promote consistency and coherence across instructional settings.

In our most recent study (Scanlon et al., 2008), intervention and classroom teachers participated in essentially the same professional development program. The program consisted of a summer workshop, a detailed handbook that reiterated and elaborated on the content of the workshop, and various follow-up activities during the ensuing school year. For kindergarten classroom teachers, the program encompassed a three-day summer workshop, while for first-grade teachers, the workshop was four days in length. At both grade levels, the workshop was followed by monthly grade-level meetings within participating schools and periodic (one-to-one) classroom observation/coaching sessions. In these sessions, the teachers were observed during their language arts instruction, and then they met with an early literacy collaborator (ELC) who is an expert in the ISA. The purpose of these sessions was to help the teacher implement the ISA in a coordinated way with the literacy curriculum that was already in place in the school/classroom. These collaboration sessions occurred, at a minimum, five times per year.

Kindergarten and first-grade intervention teachers participated in the same initial workshop as did classroom teachers plus a day or two that focused on the planning, delivery, and documentation of small-group (Tier 2) and one-to-one (Tier 3) intervention lessons. Throughout the period of professional development, both intervention and classroom teachers were repeatedly reminded that they were teaching children, not programs, and that to be optimally effective, every effort must be made to ensure that instruction did not provide students with conflicting views of the literacy process. For example, intervention teachers were encouraged to learn about and support their students' classroom language arts program so that the students who knew the least would not be asked to learn more than their classroom peers. Furthermore, intervention teachers were encouraged to learn about the phonics instruction that was being provided in the classroom and support the students' development of skill relative to that program rather than introduce an entirely different approach to teaching phonics skills.

The monthly professional development sessions for classroom teachers were planned for individual buildings and grade levels and based on teacher concerns and interests and on the ELC's sense of priorities relative to helping teachers implement the ISA in the context of the existing curriculum. However, in general, the monthly meetings tended to revolve around one of the main goals of the ISA (as described later in this chapter) and often involved revisiting the content that had been presented in the initial summer workshop.

For the intervention teachers, follow-up professional development occurred in group meetings that occurred every other week at the research center. During these meetings, the content of the workshop and handbook were revisited and intervention sessions were reviewed and discussed. Audio or video recordings of intervention sessions were periodically reviewed at these meetings. In addition, intervention teachers were periodically observed and coached by the ELC assigned to their school as they taught their small-group or one-to-one intervention sessions. Generally the individual observations occurred once every four to eight weeks, depending on the perceived need of the intervention teacher.

The observations often focused on the group or individual students whom the intervention teacher found to be most challenging to teach. These coaching sessions usually had a collaborative, student-focused, problem-solving approach, and every effort was made to avoid having the teachers feel that the purpose was evaluative.

Content of the ISA Professional Development Program

Early literacy instruction based on the ISA is intended to be highly responsive to what individual students know and are able to do and to be useful in and supportive of a variety of classroom language arts curricula. The ISA professional development program focused on the need for teachers to be knowledgeable about the potential causes of early reading difficulties and the ways in which various types of difficulties might be addressed through instruction. Early in the workshop component of the professional development program, we introduced and discussed a set of basic instructional principles that were intended to guide teachers' efforts to be responsive to and supportive of the skills and abilities of individual students. Once introduced, these basic principles were revisited throughout the duration of the professional development program and, we hoped, would serve as guiding principles throughout the teachers' careers.

The major focus of the ISA professional development program is a set of instructional goals for beginning readers. For each of the goals, teachers were provided with a brief review of the theory and research related to the goal and a more thorough discussion of how the goal might be accomplished through instructional interactions. In presenting each goal, its relationship to the other instructional goals (particularly the end goal of reading comprehension) was also discussed. Our intention was that, by using a goal structure to guide their observations of students and their resultant instructional planning and decision making, instruction would ultimately be very purpose oriented rather than activity oriented and, as a result, be much more effective in accelerating students' progress. We discuss the instructional principles of the ISA followed by the goals for the students in the sections that follow.

Instructional Principles of the ISA

Five basic instructional principles are taught and repeatedly revisited during the course of the ISA professional development program. These principles are described in the following sections. It is important to note that the principles are not necessarily ordered by importance.

Principle 1: Adopt a Vygotskian Perspective on Teaching and Learning

Vygotsky (1978) was a developmental theorist who believed that much of what a child learns is the result of extended interactions with an adult or more expert "other." From his perspective, the skills that children acquire reflect the internalization of problem solving that the child has initially done in collaboration with an adult who has provided careful verbal guidance to direct the child's thinking. Children are believed to internalize the verbal guidance initially provided by the teacher (or expert other) in such a way that it ultimately becomes a form of inner speech that guides the children's thinking when they encounter similar problem-solving situations. Because reading acquisition essentially involves the children in solving a series of cognitive problems, we feel that this characterization of the teaching–learning process is valuable, as it focuses on helping children become effective problem solvers—or strategic readers.

If we assume that the adult's speech (and through it, the adult's thinking) is, on some level, internalized by the child, then it becomes important to carefully consider instructional language. It is important to try to take the perspective of a student relative to teacher language. In the English language, there are multiple terms that can refer to the same concept and multiple concepts that are sometimes labeled with the same term. Therefore, it is easy, particularly with students who struggle with literacy acquisition, for teachers to inadvertently use terminology that carries no meaning or a different meaning for an individual student. For example, some beginning kindergartners might think a letter is something that comes in the mail, not a squiggle that is associated with a sound. It is remarkably easy to wrongly assume that students know or understand things and as a result have an instructional episode be quite confusing to them. Virtually every teacher has had this experience.

It is also important to give students the opportunity to see how to use the problem-solving processes we teach. Because problem solving is a thinking process, the only way the students can "see" the process is if we think out loud. The name for this approach to instruction is called think-aloud. It has been found to be an important component of instruction in attempts to develop strategic thinking. When we think out loud for the students, we are essentially guiding the development of their thinking. The use of think-alouds is particularly relevant when we attempt to teach students to use strategies.

Vygotsky (1978) also argued that the most effective instruction focuses on skills and abilities that are somewhat too challenging for the child to handle independently but are easy enough for the child to handle when assistance is offered at key points. The disparity between what children are able to do with and without assistance is referred to as the zone of proximal development (ZPD). To instruct in the ZPD, the teacher needs to offer learning opportunities that present some challenge, but not so much as to overwhelm the child.

Based on Vygotsky's theory, Wood, Bruner, and Ross (1976) developed the concept of scaffolding as an analogy for the role that skilled collaborators play in supporting a student's learning. Scaffolding involves the provision of temporary supports that allow students to successfully accomplish a task that is too challenging for them to accomplish on their own. Scaffolding also involves the gradual reduction of support as students demonstrate the ability to regulate their own thinking and problem solving. To do the types of assessment, modification, and scaffolding suggested earlier, it is necessary for the teacher to have a firm grasp of the developmental progression of the skills he or she is helping the students develop. The development of such expertise is a focus in much of the ISA professional development program.

Principle 2: Provide Engagement Opportunities for All Students

In general, the more reading and writing students do and the more they practice the underlying skills that are foundational for reading and writing, the more quickly they become proficient. This is true when students actually engage in the cognitive processes required to read and write. Unfortunately, students sometimes find ways of avoiding the thinking parts of instructional activities. For example, in a choral reading situation, when the entire class or group is engaged in reading the same text, some students might not be looking at the words and thinking about them. Rather, they might be simply gazing in the right direction and saying the words slightly after their friends say them. These students might look engaged, and might in fact be engaged in the meaning construction part of the process, but they are not involved in the kind of thinking that will help them learn to read on their own. They need the opportunity to read text to the teacher or to a friend to fully engage in the necessary thinking processes.

Similar types of disengagement can arise when a teacher calls on one student before asking a question, because the students who are not called on know that they are not expected to answer. If, on the other hand, the teacher asks the question without immediately calling on an individual, more students are likely to engage in the thinking that the task involves. Better still, if all the students have dry erase boards or chalkboards to write on, they could all engage in the task. During a shared writing activity, the teacher might say, "Write down the letter you think I need at the beginning of the word *dog*." This allows every student to respond, and, as a result, they are all likely to benefit from the instructional interaction. We strongly encourage teachers to incorporate opportunities for every student to respond during the course of instruction and ensure that the thinking that the students actually engage in moves them forward relative to the instructional goal of the activity.

Principle 3: Set High Expectations for All Students

At various points in the history of education, people have believed that some children are destined to have great difficulty learning to read or write and that there is little to be done to help them overcome their difficulties. Research has demonstrated that students tend to live up to the expectations we have for them. Thus, a belief that a student is unlikely to make progress has the clear potential to slow the progress made by that student. Conversely, the expectation that a student will succeed academically increases the likelihood that he or she will. In fact, research conducted in "Beat the Odds" schools, where students succeed at much higher levels than might be expected given their socioeconomic circumstances, indicates that a common characteristic of such schools is that all school staff hold high expectations for all of the students (Taylor, Pearson, Clark, & Walpole, 2000).

RTI approaches to literacy learning difficulties arose from the research demonstrating that nearly all students can make substantial progress in acquiring literacy skills if instruction is appropriately targeted to meet their needs. This research makes it easier to hold high expectations for students who initially demonstrate limited literacy skills. Every student is expected to do well in reading and writing development, and if the student is not progressing, we now know that it is more important to examine the instruction than to examine the student to try to determine what has gone wrong. Students learn what we teach them, as long as we teach them what they are prepared to learn. The challenge, of course, is that the students in any given classroom generally are not all ready to learn the same things, at least with regard to reading and writing. Nevertheless, students are all expected to attain the same grade-level standards, which is why a tiered approach to instruction and intervention is so important to promoting literacy success.

Principle 4: Interface Support Services With the Classroom Program

For students who are receiving intervention services beyond the classroom, it is important that the instruction in all settings work to mutually supportive ends. This principle was discussed earlier but warrants reiteration because so many RTI efforts seem to violate this principle. There are many ways in which classroom and supplemental instruction can be profitably interfaced. For example, at the kindergarten level, if instruction about the alphabet is sequenced in a particular way, it makes sense to sequence alphabet instruction in intervention settings to parallel the instructional sequence in the classroom. Similarly, if keywords are used in the classroom to support the learning of letter sounds, supplementary instruction should use the same keywords.

Additional suggestions include, when appropriate, teaching and practicing the same high-frequency words across settings, using at least some of the same reading materials across settings, and engaging the students in similar writing activities. By increasing the congruence between classroom and supplementary instruction, we hope to increase the instructional impact of both the classroom program and the intervention program. The students who struggle in the classroom program will be better prepared for subsequent instruction in that program if they have reviewed some of the material in another context.

Principle 5: Plan for Success

In all instructional interactions, teachers should make every effort to structure the activities so that the students experience success and the rewarding feelings that go along with success. The teachers should look for opportunities to provide genuine praise for the students' efforts and avoid negative and discouraging comments. Although teachers might sometimes feel frustrated that they have yet to find a way to help a particular student accomplish a particular objective, communicating this frustration only serves to make the student feel that his or her situation might be hopeless. If the student is not progressing in a certain area, it is important to try to determine the source of the problem. Perhaps the level of difficulty needs to be reduced. Perhaps the student is misconstruing the task. Perhaps the teacher is using terminology for certain concepts that differs from the terminology to which the student is accustomed.

Instructional Goals of the ISA

In this section, we present the five instructional goals around which we encourage teachers to build their instruction in classroom and intervention settings. During professional development workshops, we emphasize that the goals can be pursued in a variety of instructional contexts (e.g., one-to-one, small group, whole class) and components (e.g., read-aloud, shared reading, supported reading, writing). Teachers are encouraged to view instruction as a goal-oriented activity wherein they work to help students achieve identified goals using a variety of instructional formats and materials. The goals range from the relatively simple and straightforward (e.g., developing letter-name knowledge) to complex and involved (e.g., helping students become strategic and active readers).

As we discuss each goal, we highlight the importance of being able to view literacy and literacy-related skills from the perspective of a young child who is a relative novice when it comes to understanding the intricacies of written language and how it relates to spoken language. Often in our formal and informal observations of teachers working with young students, and in our own work with young students who are having difficulty learning about written language, we are struck by how difficult it is for highly literate people to take a step back and understand the complexity of reading and writing processes from the perspective of a young person who is just learning about print. It is difficult to respond to a child's confusion if one does not understand the source of the confusion.

In a forthcoming book describing the ISA (Scanlon et al., 2010), we discuss each goal in detail, review the relevant research related to the goal, and discuss why and how the goal relates to reading and writing processes more generally. We also discuss and provide sample instructional activities that can be used to help the student accomplish the goal, and where relevant, we discuss more and less challenging aspects of particular activities, often presenting a sequence of objectives within given goals. We also discuss the kinds of difficulties students might have, why they have those difficulties, and what teachers can do to alleviate those difficulties. Here, because such detail is obviously beyond the scope of a single chapter, we list each goal and briefly discuss it. With the exception of the first goal, Motivation to Read and Write, the ordering of the goals should not be taken as an indication of their importance.

Goal 1: Motivation to Read and Write

The student will develop the belief that reading and writing are enjoyable and informative activities that are not beyond his or her capabilities.

In discussing this goal, we focus on a variety of factors that contribute to motivation, such as ensuring that students face an appropriate level of challenge in literacy tasks, that they have some choice in what they read, that teachers model enthusiasm for reading and writing activities and actively engage students in thinking about and responding to texts, that read-aloud is an important and interactive part of the day, and that teachers should construe reading and writing as pleasant and rewarding activities rather than as jobs (e.g., "You *get* to finish your book before recess," rather than, "You *have* to finish your book before recess."). Related to the later point, teachers are encouraged to avoid the use of stickers or other tokens to reward engagement in literate activity, as such rewards have the potential to communicate to students that reading and writing are work that requires an external reinforcement rather than inherently rewarding activities. Early on, when teachers feel that they absolutely need some sort of reward to elicit engagement, they are encouraged to use the opportunity to play one of several literacy skill games that have proven to be quite motivating for students and that also help promote the development of foundational literacy skills.

Goal 2: Alphabetics

The student will understand the relationships between printed and spoken language and will be able to use these relationships in reading and writing.

Within this overarching goal, there are several interrelated subgoals that pertain to the development of skill with the alphabetic code.

Purposes and Conventions of Print

The student will understand that the purpose of print is to communicate. The student will also understand the most basic print conventions, such as the left-to-right and top-

to-bottom sequencing of print, where to begin reading a book, and the concepts of letter and word.

In the current iteration of the ISA, this is the first subgoal addressed in the alphabetics goal, largely because, if students do not have some insight into the purposes and conventions of print, it will be difficult for them to make much progress relative to alphabetic knowledge. Thus, the discussion of this goal is critical, albeit brief relative to the other goals addressed. The main points made are that some students experience confusion related to purposes of print and to the conventions relating to how print is organized. Therefore, in early instruction, teachers need to be explicit about these concepts.

For example, during shared reading activities, teachers of emergent readers should point to the words as they read and, on occasion, engage the students in discussions of where on the page to begin reading, which way to progress, and so on. Teachers are also encouraged to make pointed use of key terms that are potentially confusing for early literacy learners. For example, while jointly examining a page in an emergent-level text with a group of students, the teacher might talk about how many words are in the sentence, what the spaces are for, how many letters there are in a particular word, and so on. As students progress, more advanced print conventions are discussed, such as the role of punctuation marks and variations in print size.

In addressing this goal, we also discuss the areas of confusion students demonstrate at the early stages of learning to read. Because many of these areas (such as calling a *b* a *d*) were once thought to be hallmarks of reading disability or dyslexia, it is important for teachers to understand that the instructional guidance they provide when the students make such errors can help avoid long-term confusion of this sort. It is remarkable to us that, although the research community has known for decades that such confusion is due to the student's difficulty in remembering which symbol is called by which name, we have failed to effectively communicate this fact to the public at large. Thus, we still encounter some teachers and many parents who believe that these areas of confusion are caused by visual processing difficulties. Learning that a written symbol's orientation in space is a significant clue to its identity is an important convention of print that students need to learn. Because the confusion of lowercase *b* and *d* tends to be common, we encourage teachers to provide a graphic display of an upper- and lowercase *B* and *D* (see Figure 2.1), so students can check themselves when they are uncertain of the identity of the lowercase version. (Students do not tend to confuse the uppercase versions of these letters.)

Figure 2.1. Graphic Used to Prevent *b/d* Confusion

Phoneme Awareness

The student will have a conceptual grasp of the fact that words are made up of somewhat separable sound segments. Further, the student will be able to say individual sounds in simple words spoken by the teacher and blend separate sounds to form whole words.

In order for students to understand the relationships between the letters in printed words and the sounds in spoken words and effectively use that knowledge in reading and writing, they must gain some insight into the phonemic nature of spoken language. In addressing this goal, we first work to attune teachers to the phonemes in spoken language. Many highly literate adults are confused about how to segment words in which there are more letters than sounds (e.g., three = /th/-/r/-/ē/) or more sounds than letters (e.g., box = /b/-/o/-/k/-/s/), and we find the need to emphasize that, for the purpose of instruction in phonemic awareness, teachers need to think about sounds and not letters. We discuss various approaches to developing phonemic awareness, with a particular emphasis on blending (i.e., hearing separate phonemes spoken by the teacher and blending them to form a word) and segmenting (i.e., articulating the separate sounds in a word). We discuss the relative difficulty of analyzing words into different units (e.g., onsets and rimes versus individual phonemes).

We also discuss the features of phonemes that make them more and less challenging for students to attend to or manipulate. For example, some phonemes, such as the sounds represented in print by the letters *M* and *S*, can be elongated without distorting them (e.g., "mmmm" or "ssss"), thereby making it relatively easy to draw students' attention to them in spoken words. However, other phonemes, such as the sounds associated with the letters *B* and *K*, cannot be elongated without distortion. For example, the sound for *B* is typically pronounced "buh," and we have often heard teachers emphasize the sound as "buuuhhhh," which is not particularly helpful to a student trying to attend to the /b/.

We try to instill in teachers the understanding that it would be easier to draw students' attention to the sounds in the word *fin* than to the sounds in the word *dot,* because all of the sounds in *fin* can be elongated without distortion whereas neither of the consonant sounds in *dot* can be. Once teachers are secure in this understanding, it is much easier for them to plan instruction for students who have little to no phonemic analysis skill (and so need instruction that uses words comprised of stretchable sounds) and adjust instruction in accord with the differing skills of students in an instructional group. As students demonstrate a grasp of the phonemic analysis concepts for words with stretchable sounds, instruction moves on to include words in which the sounds cannot be elongated without distortion.

To document progress and guide instructional planning, teachers are encouraged to use checklists of skills. The checklist for phonological skills is presented in Figure 2.2. This version provides space for teachers to record their observations of phonological skills for students in a small group (up to five). The checklist is organized around the major skills that are the focus of instruction and, within each major objective, the progression that would be followed in helping students achieve that objective.

To limit the paperwork burden, teachers are encouraged to use the notational system provided at the bottom of the form that involves marking a single slash to indicate that instruction has begun to address a particular objective, crossing that slash (to form an *X*) when the student appears to be making progress in accomplishing the skill or objective, and adding a third line (to form an asterisk) when, in the teacher's judgment, the student has a firm grasp of the skill or concept and no longer needs instruction on that particular objective. Using such a system, it is easy for teachers and their supervisors to identify students who are making substantially less progress than their peers. There is also a clear connection between the documentation of student progress and instructional planning. Further, these checklists can be compared to determine whether there are discrepancies in progress between instructional groups that may require attention.

Letter Identification

The student will be able to name, rapidly and accurately, all 26 letters of the alphabet, both upper- and lowercase versions.

For students who know very little about the alphabet, initial instruction focuses on teaching the names of letters rather than teaching simultaneously about the

Figure 2.2. Group Snapshot for Phonological Skills

Group Snapshot: Phonological Skills					
Student Names					
I. Sensitivity in Text					
Completes rhyme in known text					
Identifies rhyme in text					
Identifies alliteration in text					
II. Sound Sorting					
Beginning sound					
Rhyme					
Ending sound					
Medial vowel					
III. Sound Blending					
Onset–rime with pictures					
Onset–rime without pictures					
Single phoneme with pictures					
Single phoneme without pictures					
IV. Sound Counting/Segmentation					
Two phonemes, with stretchable consonants					
Two phonemes, with stop consonants					
Three phonemes, with stretchable consonants					
Three phonemes, with stop consonants					
Words with consonant blends					

◨ Beginning   ⊠ Developing   ⊠ Proficient

letters' names, sounds, and keyword mnemonics as is often done in kindergarten programs. Students with very limited knowledge are likely to become overwhelmed if asked to learn all of that at once. In rationalizing the initial focus on letter names, we focus on how young children often rely on the names of the letters as an aid to remembering their sounds. For example, the sound for the letter *B* is the first phoneme in its name (/b/). Thus, if students know the name of the letter, it will be easier for them to remember the sound of the letter. This relationship between the letter name and the letter sound works for most but not all of the letters of the English alphabet.

We stress the importance of teachers developing sensitivity to young students' inclination to use letter names to derive letter sounds because understanding what the students are doing influences the feedback that teachers provide. For example, if a student wrote the word *chip* as *HP*, a teacher might well respond by trying to help the student analyze the beginning sound in the word *chip*, thereby confusing the student who selected the *H* to represent the /ch/ because the name of the letter "aich" includes the phoneme /ch/—just as the name of the letter *M* includes the phoneme /m/.

In discussing this goal, we also begin to address fluency with foundational skills as an important contributor to reading comprehension. We stress that automaticity with letter identification is important to free up cognitive resources for higher level skills. To promote fluency with letter identification, we stress the importance of having the students use the letter names frequently during the course of the various activities used to promote letter-name knowledge.

Letter–Sound Association

The student will be able to associate the most common sounds of individual letters with their printed representations.

In discussing this goal, we continue to focus on the relationship between letter names and letter sounds, how to take advantage of that relationship, and how to address the areas of confusion that arise for those letters where the relationship does not hold (i.e., the consonants *H*, *W*, and *Y* and most of the short vowels). We discuss the importance of using keywords to help students remember letter–sound correspondences, using the same keywords across instructional settings and grade levels, and explicitly teaching students how to use the keywords when reading and writing. In contrast to these recommendations, our observations in kindergarten and first-grade classrooms have revealed that teachers often have multiple alphabet strips on display that are used inconsistently, if at all, and the students are rarely taught how to use the keywords independently. Moreover, some of the keywords used are poor exemplars of the sounds they are supposed to represent. For example, the words *train* and *truck* are sometimes used as keywords for *T*, although when pronounced, both sound like they begin with a /ch/ as in *chrain* and *chruck*.

The Alphabetic Principle
The student will understand that the letters in printed words represent the sounds in spoken words and will understand how to use the alphabetic code to read and spell words.

In discussing this goal, we follow a progression from an early understanding about how the letters in printed words represent the sounds in spoken words, initially focusing on beginning sounds, then ending sounds, and then the interior parts of words. As the students progress, they are taught about consonant digraphs (e.g., *sh*, *ch*, *th*) and learn to decode consonant blends through a process of sounding each consonant and then blending the sounds together.

In teaching about vowel sounds, each vowel is taught individually. For each vowel, its two most common sounds are taught simultaneously, with the logic being that this requires the students to learn only one new association for the vowel because they will have already learned the name of the letter, hence its long-vowel sound. Additional logic, and the most important one, for this approach to teaching vowel sounds is that many of the spelling–sound inconsistencies that characterize the English writing system involve the vowels. We argue that if students come to view vowels as decision points and learn to be flexible about the vowel sounds they try as they are attempting to puzzle through unfamiliar words encountered in text, they will be able to successfully identify a higher number of the words encountered.

For example, if a student encounters the sentence "The boy saw a wild dog," and initially decoded the *i* in *wild* as a short *I*, the result would be a nonsensical sentence: "The boy saw a willed dog." However, assuming that the student was attending to meaning and therefore was alerted to the decoding problem, the student's awareness of the need to be flexible with the vowels (i.e., try alternate sounds) is apt to allow him or her to accurately identify the word *wild*, thus allowing the student to comprehend the sentence and helping add the word *wild* to the body of words that he or she can identify automatically.

It is interesting to note that several of the teachers with whom we have worked over the years were initially reluctant to teach their students about the vowel-flexing strategy, because they thought it would be too difficult and confusing for them. However, once they tried it, they reported success and surprise at how effective it was in facilitating students' word-solving attempts. The use of vowel flexing while reading connected text is discussed in greater detail in Goal 3.

With regard to the alphabetics goal, however, it is important to note that the vehicle used for helping students become facile with the alphabetics skills discussed thus far is to engage students in exercises focused on isolated words. Such exercises include word building, in which students use a limited set of letter tiles to build words dictated by the teacher; word reading, in which the teacher makes words with letter tiles and the students read them; and word writing, in which students write words dictated by the teacher without the support of having a limited set of letter tiles (as in word building).

In these activities, minimal changes are made from one word to the next so that the students' attention can be focused on the part(s) of the words that are under study. For example, when the students are learning about vowels, most of the changes involve alternations between the long and short sounds for a particular vowel. For instance, students might be taught the two sounds for *A* and the vowel-consonant-e (VCe) long-vowel spelling pattern and then be asked to build the following words, one after the next: *mat, mate, fate, fat, hat, hate, rate, rat,* and so on. Once students are facile with building, reading, and writing words that include the two sounds of *A*, the long and short sounds of another vowel would be taught and practiced (e.g., *bit, bite, kite, kit, dim, dime*). Later, the two vowels would be used in practice activities (e.g., *bit, bat, fat, fate, fame, tame, time, Tim*). The point of these practice activities is to help students become so flexible with the vowel sounds that they can readily draw on this knowledge when encountering unfamiliar words in text.

The Development of More Extensive Decoding and Encoding Strategies
The student will develop the ability to use both single-letter phonics and a variety of spelling patterns (e.g., phonograms, prefixes, suffixes) to decode and spell individual words.

Although it is fairly common practice for teachers to instruct beginning readers on the use of phonograms, or word families, as decoding elements, we find that this instruction is often not as effective as it could be, because the instructional technique most often used involves having the students work with only one word family at a time. For example, the teacher might teach the -ight word family and engage students in making and reading the words *might, sight, bright, light, tight,* and so on. In this activity, all students really need to attend to is the beginning part of the words, as that is the only part that changes. As a result, at least for some students, little is learned about the word family.

As an alternative, we have found it useful to have students working with at least two word families at a time. For example, once a new word family has been introduced and practiced, additional practice is provided with it in combination with one or more previously taught word families. Thus, the students might be engaged in building, reading, and writing the words *might, make, take, tight, fight, fake,* and so on. As for other decoding skills, we stress teaching and practicing each new coding skill in isolation prior to providing the opportunity for application in context. Thus, the new word family a teacher chooses to teach in a particular lesson would be drawn from a book that includes several instances of words in that family.

In first grade, we also teach students tactics for puzzling through words that are comprised of more than one syllable. Often this instruction occurs when the words are encountered in context, but for students who frequently struggle with such words, some isolated practice may also be provided. In first grade, the most commonly encountered multisyllabic words are those with inflectional endings (e.g., *running, wanted*). For these, we teach students to notice and temporarily ignore the endings (perhaps by covering up the ending with a finger), then decode the rest of the word, and then add the ending. We also teach breaking a word between double consonants and decoding each part, and we teach the C+le syllable pattern to provide the students with the logic for decoding words like *little, apple,* and *twinkle.*

Throughout our discussion on the alphabetics goal, teachers are reminded that opportunities to apply skills in context are important. Further, we encourage teachers to think through how instruction should proceed by considering what makes a decoding task more or less challenging and what materials the students will be reading. We also stress the benefits of guiding students to be strategic in using resources such as the keywords and word family charts to assist them in decoding and encoding activities.

Goal 3: Word Learning and the Development of Sight Vocabulary
The student will learn to effortlessly identify a large number of words.

To comprehend written material, readers need to be able to identify most of the words in the text with relative ease. This allows readers to devote most of their cognitive resources to the meaning-making enterprise. Thus, a major goal of early literacy instruction is to help students build their sight vocabularies as quickly as possible. In discussing the development of sight vocabulary and how to facilitate its growth, we make a distinction between high-frequency words (e.g., *the, of, and, is*) and words that have a lower frequency of occurrence (e.g., *hop, swim, horse*) in both print and spoken language.

In the ISA, teachers are encouraged to teach high-frequency words directly and explicitly, because knowing these words to the point of automaticity will enable students to read approximately 50% of the words they encounter in just about any text. With regard to less frequently occurring words, however, a different tactic is needed. There is no way that teachers could possibly teach the tens of thousands of words that readers ultimately come to know as sight words. Therefore, students need to learn these words pretty much on their own through extensive reading of texts that provide some but not too much challenge and by effectively puzzling through and accurately identifying unfamiliar words encountered in text.

Share (1995) suggests that the ability to figure out unfamiliar words serves as a self-teaching mechanism. The notion that readers teach themselves most of the words in their sight vocabularies is a pivotal concept in the ISA, as it provides the logic for the heavy emphasis we place on explicitly teaching students to be strategic and active word solvers. In the ISA, teachers are taught two basic approaches to promoting the development of sight vocabulary: a strategic word-learning approach that aims to help students develop a self-teaching mechanism and a direct-teaching approach for high-frequency words that is used to speed the process of establishing these important words in the students' sight vocabularies. Thus, there are two word-learning subgoals, each of which focuses on a different vehicle for word learning.

Strategic Word Learning

The student will develop flexibility and independence in applying a variety of strategies to facilitate the identification of unfamiliar words encountered in text.

The development of word-learning strategies is an important goal of the ISA and one of the most prominent ways in which it differs from other approaches to early literacy instruction and intervention. Instead of simply encouraging students to access a variety of sources of information in attempting to decode and confirm the identity of unfamiliar words encountered while reading, in the ISA we explicitly teach students to use a specific set of word-identification strategies (see Figure 2.3). The strategies include four code-based strategies (the second,

Figure 2.3. ISA Word Identification Strategy List

To figure out a word:

 Check the pictures.

fun   Think about the sounds in the word.

??   Think of words that might make sense.

sat   Look for word families or other parts you know.

 Read past the puzzling word.

 Go back to the beginning of the sentence and start again.

a e i o u   Try different pronunciations for some of the letters, especially the vowel(s).

Look / ing   Break the word into smaller parts.

---

third, seventh, and eighth strategies on the list) and four meaning-based strategies (the four other strategies on the list). The strategies are taught one at a time in preparation for reading a book in which a strategy is likely to be particularly useful.

Teachers follow a gradual release of responsibility procedure (Pearson & Gallagher, 1983) and begin by explaining what the strategy is, why it is useful, and how it is used. Then, they model the use of the strategy using a think-aloud procedure. For example, while reading a portion of text, the teacher might say,

> I am going to pretend that I don't know this word, and I'll use our new strategy to figure it out. Our new strategy is, "Look for word families or other parts you know." We know that we can find word families by looking for the vowel and what comes after it. So, I find the vowel *I* and look at the next couple of letters: *g, h, t*. I-g-h-t! That is a word family we have learned: -ight. So, all I have to do is blend -ight with the first sound, /m/, and I get *might*. Then, I have to read the sentence to see if might makes sense. "Mom said she might let us stay up late." That makes sense, doesn't it? So, looking for the word family helped us figure out that word.

As each new strategy is taught, students are encouraged to use the strategy in an interactive and confirmatory way in conjunction with previously learned strategies. Early on, students are encouraged to use as much of the code-based information as they are able to use (based on the teacher's observations of the students' skills during alphabetic activities) and confirm or reject their initial hypotheses about the identity of a word using context-based strategies. For strategies that are new to the students, the teacher prompts them to use the strategy when they are fairly certain that the strategy will work in a particular context. As the students experience success in using the strategies when prompted, the teacher gradually withdraws his or her support in an effort to have the students take responsibility for word solving and confirming hypotheses about a word's identity.

Until students clearly demonstrate that they are routinely and effectively strategic in word solving, strategies are discussed before, during, and after the students engage in reading. Thus, before reading, the teacher might teach a new strategy or engage the students in reviewing the strategies that have recently been taught. During reading, the teacher might prompt a student to use a particular strategy or, depending on the student's point in development, ask, "What can you try?" when the student encounters a puzzling word. If necessary, the teacher might suggest that the student check his or her strategy list. On occasion, the teacher would engage the students in reflecting on their word-solving successes. For example, when a student hesitates on a word and then identifies it, the teacher might say, "I saw you thinking about that word. How did you figure it out?"

An important objective for teachers in this instructional interaction is to be sure to give students as much responsibility for word solving and confirming as they are ready to handle. We have found this to be a bit of a challenge for teachers who are, by nature, helpful. We often encounter teachers who are new to the ISA doing too much of the thinking for the students. For example, when a student has been puzzling over a word and finally pronounces it correctly, the teacher would jump in and confirm the identification (e.g., "Uh-huh!" "Nice job!"). In doing so, the teacher deprives the student from engaging in the final step of the word-solving process—confirming that the identified word fits the sentence and that the sounds in the word match the letters.

Another teacher behavior that we try to retrain during the course of professional development is the habit of alerting students to word-identification errors by asking, "Does that make sense?" Because many teachers use this question only when something does not make sense, the question is interpreted by students to mean there is something wrong. Because we want students to be alert to meaning-disrupting errors/miscues, it is important to ask that question both when the sentence does make sense and does not, as this will help the students do the monitoring on their own.

As teachers listen to students read, they make note of the strategies the students use either spontaneously or with prompting. This information helps inform their future planning around word-identification strategy instruction. Planning for future instruction is also facilitated by the reflection on strategy use that occurs after the students have finished their reading. At this point in the lesson, the students and the teacher might engage in reflecting on the strategies that the students used, where they used them, which ones they still need to practice, and so forth.

The list of strategies provided in Figure 2.3 is gradually developed as the strategies and the mnemonic value of the symbol to the left of each strategy are taught. Students are encouraged to refer to the strategy list as a resource to remind them of the kinds of things they can do when puzzling over an unknown word. The rationale for teaching a small set of strategies explicitly is that, in doing so, we hope to provide students with a useful tool for self-prompting. In other words, with only a small set of strategies to think about, we expect that the students will ultimately be able to internalize them and independently guide their word-solving attempts.

Of course, there is a clear connection between the word-solving strategies taught and the approach to alphabetic instruction (as described earlier) and the emphasis on meaning making (as we describe later). Only when a student has the foundational alphabetics knowledge and the clear understanding that text is supposed to make sense will the interactive and confirmatory use of strategies be possible. To promote coordinated use of these multiple knowledge sources, teachers are encouraged to help students see the connections between and among the various components of instruction. For example, in teaching a decoding skill, the teacher would typically explain that the students will be able to use the skill when they are reading and come to an unfamiliar word that contains that particular pattern. While engaging students in meaning-focused activities such as interactive read-alouds, the teacher would model the use of some of the meaning-based word-identification strategies. For example, on occasions when the teacher inadvertently misidentifies a word, he or she might say, "That doesn't make sense! I need to go back and start again!"

As for other aspects of early literacy development, teachers are provided with checklists to use in documenting students' progress in becoming effective word solvers. Figure 2.4 provides an example of a record form that might be used in small-group instruction. These forms are referred to as "snapshots" because they provide teachers with a quick picture of where students in an instructional group are and where they are ready to go.

High-Frequency Words

The student will be able to quickly and accurately identify a large number of high-frequency words.

The most frequently occurring words tend to be difficult to learn because of their irregular spellings (e.g., *the, was, of, said*) and their abstract nature (e.g., how would you define *the*?). Therefore, we encourage teachers to explicitly teach and provide practice with these words. The first few words should be taught one at a time and in conjunction with having students read an emergent-level book that contains that word several times. After reading and reacting to the book, we would have the students go back into it to find and name the word each time it occurs. Later, the word would be used along with other previously taught words in gamelike practice activities.

Figure 2.4. Record Form for Strategic Word Learning: Use of Word-Identification Strategies

Group Snapshot: Strategic Word Learning Use of Word-Identification Strategies							
		Student Names					
Strategy							
CP—Check the Pictures							
TS—**T**hink about the **S**ounds in the word	First						
	Last						
	Medial						
MS—Think of words that might **M**ake **S**ense							
WP—Look for **W**ord families or other **P**arts you know							
RP—**R**ead **P**ast the puzzling word							
SA—Go back to the beginning of the sentence and **S**tart **A**gain							
DP—Try **D**ifferent **P**ronunciations for some of the letters, especially the vowel(s).							
BW—**B**reak the **W**ord into smaller parts							
IC—Use multiple strategies in an **I**nteractive and **C**onfirmatory way							

Use the markings below to characterize the students' level of proficiency for each word-identification strategy.

◻ **Beginning**   ⊠ **Developing**   ⊠ **Proficient**

Beginning indicates that instruction has addressed the strategy, but the student has only a preliminary understanding or capability with regard to its use.

Developing indicates that the students has some understanding of the strategy, but does not reliably or spontaneously use the strategy.

Proficient indicates that the student reliably and spontaneously demonstrates use of the strategy.

For example, the students might play tic-tac-toe with high-frequency words. Each student gets a different color marker, and on an individual's turn, he or she draws a word card from a deck, reads the word, and then writes it in the chosen space on the game board. The winner is determined by having three words of the same color in a row. Activities of this sort help stabilize the words' identities in the students' memories because they are naming and writing the words and, therefore, attending to their internal structure.

For the purpose of building high-frequency sight vocabulary, we have found it useful to employ books that build vocabulary in a cumulative way (i.e., a word that occurs frequently in the first book reappears in the second book but not as frequently, and again in the third book, and so on). Also, we have found that various series for books designed to help build high-frequency sight vocabulary can be differentially useful. For example, when a book uses a consistent and repetitive pattern (e.g., "I see the," "I see the," "I see the") from one page to the next, the students quickly memorize the pattern and, therefore, have little need to attend to the words. However, for a book in which the words are switched around a little, there is more of a need for the students to attend to the words, and as a result, students acquire the words more quickly. Figure 2.5 presents two renditions of a teacher-created book called *See My Pets*. The version on the left is more likely to help students learn the words *I*, *my*, and *see* than is the version on the right because the pattern is not entirely repetitive. The Short Books (myshortbooks .com/Default.aspx) are particularly good examples of the kinds of books we have found to be useful for developing skill in identifying the most frequently occurring words. However, virtually any of the sight word readers on the market can be modified in a way that would make them more useful for the purpose of building high-frequency sight vocabulary by using removable labels, a good primary font, and a printer.

For students who are further along in their reading development but continue to struggle with building high-frequency sight vocabulary, we have found that using books that include many repetitions of high-frequency words help to facilitate the development of this skill. For example, books by Margaret Hillert and Babs Bell Hajdusiewicz are particularly helpful. To keep the book easy and build in the desired repetition of high-frequency words, the language structures in these books tend to be rather unnatural. However, because the stories are supported by pictures and word repetition, students are able to read these books quite comfortably after the first few pages. We have encountered many students who were initially slow in acquiring high-frequency sight words who showed

Figure 2.5. Two Renditions of a Teacher-Created Book Called *See My Pets*

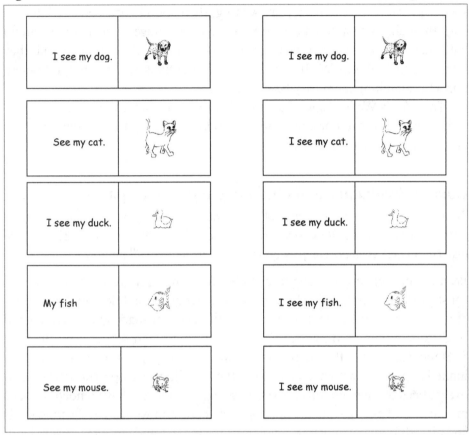

rapid gains in this aspect of reading when given the opportunity to read some of these books.

In working in small-group or one-to-one contexts with young struggling readers, we have also found it useful to maintain a "Words We [I] Know" chart that follows the format of a word wall but contains only the high-frequency words that the students in the group or the individual student knows. This chart is used for practice activities (e.g., reading all the words under the letter T) and as a reference for the students when they are reading and writing. Because our goal is for students to become automatic in their ability to identify high-frequency words, we encourage them to spell the words they know (i.e., the words on their chart) conventionally when they write by referring to the chart.

The logic here is that if students can read the word *was*, for example, but then spell it as *yz* or *wuz* when they are writing, their sound spellings will interfere with their ability to automatize the word. We encourage teachers to be careful with their wording when imposing this expectation. Telling students that they *get* to use their Words We [I] Know chart for the book spelling has a different impact than telling them they *have* to use it.

The Words We [I] Know chart can also be used as a form of progress monitoring for students in one-to-one intervention by tallying the number of words on the chart every week or two.

Goal 4: Vocabulary and Oral Language Development

The student will learn the meanings of new words encountered in instructional interactions and be able to use those words conversationally. Further, the student's ability to understand and use more complex grammatical structures will improve.

Reading and writing are language skills, therefore, to a great extent, they are constrained and determined by students' oral language abilities. Students' levels of vocabulary development measured in the early primary grades are a good predictors of their reading comprehension through high school (Cunningham & Stanovich, 1997). If students have limited knowledge of word meanings or limited experience with book language, their reading development will be negatively affected. Interventions for young struggling readers have tended to focus primarily on helping students develop alphabetic and word-identification skills and placed comparatively little emphasis on language and comprehension. Until our most recent intervention study (Scanlon et al., 2008), we too were guilty of this shortsightedness. However, because the 2008 study focused on schools that served a high percentage of students living in poverty, and thus more likely to have limited language skills (Hart & Risley, 1995), we began to address vocabulary and language skills more intentionally in our work with classroom and intervention teachers.

In this most recent study, we were frequently struck by the number of times students struggled to identify a word not because they could not figure out how it sounded but because they did not know the meaning of the word. Thus, students might precisely decode a word or come up with a close approximation of the word's pronunciation but be unable to confidently identify (confirm) it, because they had no word stored in verbal memory that matched it. At least for students living in poverty, it appears that limitations in vocabulary knowledge play a much greater role in early literacy development than is commonly recognized. Of course, influencing vocabulary development is a much larger undertaking than improving decoding skill, and we certainly do not feel that we have found an optimal way to address this daunting problem. Most studies that have specifically studied the effects of vocabulary interventions have found positive effects only for the words taught. They do not show generalized positive outcomes on word knowledge. Our results are no different. Nevertheless, because vocabulary knowledge plays such a pervasive role in reading comprehension and word learning, we are certain that teachers need to be more attuned to the role of vocabulary knowledge in early and long-term reading development and prepared to recognize and address difficulties that arise from limitations in vocabulary. Because vocabulary development is a gradual and ongoing process and most interventions for vocabulary and language skills have been of fairly limited duration, we remain hopeful that sustained and prolonged efforts to enhance these important language skills will, ultimately, prove to be effective.

In our 2008 intervention study we focused on interactive read-alouds as one of the most powerful means by which to enhance the vocabulary and language development of young children. Although, as noted previously, the professional development provided for classroom and intervention teachers was pretty much the same, we particularly stressed the role of interactive read-alouds in the classroom context, because they are a common practice in primary-level classrooms and support for vocabulary and language development can be more readily instituted in a classroom where the teacher has the students for most of every day. In working with teachers, we emphasize the fact that vocabulary is not effectively acquired in discrete lessons that focus on word learning. Rather, word meanings are acquired gradually through repeated encounters with a word in a variety of contexts. Therefore, classroom teachers are better positioned to support vocabulary acquisition and development more generally.

In the professional development for both classroom and intervention teachers, we relied heavily on the work of Beck, McKeown, and Kucan (2002) to structure participants in thinking about how to select words for instruction, how instruction should proceed, and the importance of using targeted words repeatedly, in a variety of contexts, and over an extended period of time. In accord with Beck et al.'s recommendations, the power of interactive read-alouds was stressed. In addition, teachers were encouraged to provide students with ample opportunities to engage in extended conversations with adults and peers to promote the development of more general oral language skills.

Goal 5: Comprehension

The student will develop comprehension skills and strategies that will enhance his or her ability to construct the meaning of texts heard or read.

In discussing this goal, we begin by attuning teachers to the constructive nature of comprehension and the fact that understanding the meaning of a text requires the reader to attend to the author's words and ideas and to what the reader already knows that is relevant to the topic. Across several studies, we have waffled a bit on the appropriateness of explicitly teaching comprehension strategies to young struggling readers. Although there is some evidence that doing so has a positive impact on comprehension (Roberts & Duke, 2010), we have been concerned that, because students in the ISA are focused on developing word-identification strategies, the addition of another layer of strategic thinking might be too much for them to handle. Therefore, we currently encourage teachers to rely on the research on comprehension strategies to guide their interactions with students around texts but not to explicitly teach comprehension strategies at least until the students are effective and independent word solvers.

For students in the early primary grades, the development of comprehension skills and strategies is discussed mainly in the context of read-alouds. We advocate active engagement of the students in discussions of texts. Teachers are encouraged to model various strategies and prompt the students to use them (e.g., "I think he's going to get a puppy for his birthday. What do you think he's going to get? Why?"). In addition, we discuss the value of reading and discussing informational texts to help build the critical knowledge base on which comprehension depends. As students begin to read texts on their own, we stress the importance of engaging students in discussions of what they are reading, as we have encountered many students who read quite fluently but have little recollection of what they read. Especially in light of the fact that many intervention studies have not been successful in boosting comprehension skills, we feel that it is important to focus on encouraging active engagement with the meaning of text from early on.

What Does ISA-Based Instruction Actually Look Like?

Because of the goal-oriented nature of the ISA, we have described instruction in a way that may seem fragmented, so we want to conclude by pulling things together. The instructional goals and principles described earlier can be effectively integrated into the context of both whole-class language arts instruction and small-group and one-to-one intervention settings. Table 2.1 illustrates this integration. Each of the goals is listed across the top, and the typical components of language arts instruction appear in the left column. The checkmarks reflect the

Table 2.1. Intersection of the Goals of Instruction and the Components of Language Arts Instruction

| Language Arts Components | Instructional Groupings | Motivation | Alphabetics | | | Word Learning | | Language and Vocabulary | Knowledge and Comprehension |
			Print Concepts	Phonological Analysis	Alphabetic Coding Skills (letter names, sounds, alphabetic principle, etc.)	Strategic Word Identification	High-Frequency Words		
Read-aloud	WC, SG, 1-1	✓✓		✓	✓	✓		✓✓	✓✓✓
Shared reading	WC, SG, 1-1	✓	✓✓	✓	✓✓	✓✓	✓✓	✓	✓
Independent and buddy reading	WC, SG, 1-1	✓	✓✓	✓	✓✓	✓✓	✓✓	✓✓	✓✓
Writing and composition	WC, SG, 1-1	✓	✓✓✓	✓✓	✓✓	✓	✓✓	✓✓	✓✓
Oral language	WC, SG, 1-1	✓		✓✓	✓	✓		✓✓✓	✓✓
Foundational skills	WC, SG, 1-1	✓	✓✓	✓✓✓	✓✓✓	✓	✓✓	✓	✓
Supported reading group	SG, 1-1	✓✓	✓✓	✓✓	✓✓✓	✓✓✓	✓✓✓	✓✓	✓✓

Note. Checkmarks represent the degree to which each instructional goal can be addressed in the context of given components of language arts instruction. ✓= goal can be addressed to some extent, ✓✓ = goal can be strongly addressed; ✓✓✓ = goal can be strongly addressed. 1-1 = one-to-one; SG = small group; WC = whole class.

degree to which a given goal can be addressed in the context of a particular language arts component. The more useful a particular language arts component might be in addressing the goal, the more checkmarks there are. Although there is certainly room for debate regarding how many checkmarks might be placed in the given cells of this matrix, the general point should be clear—most of the goals can be effectively addressed in most language arts contexts. This does not, of course, mean that every goal should be addressed in every instructional interaction. Rather, our purpose in presenting this table is to reinforce the notions that instruction should be purposeful (goal oriented) and teachers should be constantly evaluating whether the instructional activities they use in language arts instruction actually move the students toward achieving the goals.

For purposes of meeting the needs of students who are at risk of experiencing reading difficulties, small-group (in and beyond the classroom) and one-to-one instruction that specifically address the students' current levels of understanding and specific instructional needs is a critical component in addressing and preventing long-term learning difficulties. In kindergarten, small-group intervention in the classroom (Tier 1) and beyond the classroom (Tier 2) might look similar. The major differences between the two are the size of the instructional group (i.e., Tier 2 groups are likely smaller than Tier 1 groups) and the degree to which instruction was appropriately targeted and responsive. Because Tier 2 groups are smaller and perhaps taught by a teacher with greater expertise in addressing the needs of struggling literacy learners, instruction at Tier 2 should be more explicitly focused on meeting the specific needs of the students in the group.

A typical small-group intervention lesson in kindergarten (Tier 1 or Tier 2) consists of the following components:

- *Reading/rereading*—Depending on the students' point of development, teachers either read to the students or engage them in reading one or more emergent-level texts that were read in previous lessons.

- *Phonological analysis*—Teachers evaluate the students' status on phonological analysis skills, using a phonological skills snapshot as a guide, to determine the appropriate focus of instruction for the group. For students having some skill in phonological analysis and some familiarity with letter names and letter sounds, the phonological analysis and alphabetic segments of the lesson would be integrated.

- *Alphabetics*—Instruction follows the developmental progressions described under the alphabetics goal. Depending on the skills of the students in the group, initial instruction focuses on learning letter names and proceeds to instruction on letter sounds, word families, and other orthographic units. All skills taught in the alphabetics segment are skills that could be applied in the book(s) that the students read in the reading segment of the lesson.

- *Reading*—In every intervention session, students read one or more emergent-level texts. This segment of the lesson provides teachers with the opportunity guide the development of the students' word-solving skills and encourage active engagement in the construction of the meaning of texts read. Prior to reading the new book for the day, teachers engage the students in thinking and talking about strategies to use in word identification. Teachers also prepare the students for reading the book(s) in a variety of ways depending on the characteristics of the book(s) and the skills of the students. Thus, teachers might provide a fairly elaborate book introduction for books that they expect will be more challenging or a more limited introduction if they believe that the students have the skills to solve the problems they will encounter while reading.

  Following the book introduction, each student reads the book, and the teacher makes every effort to ensure that each student is, in fact, reading, rather than shadowing his or her neighbor's reading. As the students read, the teacher moves from student to student, engaging in brief discussions of the meaning of the text or coaching the students in the use of word-identification strategies. An overarching goal is for each student to have maximum opportunity to do the thinking that early reading entails. The teacher's varied conversations with different students convey the distinct impression that reading is not to be done in unison.

  The selection of books for students to read is determined by the teacher's perceptions of what the students are able to do and what they need more practice with. In our intervention studies, we have made frequent but not exclusive use of the Ready Readers series because it systematically develops decoding skills and high-frequency sight vocabulary. Teachers reported that the progressions incorporated in these books eased the tension of selecting the right book for a given group, but at times, the series moved too fast for the students they were teaching, and they needed to seek additional books to meet their students' needs.

- *High-frequency word practice*—A small segment of each lesson is devoted to teaching and practicing high-frequency words. A variety of games are used for this purpose as is periodic review of the Words We [I] Know chart.

- *Writing*—Each lesson involves the students in a writing activity. Early on, the teacher does the writing and engages the students in as much of the writing process as possible. Thus, he or she might engage them in constructing the message, analyzing the sounds in the words to be written, deciding which letters to use to represent sounds, consulting the Words We [I] Know chart for the conventional spelling of a high-frequency word, as so on. As the students progress, the teacher turns over more of the responsibility to them.

The order of the lesson components is not fixed and is allowed to vary on the basis of teachers' perceptions of what would be optimal for the students in their groups. However, teachers are encouraged to strive to include all of the components in every small-group lesson. Most teachers have tended to follow the sequence previously described.

One-to-one intervention lessons for first graders generally consist of many of the same elements as the small-group lessons. The first major difference is that each lesson begins by engaging the students in reading one or more texts that were read in previous lessons. One purpose of the rereadings is to build fluency and confidence and thereby promote enjoyment of the reading process. The second major difference is that, for most students, the phonological analysis and alphabetic skills portions of the lesson are combined. Research suggests that once students have some insight into each aspect of the process, maximum progress is made when the processes are integrated (National Institute of Child Health and Human Development, 2000). The third major difference is that when students are reading shorter, emergent-level texts, they often read four or more books in a single lesson (e.g., two rereads and two new books). The teachers are frequently reminded that the more appropriately challenging reading students do, the faster they will grow as readers.

Concluding Thoughts

The ISA represents an instructional approach appropriate for use in an RTI model, because the research evidence demonstrates its success among the types of students who often struggle in the early stages of learning to read. Research on the approach, to date, indicates that it is effective when used in the early primary grades in classroom, small-group, and one-to-one intervention settings. A unique aspect of the approach, relative to many of the models of instruction proposed for use in RTI contexts, is the stress placed on the need for instruction to be consistent and coherent across instructional settings. Further, stress is placed on the importance of teaching foundational skills, especially phonics skills, for the purpose of facilitating text reading. Thus, the phonics skills are directly taught are taught in preparation for a book that the students will read the same day. As a result, students understand very well the use of the skills they learn in these more isolated activities.

Another unique feature of the ISA is the explicit instruction provided to support students' word solving in context and, thereby, their word learning. By explicitly teaching a small set of code-based and meaning-based strategies for word solving, and teaching students to use the strategies in an interactive and confirmatory way to become independent in the use of these strategies, we hopefully provide students with an approach to reading that will allow them to grow as readers every time they read. As discussed previously, the ability to effortlessly identify most of the words encountered in text allows readers to devote most of their cognitive energy to constructing the meaning of the text.

Instruction in the use of the word-solving strategies has helped students feel empowered as readers. It is common for us to observe students new to the ISA move from a dependent stance, wherein they frequently appeal to the teacher for assistance when they encounter a puzzling word, to a point where they are persistent and productive in their word-solving attempts and at times rather indignant if the teacher tries to step in to help them puzzle through a word ("No, no! Don't tell me!"). Of course, to engage in effective word solving, students need to actively attend to both the alphabetic information contained in the word and the meaning of the text. We feel that the need to draw on both sources of information enhances students' word solving and their understanding of text more generally.

NOTES

The studies of the ISA were supported by grant funds provided by the National Institute of Child Health and Human Development. The earliest study (Vellutino et al., 1996) was implemented under the auspices of a special center grant (#P50HD25806) awarded to the Kennedy Krieger Institute of Johns Hopkins University. Martha B. Denckla was the principal investigator overseeing the various projects initiated under the grant. The second project (Scanlon et al., 2005) was supported by grant #1R01HO34598. The third (Scanlon et al., 2008) was supported by grant #1R01HD42350. We wish to acknowledge the contributions and cooperation of collaborators in these projects: Christopher Schatschneider, Diane Fanuele, Frank Vellutino, Joan Sweeney, Lynn Gelzheiser, and Sheila Small (alphabetized by first name). We are also indebted to the teachers and students who participated in the various studies and to the administrators and clerical staff in the schools who facilitated the conduct of the research.

REFERENCES

Beck, I.L., McKeown, M.G., & Kucan, L. (2002). *Bringing words to life: Robust vocabulary instruction.* New York: Guilford.

Cunningham, A.E., & Stanovich, K.E. (1997). Early reading acquisition and its relation to reading experience and ability 10 years later. *Developmental Psychology, 33*(6), 934–945. doi:10.1037/0012-1649.33.6.934

Dorn, L.J., & Schubert, B. (2008, Spring). A comprehensive intervention model for preventing reading failure: A Response to Intervention process. *Journal of Reading Recovery, 7*(2), 29–41.

Fuchs, D., & Fuchs, L.S. (2006). Introduction to Response to Intervention: What, why, and how valid is it? *Reading Research Quarterly, 41*(1), 93–98. doi:10.1598/RRQ.41.1.4

Good, R.H., Kaminski, R.A., Smith, S., Laimon, D., & Dill, S. (2001). *Dynamic Indicators of Basic Early Literacy Skills* (5th ed.). Eugene: University of Oregon.

Hart, B., & Risley, T.R. (1995). *Meaningful differences in the everyday experience of young American children.* Baltimore: Paul H. Brookes.

Individuals With Disabilities Education Improvement Act, Pub. L. 108-466. (2004). Retrieved January 20, 2010, from idea.ed.gov/

Invernizzi, M., Meier, J., & Juel, C. (2003–2007). *PALS: Phonological awareness literacy screening.* Charlottesville: University of Virginia.

Mellard, D.F., & Johnson, E. (2008). *RTI: A practitioner's guide to implementing Response to Intervention.* Thousand Oaks, CA: Corwin.

National Institute of Child Health and Human Development. (2000). *Report of the National Reading Panel. Teaching children to read: An evidence-based assessment of the scientific research literature on reading and its implications for reading instruction* (NIH Publication No. 00-4769). Washington, DC: U.S. Government Printing Office.

Pearson, P.D., & Gallagher, M.C. (1983). The instruction of reading comprehension. *Contemporary Educational Psychology, 8*(3), 317–344. doi:10.1016/0361-476X(83)90019-X

Roberts, K.M., & Duke, N.K. (2010). Comprehension in the elementary grades: The research base. In K. Ganske & D. Fisher (Eds.), *A comprehensive look at reading comprehension.* New York: Guilford.

Scanlon, D.M. (in press). Response to Intervention: The role of instruction and assessment in the prevention and identification of reading disabilities. In R. Allington & A. McGill-Franzen (Eds.), *Handbook of reading disabilities research.*

Scanlon, D.M., Anderson, K.L., Gelzheiser, L.M., & Vellutino, F.R. *The effects of implementation of the Interactive Strategies Approach in classroom, small group and one-to-one settings.* Manuscript in preparation.

Scanlon, D.M., Anderson, K.L., & Sweeney, J.M. (2010). *Early intervention for reading difficulties: The Interactive Strategies Approach.* New York: Guilford.

Scanlon, D.M., Gelzheiser, L.M., Vellutino, F.R., Schatschneider, C., & Sweeney, J.M. (2008). Reducing the incidence of early reading difficulties: Professional development for classroom teachers versus direct interventions for children. *Learning and Individual Differences, 18*(3), 346–359. doi:10.1016/j.lindif.2008.05.002

Scanlon, D.M., Vellutino, F.R., Small, S.G., Fanuele, D.P., & Sweeney, J.M. (2005). Severe reading difficulties—can they be prevented? A comparison of prevention and intervention approaches. *Exceptionality, 13*(4), 209–227. doi:10.1207/s15327035ex1304_3

Share, D.L. (1995). Phonological recoding and self-teaching: *Sine qua non* of reading acquisition. *Cognition, 55*(2), 151–218. doi:10.1016/0010-0277(94)00645-2

Taylor, B.M., Pearson, P.D., Clark, K., & Walpole, S. (2000). Effective schools and accomplished teachers: Lessons about primary-grade reading instruction in low-income schools. *The Elementary School Journal, 101*(2), 121–165. doi:10.1086/499662

Tivnan, T., & Hemphill, L. (2005). Comparing four literacy reform models in high-poverty schools: Patterns of first-grade achievement. *The Elementary School Journal, 105*(5), 419–441. doi:10.1086/431885

Vellutino, F.R., & Scanlon, D.M. (2002). The Interactive Strategies approach to reading intervention. *Contemporary Educational Psychology, 27*(4), 573–635. doi:10.1016/S0361-476X(02)00002-4

Vellutino, F.R., Scanlon, D.M., Sipay, E.R., Small, S.G., Pratt, A., Chen, R., et al. (1996). Cognitive profiles of difficult-to-remediate and readily remediated poor readers: Early intervention as a vehicle for distinguishing between cognitive and experiential deficits as basic causes of specific reading disability. *Journal of Educational Psychology, 88*(4), 601–638. doi:10.1037/0022-0663.88.4.601

Vygotsky, L.S. (1978). *Mind in society: The development of higher psychological processes* (M. Cole, V. John-Steiner, S. Scribner, & E. Souberman, Eds. & Trans.). Cambridge, MA: Harvard University Press.

Wood, D., Bruner, J.S., & Ross, G. (1976). The role of tutoring in problem solving. *Journal of Child Psychology and Psychiatry, 17*(2), 89–100. doi:10.1111/j.1469-7610.1976.tb00381.x

Spotlight on the Interactive Strategies Approach: The Case of Roosevelt Elementary School

Kimberly L. Anderson

University at Albany, State University of New York

As a participant in the two most recent studies of the Interactive Strategies Approach (ISA), I developed some expertise in the approach and a strong commitment to the idea of taking steps to prevent reading difficulties beginning in kindergarten. When the research projects ended, I returned to my position as a reading specialist at Roosevelt Elementary School. This chapter describes my experiences in attempting to implement aspects of the ISA in that school with the support of and in collaboration with a dedicated principal and dedicated classroom teachers.

Roosevelt Elementary School is a large (approximately 1,000 K–5 students) elementary school in the state of New York. Although the school would be characterized as low need overall, about 20–25% of the students in kindergarten typically qualified for supplementary support in reading at the beginning of the school year. Because of the principal's commitment to early intervention and because of my experience with the ISA, she assigned me to work mainly with students from the eight kindergarten classrooms. A small amount of my time was also devoted to first grade to cover needs that arose throughout the year.

In the sections that follow, I describe how we organized and provided instructional support for kindergartners determined to be at risk for early reading difficulties. The focus is on kindergarten because of our collective belief that interventions should begin as early as possible. I start with the big picture, describing such aspects as how students qualified for intervention, scheduling, movement through the tiers, and the importance of a team approach. I then describe the instructional components of the intervention and the importance of encouraging consistency between intervention and classroom instruction.

Throughout this description, I emphasize that the development of an efficient and effective early literacy program is highly dependent upon a close working relationship and shared philosophy between all parties, including the principal, the reading specialist, classroom teachers, and parents.

As with the research on the ISA that is referenced throughout Chapter 2, my experiences in providing small-group (Tier 2) intervention at Roosevelt Elementary School predate the more formal implementation of RTI procedures that are currently recommended. Nonetheless, this case study should help clarify just how the various pieces of the process fit together and, more important, how those pieces and the instruction the students receive can and must be adapted to meet the needs of both the students and their teachers in a particular school.

Selection of Students for Intervention and Assessment

Assessment of the kindergartners' early literacy skills typically began during the second or third week of school, allowing the students a short time to acclimate to their new surroundings. I completed most of the kindergarten assessments myself, with some additional time provided by other reading specialists as their schedules allowed. This arrangement allowed the classroom teacher to attend to the needs of 18–20 kindergartners as they learned and adjusted to the daily routines. At the beginning of the year, I used the Phonological Awareness Literacy Screening (PALS; Invernizzi, Meier, & Juel, 2003–2007) to assess students' incoming skills in lowercase letter identification, letter–sound association, spelling, matching rhyming words, and matching words with the same beginning sounds. Students who were close to or below the fall benchmark of 28 were considered for the early intervention program, with a final determination based on both the assessment and the students' performance in the classroom program.

In a more formal RTI context, the same measure would likely be administered to all students at least two more times: typically at midyear and at the end of the year. At Roosevelt Elementary School at this time, however, students were assessed with a district-designed early literacy measure at the end of each marking period. The district assessment included measures of rhyme recognition and rhyme generation, blending and segmenting with onsets and rimes, blending and segmenting with individual phonemes, upper- and lowercase letter identification, letter–sound association, high-frequency word reading, and in the last two administrations, a benchmark reading assessment. I also readministered the PALS spelling assessment at the end of the year.

The district assessment was set up in such a way that students did not complete all items in any one assessment cycle. For example, students who did not reach the criterion of six items correct out of eight for segmenting onsets and rimes were not asked to segment by individual phonemes, students were not asked to provide letter sounds for any letters that they could not first identify by name, and so on. Similarly, students who met mastery on a given task did not repeat that task during a subsequent administration. Student performance on these assessments, in conjunction with less formal documentation of progress that occurred in the classroom and intervention settings, was used to make decisions about whether students should continue in intervention and whether students who were not in intervention should be considered for inclusion. All such decisions were always jointly made by me in collaboration with the classroom teacher and took into consideration the student's day-to-day performance in both large- and small-group settings.

It is important to note here that there were several students who entered kindergarten with Individualized Education Programs (IEP). These students, as per their IEPs, received small-group or individualized reading instruction from a special education teacher in addition to their classroom instruction. The special education teacher and I shared a classroom and materials and worked closely together throughout the year, but I did not personally work with these students.

Time Frame and Schedule for Intervention

The intervention for kindergarten began early in the school year, generally around the second week in October, and ran through about the end of May. End-of-year assessments typically began after the Memorial Day break and continued through mid- to late June. Timing at the beginning of the year was of particular importance, as parents needed to be informed of the assessment results and given the opportunity to meet with me or the classroom teacher concerning their child.

Once students were selected for intervention, the sometimes challenging task of setting up a schedule got underway. Unlike in first grade, when literacy instruction is likely to be largely concentrated within a 90–120 minute block, literacy instruction in kindergarten is more likely to be woven into ongoing activities throughout the day. As such, it can be more difficult to avoid taking students out of the classroom for intervention during literacy-related instruction. As in many schools, students at Roosevelt Elementary School could not be taken out of special area classes (e.g., art, music) for academic support, nor was it considered wise to schedule intervention during free-play times either indoors or outdoors.

Because most of the kindergarten teachers had a fairly regular routine in how their day was structured, the intervention times for any given group varied across the week. That way, no group of students missed the same instructional activity more than once during the week, and no teacher had to always accommodate to a less-than-convenient pull-out time. The classroom teachers and I worked together to establish and maintain a schedule that worked for everyone, with the realization that there might be a need for flexibility on any given day and the schedule would probably need some reworking whenever groups shifted a bit (typically at the quarter marking periods).

Most kindergarten intervention groups in this school were comprised of students from the same classroom. This allowed me to offer support that was closely matched to what was happening in the classroom and limited the impact of the pullouts on the classroom teachers' programs. Exceptions to this were made, however, especially as the year went on, to accommodate the needs of particular students. The goal for group size was three students, but this necessarily varied as well, depending on the number of students from a given classroom who had been identified as in need of support.

At the beginning of the year, groups were scheduled to meet three times per week for 30-minute sessions. Including time set aside for working with first grade, I began the year with eight or nine 30-minute blocks of instructional time on any given day.

This schedule changed considerably throughout the year. As mentioned, students were formally reassessed at the end of every quarter and, more informally, on an ongoing basis both in the classroom and in intervention. At the breaks between marking periods, it was not uncommon for a student's level of support through the intervention program to increase or decrease, for students to be shifted around between groups when there was more than one group from a particular classroom, or for a new student to be added to an intervention group.

Less commonly, students who were making minimal progress were provided with one-to-one instruction, which, given the limited number of instructional blocks available, meant reducing time for other students. This was not always an all-or-none situation, and it varied according to the needs of the students and, to some extent, what the schedule could bear. For example, if one student within a group needed substantially more support than the other two, one possibility was to reduce the time for the two stronger students to two times per week, leaving a one-to-one time for the student with greater needs. Typically, this meant meeting with the individual student in the earliest session of the week, then with all three students in the two sessions that followed. Alternatively, a fourth time might be found for the student with the greater needs either by himself or herself or with a student with similar needs from another classroom. On rare occasions, I met individually with students who were making minimal progress for all of their intervention time.

Moving Students In and Out of Intervention

As I alluded to earlier, there was a reasonable amount of movement across the year as to the amount and intensity of support students received through the intervention program. Using a somewhat conservative approach, all students identified as at risk for early reading difficulties began the year with me in small-group intervention (Tier 2) and were included in classroom literacy instruction (Tier 1) as well. Students who made fairly rapid progress typically had their intervention time reduced or had exited from the small-group intervention by the end of the second marking period. However, I continued to monitor the progress of these students throughout the year, and in all but a few cases, they continued to receive a weekly take-home folder that included activities and leveled readers, or "little books."

In a year, about 25% of the students exited from the small-group intervention during the school year, with about an equal number of students added to the small groups generally at the beginning of the third or fourth marking period. Students moving into the intervention program later in the kindergarten year were often new students to the school. On occasion, however, students who appeared to have adequate skills early on did not make the anticipated progress in applying those skills in reading or writing and were moved into the intervention program as those difficulties became evident. A smaller number of students, approximately 10% of the intervention group, or 2.5% of the total number of kindergartners in any one year, were seen one to one for at least some portion of their literacy instruction. Thus, some kindergartners' programs resembled more of a Tier 3 plus Tier 1 combination, while the programs for a few included aspects of all three tiers.

Working Together as a Team

Although open and ongoing communication with parents is always essential, this is especially true when dealing with the parents of kindergartners. At Roosevelt Elementary School, communication about the kindergarten intervention program began at kindergarten screening in the spring before the children entered kindergarten and continued throughout the kindergarten year. Kindergarten screening was generally held in April. I participated as part of the screening team, administering the portion of the assessment that was related to early literacy and language.

After each child was screened, the principal or another reading specialist (who had formerly been a kindergarten teacher) met with the parents of each incoming student to discuss their child's screening results and briefly describe, if appropriate, the kinds of programs that were available in kindergarten for students who might be in need of instructional support. Parents were also provided with some ideas for at-home activities focused on language development, early literacy skills, and gross and fine motor development. A few weeks later, parents came in to school for an evening kindergarten orientation program led by the principal. As one of several speakers at this program, I described both the classroom literacy curriculum and the intervention program. I emphasized the expectations for literacy development during the kindergarten year and the kinds of instructional activities and supports that would be used in helping all students realize these expectations.

Communication with parents continued into the kindergarten year. In September, I visited each kindergarten classroom during open house night, speaking for just a few minutes again about the early intervention program, informing parents that they might be receiving a letter if their child had been selected for the program, and inviting them to stop by with any questions or concerns about their child's assessment results. Several weeks later, after the small-group sessions were underway, I held a separate open house for the parents of students in the intervention program. At this open house, I provided a more thorough description of the intervention program and showed a videotape of a small-group lesson so that parents could see what their children were actually doing in intervention. Throughout these meetings with parents, the preventative nature of the intervention program was highlighted. The combination of these activities served to keep the parents well informed as to what was happening with their children and why and to avoid the potential anxieties that might arise if parents were to be suddenly told at the beginning of the year that their kindergartner was at risk for early reading difficulties and was being placed in a reading intervention program.

Communication with parents was a continued theme throughout the school year, and the kindergarten teachers and I made every effort to include the parents as partners in their children's learning. As the reading specialist, I participated in the first-quarter report card meeting with the parents of each student in the intervention program and was also available for report card conferences on any other students about whom teachers or parents had concerns related to literacy. Face-to-face conferences with parents at the end of subsequent marking periods were generally held only when a student was experiencing difficulty or there was a plan to change the student's instructional program to include more or less support in early literacy. These conferences could be requested by me, the classroom teacher, or the parent.

As one way of keeping parents abreast of what was happening in the early literacy program, the classroom teachers and I worked together to plan a Kindergarten Literacy Night about midyear and invited the parents of all kindergartners to this event. The evening was set up for parents in much the same way that center time might be for their children. Kindergarten teachers worked in pairs to plan and present information on early literacy, demonstrate what the students were learning in their classrooms, and provide gamelike materials that the parents could take home to use with their children. The parents rotated in groups throughout the kindergarten classrooms, learning about topics such as phonological awareness, letter–sound knowledge, high-frequency word learning, and supported reading with little books. The focus of each presentation was on the kinds of things that parents could do at home to support what was happening in the classroom.

Parents were also recruited to work as volunteers in their children's kindergarten classrooms during center time or to volunteer their time to work one to one with a kindergartner in need of extra support. Finally, I prepared a weekly take-home folder for each student in the intervention program; contents of the folder informed parents of the specific skills and strategies their child was working on that week, provided specific suggestions for activities that could be carried out at home, and included little books that had been read in school and could be reread at home for the purpose of building sight vocabulary and reading fluency.

Although there was no formal professional development on the ISA provided for the kindergarten teachers, three of the teachers chose to learn more about the ISA as their professional development plan for the year. To accomplish this goal, the teachers read chapters from a version of the ISA book that was developed for the previously mentioned professional development study (Scanlon & Sweeney, 2004), and we met on a monthly basis to discuss a particular aspect of early literacy instruction (e.g., purposes and conventions of print, phonological awareness) and how it could be addressed in both small- and whole-group contexts. All of the kindergarten teachers were encouraged to use leveled readers available in the reading room to supplement the texts provided in the core curriculum, and many of the teachers did so on a regular basis, particularly as the year progressed.

Structure, Planning, and Documentation of the Intervention Lessons

As described in Chapter 2, the intervention lessons were designed to address multiple aspects of early literacy development and included the reading and re-reading of little books, writing activities, and activities focused on the development of phonological analysis skills, alphabetic knowledge, and high-frequency sight vocabulary. I used the small-group lesson sheet developed for the kindergarten intervention study (Scanlon, Vellutino, Small, Fanuele, & Sweeney, 2005) to both plan instruction and document student progress on a day-to-day basis (see Figure 3.1). Directions on how to use the Daily Kindergarten Small-Group Lesson Sheet can be found in Figure 3.2.

Although this lesson sheet appears formidable on first encounter, using it along with a set of codes (see Figure 3.3) to describe the instructional activities and the same beginning, developing, and proficient designations used on the group snapshots described in Chapter 2 actually streamlined the planning process, provided a ready data source for informing communications with classroom teachers and parents, and, most important, served as a daily reminder to me of the various literacy components that needed to be addressed.

Figure 3.1. Daily Kindergarten Small-Group Lesson Sheet

Date _____ Session # _____

Student 1 _____ Student 2 _____ Student 3 _____

Component 1: Read-Aloud/Shared Reading or Rereading		
Title (and Level):		
Text Comprehension: GU, AE, RET, PC, CON		
Word Identification Strategy: Code (TSF, TSL, TSM, WP, DP, BW), Meaning (PIC, MS, RP, SA), Interactive & Confirmatory (IC)		
Letter/Sound: REC, ID		
Print Concepts: LR, TB, CW, CL, COM, PUN, 1-1		
High-Frequency Words: REC, ID		
Phoneme Awareness: CR, IR, IA		
Vocabulary		
Comments/Notes for Next Session:		

(continued)

Figure 3.1. Daily Kindergarten Small-Group Lesson Sheet (*continued*)

Student 1 _____ Student 2 _____ Student 3 _____

Component 2: Phoneme Awareness		
Sound Sorting: RH, BEG, END, MID		Stretch?
Sound Blending: Onset–Rime, Single Phonemes: w/pics, w/o pics		Stretch?
Sound Counting/Segmentation of 2 and 3 Phonemes		Stretch?
Comments/Notes for Next Session:		

Component 3: Letters & Sounds, Alphabetic Mapping, Word Families, Decoding		
Letter Names: REC, ID, PR		
Letter Sounds: LS, CS-B, CS-E		
Other Decoding Elements: SV, VCe, Di, Bl		
Word Building		
Word Reading		
Written Spelling		
Comments/Notes for Next Session:		

(continued)

Figure 3.1. Daily Kindergarten Small-Group Lesson Sheet (*continued*)

Student 1 _____ Student 2 _____ Student 3 _____

Component 4: Reading		
Title (and Level):		
Text Comprehension: GU, AE, RET, PC, CON		
Word-Identification Strategy: Code (TSF, TSL, TSM, WP, DP, BW), Meaning (PIC, MS, RP, SA), Interactive & Confirmatory (IC)		
Letter/Sound: REC, ID		
Print Concepts: LR, TB, CW, CL, COM, PUN, 1-1		
High-Frequency Words: REC, ID		
Phoneme Awareness: CR, IR, IA		
Vocabulary		
Comments/Notes for Next Session:		

(*continued*)

Figure 3.1. Daily Kindergarten Small-Group Lesson Sheet (*continued*)

Student 1 _____ Student 2 _____ Student 3 _____

Component 5: Writing		
Writing Prompt or Dictated Sentence:		
Letter/Sound: PR, LS, BS, ES, CS-B, CS-E Other Encoding Elements: SV, VCe, Di, Bl		
Print Concepts: LR, TB, CWL, CLW, COM, PUN, 1-1		
High-Frequency Words: CP, CS		
Comments/Notes for Next Session:		

Component 6: High-Frequency Words		
Practice Plan:		

Figure 3.2. Directions for Using the Daily Kindergarten Small-Group Lesson Sheet

The Daily Kindergarten Small-Group Lesson Sheet can be used to organize and record information regarding each day's lesson. The major components of the lesson are listed on the Lesson Sheet along with a section to record information about high-frequency sight word practice activities and assessment.

The Reading and Writing components of the lesson are broken down into several different areas that may be the focus of instruction on a particular day depending on the needs of the students; only a few of these areas will be focused on in any given lesson. Similarly, within a selected component, only a few of the possible objectives will be addressed in any one lesson. For example, within Read-Aloud/Shared Reading or Rereading (Component 1), the teacher might choose to use a particular text to focus on comprehension, word-identification strategy, and print concepts, but not on letter/sound, high-frequency words, or phoneme awareness. Further, within text comprehension, the teacher might focus on general understanding and picture cues but not on active engagement, retelling, or connections.

In preparation for each lesson, the following items should be completed on the daily lesson sheet:

• The names of each of the students in the group should be listed as column headers: Student 1, Student 2, and Student 3.

• The text(s) that will be read to or with the students on a given day should be recorded next to the word Title (and Level) for Components 1 and 4.

• The codes for the objectives that are planned for either Introduction and Practice (I/P) or Review (R) should be recorded in the blank space next to the objectives. [Example: A teacher using shared reading to focus on print concepts might be reviewing the left-to-right and top-to-bottom progression of print but introducing concept of word for the first time. In the space beneath the objective Print Concepts in Component 1, the teacher would write the codes LR(R), TB(R), and CW(I/P).]

During the course of a lesson, brief notes concerning the responses of the individual students should be made in the columns headed with their names. At the very least, each student's progress toward accomplishing the listed objectives should be recorded using beginning (B), developing (D), and proficient (P) designations. More expanded notes and thoughts for planning the next lesson can be recorded in the Comments/Notes for Next Session box at the end of Components 1–5.

Figure 3.3. Codes for Lesson Objectives

READ-ALOUD, SHARED READING (Component 1)

Text Comprehension
AE: active engagement
CON: connect to existing knowledge
GU: general understanding
PC: picture cues
RET: retell

Word-Identification Strategy
BW: break word
DP: different pronunciation
IC: Interactive & Confirmatory
MS: make sense
PIC: picture cues
RP: read past
SA: start again
TS: think about the sounds
TSF: first sound(s)
TSL: last sound(s)
TSM: medial sound
WP: word part

Letter/Sound
ID: identify
REC: recognize

Print Concepts
1-1: voiceprint match
CL: concept of a letter
COM: print as communication
CW: concept of a word
LR: left-to-right directionality
PUN: punctuation
TB: top-to-bottom directionality

High-Frequency Words
ID: identify
REC: recognize

Phoneme Awareness
CR: complete rhyme
IA: identify alliterative words
IR: identify rhyming words

PHONEME AWARENESS (Component 2)

Sound Sorting
BEG: beginning
END: ending
MID: medial vowel
RH: rhyme

Sound Blending
w/ Pics: with pictures
w/o Pics: without pictures

LETTERS & SOUNDS, ALPHABETIC MAPPING, WORD FAMILIES, DECODING (Component 3)

Letter Names
ID: identify
PR: print or produce
REC: recognize

Letter Sounds
CS-B: consonant substitution-beginning
CS-E: consonant substitution-ending
LS: letter–sound association

Other Decoding Elements
Bl: blend
Di: digraph
SV: short vowel
VCe: vowel-consonant-e

(continued)

Figure 3.3. Codes for Lesson Objectives (*continued*)

READING (Component 4)

Text Comprehension
AE: active engagement
CON: connect to existing knowledge
GU: general understanding
PC: picture cues
RET: retell

Word-Identification Strategy
BW: break word
DP: different pronunciation
IC: Interactive & Confirmatory
MS: make sense
PIC: picture cues
RP: read past
SA: start again
TS: think about the sounds
TSF: first sound(s)
TSL: last sound(s)
TSM: medial sound
WP: word part

Letter/Sound
ID: identify
REC: recognize

Print Concepts
1-1: voiceprint match
CL: concept of a letter
COM: print as communication
CW: concept of a word
LR: left-to-right directionality
PUN: punctuation
TB: top-to-bottom directionality

High-Frequency Words
ID: identify
REC: recognize

Phoneme Awareness
CR: complete rhyme
IA: identify alliterative words
IR: identify rhyming words

WRITING (Component 5)

Letter/Sound
BS: beginning sound
CS-B: consonant substitution-beginning
CS-E: consonant substitution-ending
ES: ending sound
LS: letter–sound association
PR: print or produce

Other Encoding Elements
Bl: blend
Di: digraph
SV: short vowel
VCe: vowel-consonant-e

Print Concepts
1-1: voiceprint match
CL: concept of a letter
COM: print as communication
CW: concept of a word
LR: left-to-right directionality
PUN: punctuation
TB: top-to-bottom directionality

High-Frequency Words
CP: copy from resource
CS: correct spelling without model

HIGH-FREQUENCY WORDS (Component 6)

No codes

By quickly reviewing a week's worth of daily lesson sheets, I could see where individual students were or were not making progress and also could take notice if certain aspects of instruction were being neglected. For example, I sometimes suffered from overplanning, which resulted in not getting all the way through the lesson sheet on any given day. Because I usually planned the writing component for the end of the lesson, this meant that writing might not always get the attention it deserved. By reviewing the lesson sheets regularly, I remained alert to this problem and occasionally moved the writing component to earlier in the lesson to be sure that I would get to it regularly. The lesson sheet also served as a reminder of the sequence of skills to be pursued within some components and helped me think about how to differentiate instruction for students within a group. For example, when working on a sound-blending task (e.g., phoneme awareness component), some students might be blending at the level of onset and rime while others were ready to blend by individual phonemes. I found the comments/notes section to be useful for planning the next lesson for each group and, within each group, for planning for individual students.

Maintaining Consistency With the Classroom Program

In the school year referred to in this case study, the district had just adopted a new core reading curriculum, replacing one that had been in use for the previous 10 years. At the kindergarten level, the new program differed from the old primarily in that it had a much more prescribed sequence for skill introduction, had a more explicit focus on phonological awareness, included both big books for shared reading and leveled readers for small-group instruction for each of the themes throughout the year, and introduced more high-frequency sight words. Although all teachers were expected to use the new program as the core for their classroom reading instruction, they were given some latitude as to the specific components of the program they would use and how they would integrate that use within their already established routines.

I was provided with a set of the kindergarten materials as well, but I was not required to use them in any particular way. These materials, particularly the teacher's manual, provided a handy reference point as to the expectations for literacy development across the kindergarten year. In addition, I met with each of the teachers at least once a week to discuss more specifically what was happening in each classroom and share concerns and notes of progress regarding students in intervention or other students in the class. Although attempts were made to schedule these meetings during common planning times, more often than not they happened either before or after school. Fortunately, I had been working with most of these teachers for a couple of years at this point, and we had established an easygoing, open-door policy in both directions.

Because the students in the intervention program met with me, on average, no more than 90 minutes per week, my primary goal was to provide instruction that would enhance the students' ability to benefit from their classroom literacy instruction. Toward this end, I used some of the same materials used in the kindergarten classroom and followed the same general sequence for skill introduction. For example, to help the students learn letter–sound associations, I used the same keywords that were used in the classroom. I also followed the same order as the classroom teacher for introducing letters and high-frequency words and made a point of aligning the language I used with the language the students heard in the classroom. For example, one kindergarten teacher commonly referred to the spaces between letters and words as "spaghetti" and "meatball" spaces, respectively, so these terms were used in the intervention setting as well.

When possible, I arrived at the students' classroom a few minutes before their scheduled intervention time, which gave me an opportunity to observe or interact with them, and sometimes their peers, in the classroom setting. Being aware of the daily expectations in the classroom and observing how other students were meeting those expectations provided an important reference point for me and, in conjunction with ongoing assessment and documentation of progress, helped me avoid overly optimistic impressions based simply on the fact that the students in intervention were, indeed, making progress.

Early in the year especially, I sometimes used the same big books and charts that were used for shared reading in the classroom. Using the same materials in the small group allowed for a greater level of participation for each student and, particularly for students who had very limited experiences with print prior to entering kindergarten, served as good preparation for classroom participation. In the small group, explicit guidance as to what the students should be attending to and thinking about could be more readily provided, and expectations for behavior during these instructional contexts could be established more easily, increasing the likelihood that the students would benefit from similar shared-reading experiences in the classroom. Moreover, use of the same materials early on helped establish the connection between the two settings in the students' minds. It was not unusual, for example, for a student to spot a big book on the easel in my room and proclaim excitedly, "Hey, my teacher has that book, too!"

Focusing on Student Needs

Beyond the cited examples, however, most of the materials and instructional activities I used in the intervention setting differed from those used in the classroom and depended on the needs of the students in each group. Although instruction was aligned with what was happening in the classroom and was designed to support it, it was not a replication. For example, although I used the same keywords for letter–sound associations that were used in the classroom, instruction and practice in the use of the keywords was likely to be more explicit and more frequently occurring in the intervention setting. Similarly, although I taught the same decoding skills that the kindergarten teachers were teaching, instruction in the intervention setting typically featured more extensive use of the word-building, word-reading, and word-spelling activities described in Chapter 2.

Little Books

The aspect of the intervention program that varied the most from the core curriculum in the classroom was probably the amount of time students were engaged in the reading of little books and the emphasis that was placed on the development of a strategic approach to figuring out unfamiliar words encountered in text. The core curriculum used in the classroom included a set of decodable books, one for each week of the school year, beginning at about week six. Each book featured the letter–sound or decoding skill and high-frequency word(s) being taught that week and provided some practice with previously taught skills. Although the quality of these books improved as the year went on and more skills and high-frequency words were introduced, the language patterns tended to be stilted and the story lines somewhat disjointed. Because they did not lend themselves very well to discussion and because the students were practicing decoding skills and high-frequency words in other contexts, I seldom used these books in intervention. Although the decodable texts were used in many of the kindergarten classrooms, this was typically in combination with various leveled readers that the teachers had in their classroom collections. As the year progressed, all of the kindergarten teachers used little books for small-group instruction during center time and sent books home with their students on a weekly basis.

A variety of little books were used in the intervention setting, depending on the time of year and the current skills and strategies of the students in the groups. I used books with predictable patterns and familiar themes at the beginning of the year to establish a motivation for reading as well as an understanding of the basic conventions of print. These books, which were generally about such topics as families or playtime activities, provided opportunities for the students to make connections to their own lives and see reading as a meaningful and enjoyable activity. The close match between the pictures and the words plus the predictable nature of these books served to build the students' confidence in themselves as readers.

Because such books allow students to read without really attending to the print, however, I used them sparingly after the first few weeks of intervention. Instead, I used a combination of the sight-word readers described in the previous section and what we refer to in the ISA as "strategy-promoting texts." Unlike the predictable or decodable books described earlier, strategy-promoting texts encourage the use of information from a variety of sources for figuring out unfamiliar words. Thus, rather than relying primarily on one source of information, the reader is called on to make use of a combination of letter–sound/decoding knowledge, pictorial support, and the general context. These books are particularly conducive to promoting the kind of interactive strategy use taught in the ISA. Students in the intervention groups read at least three and as many as five new titles each week and also engaged in frequent rereading of familiar texts.

Word-Solving Strategies

In support of this reading, explicit instruction in the use of multiple strategies for figuring out words was a focal point of the intervention program. From the beginning of the year, students were taught to use both code-based and meaning-based strategies in interactive ways for figuring out words. Early on, this typically meant thinking about the sounds in the word with a focus on the beginning sound, checking the picture, and thinking about what made sense. Later strategies for kindergarten included going back to the beginning of the sentence and starting again, using letter–sounds from the final position in words (and eventually medial sounds), looking for word families, and, for some students, reading past the puzzling word to the end of the sentence and then returning to it. I introduced the code-based strategies in conjunction with the alphabetic skills that were being addressed in the classroom. For example, when word families were introduced in the classroom, the strategy of looking for word families in unfamiliar words was introduced as well.

I introduced and taught each new strategy separately; students then practiced using the new strategy in combination with those that were previously taught. To create a group strategy list, I used a tabletop pocket chart and added a sentence strip featuring each new strategy to the chart as appropriate. I reproduced the icons used to represent each strategy on index cards and placed each icon next to the matching printed strategy in the pocket chart. Having the icons on separate cards allowed for some practice in matching the icons with the strategies, which, in turn, helped the students remember what the various strategies were (because, in most cases, they could not yet actually read the words on the printed strategy list). Use of the strategy list was explicitly modeled, and the students were encouraged to refer to it when they encountered an unfamiliar word in a book or other text they were reading.

Most intervention sessions included a review of the strategies that had been taught, use of the strategies in reading continuous text, and a reflection on the strategies used by one or more students in the group. For example, I would take note of which strategies students were observed to be using while rereading and then, while holding up a book open to a particular page, say something like, "I noticed Spencer using two strategies when he was reading this page. He looked at the picture and thought about the sound for the letter F. I heard him say 'ffff,' and he read, 'I see the fox.'" Such comments invariably prompted other students to say that they had done the same thing or indicate other places where they had also used strategies.

To promote more independent use of and reflection on strategy use, I reproduced smaller versions of the strategy icons and attached them to sticky notes. On occasion, the students used the sticky notes to mark places in their books where they used a particular strategy or combination of strategies for figuring out a word. This activity helped the students consciously attend to their use of strategies as they were reading and provided a visual reminder of which strategies they had used. Students could then refer to the sticky notes during a group sharing time and talk about which strategies they used to figure out which words. For example, in a story about a birthday party, a student might think about the /k/ sound for the letter C, check the picture (which might show presents, a cake, and balloons), or use what he or she knows about birthday parties to puzzle through the last word in the sentence, "I see the cake." The student would then place the corresponding sticky notes on that page next to the word *cake*. After all students had finished reading, each would turn to a page in their book with one or more sticky notes and talk about the strategies they had used. Because students were eager to use the sticky notes and share how they had used them, they actively thought about the strategies and how more than one could be used to help them figure out a given word.

Because the use of strategies for word identification was a central part of the intervention program and was not a component of the core curriculum, a special effort was made to include the strategies in classroom instruction and make parents aware of their use. I videotaped several lessons featuring strategy instruction and shared these videos with kindergarten teachers during morning breakfast meetings and with parents during evening get-togethers. I sent the strategy list home in the intervention students' weekly folders so that parents could encourage the use of the strategies, and several of the classroom teachers began to send the list home in weekly book bags with all of the students in their classes. Quarterly report cards indicated which strategies had been introduced and addressed the students' ability to use the strategies in both supported and independent reading contexts. During the Kindergarten Literacy Night described earlier, a classroom teacher and I led the session devoted to reading little books. We focused on the enjoyment and comprehension of books and on supporting the students in their use of multiple strategies for identifying words.

Concluding Thoughts

Although the case study described in this section does not reflect all of the formalized procedures that have come to be associated with implementing RTI, what it does reflect is a focus on instruction—a focus on meeting the needs of individual students, right from the beginning of their educational careers, and doing so in such a way that includes and values, and indeed depends upon, a close working relationship and a shared philosophy and knowledge base among administrators, classroom teachers, intervention teachers, and parents. It also reflects the importance of developing a strategic stance toward word solving among beginning readers, which is a hallmark of the ISA.

Although the ISA places a high priority on the development of foundational skills such as phonological awareness and alphabet knowledge, these skills are viewed within the context of their facilitative effect on the development of word solving, word learning, and text reading. Without these foundational skills, and without the explicit instruction some students need to acquire them, development of a strategic approach to word solving that involves the interactive use of both code-based and meaning-based strategies would be all but impossible. Similarly, the development of such a strategic approach would also be challenging, and indeed pointless, without a focus on meaning and enjoyment and without the expectation on the part of the students that what they read can and should make sense.

REFERENCES

Invernizzi, M., Swank, L., & Juel, C. (2007). *PALS-K: Phonological awareness literacy screening—kindergarten* (6th ed.). Charlottesville: University of Virginia.

Scanlon, D.M., & Sweeney, J.M. (2004). *Supporting children's literacy development in the primary grades*. Unpublished manuscript, Child Research and Study Center, University at Albany, State University of New York.

Scanlon, D.M., Vellutino, F.R., Small, S.G., Fanuele, D.P., & Sweeney, J.M. (2005). Severe reading difficulties—can they be prevented? A comparison of prevention and intervention approaches. *Exceptionality, 13*(4), 209–227. doi:10.1207/s15327035ex1304_3

CHAPTER 4

The Comprehensive Intervention Model: A Systems Approach to RTI

Linda J. Dorn

University of Arkansas at Little Rock

Shannon C. Henderson

University of Arkansas at Little Rock

In 2002, the President's Commission on Excellence in Special Education (2002) reported that up to 40% of struggling readers in the United States end up in special education classes. This finding was unnerving considering that research suggests that only 1.5–2% of the student population has a cognitive reading disability (Clay, 1990; Vellutino et al., 1996). Of further concern, research revealed that struggling literacy learners, when provided with instruction matched to their needs, were able to make significant progress (Brown, Denton, Kelly, & Neal, 1999; Center, Wheldall, Freeman, Outhred, & McNaught, 1995; Mathes et al., 2005; Phillips & Smith, 1997; Scanlon & Vellutino, 1996; Torgesen et al., 2001; Vaughn & Linan-Thompson, 2003; Vellutino, Scanlon, & Lyon, 2000). As a result, many educators began to question whether a large percentage of students identified as needing special education services were instructionally rather than cognitively disabled and whether they may have attained grade-level standards with appropriate instruction (Spear-Swerling & Sternberg, 1996; Vellutino et al., 1996).

To respond to what appeared to be the overidentification of struggling readers into special education classes, the Individuals With Disabilities Education Improvement Act of 2004 introduced provisions that allowed for documentation of student response to interventions as an alternative means of diagnosing learning disabilities. As a result, struggling readers may now receive instructional interventions early in their academic years—a welcome alternative to the pervasive "wait-to-fail" model found in many schools.

From a systems perspective, RTI is viewed as a schoolwide effort that changes perceptions and practices regarding struggling readers, thus influencing the literacy achievement of the entire school. A systems approach is grounded in the belief that teachers are the agents of school improvement and that school-embedded professional development creates an authentic context for developing teacher expertise, refining the craft of teaching, and thus increasing student achievement. Within this framework, teachers are provided with evidence-based resources and specialized training that enables them to make data-driven decisions about students' learning. A systems design focuses on changing the culture of a school by institutionalizing structures that promote teacher collaboration and comprehensive approaches to student learning.

In *Reading Today*, a publication of the International Reading Association (IRA), Farstrup (2007) describes how "RTI has the very real potential of promoting cooperation and comprehensive approaches to solving students' reading problems before the corrosive and insurmountable effects of repeated failures set in" (p. 17). From a systems point of view, RTI covers four unique goals:

1. An assessment method for identifying students at risk of reading failure
2. A framework for providing evidence-based interventions
3. A structure for increasing teacher expertise and collaboration
4. A design for coordinating and monitoring schoolwide comprehensive literacy improvement

In this chapter, we describe the Comprehensive Intervention Model (CIM) as a systems approach to RTI. The chapter is divided into three sections. First, we provide a rationale for a systems approach, including issues related to the identification of learning disabled students. Next, we describe the CIM as a systemic RTI approach, including how layers of intervention are delivered within a four-tier design. Subsequently, we present the research basis for CIM and describe the CIM portfolio of interventions. Also, we explain how schools engage in a process of learning and collaboration using an assessment wall for measuring growth over time at the system level. We conclude with a description of the training model as a university–school partnership that focuses on developing teacher expertise for teaching struggling readers.

A Brief Historical Perspective

Since the establishment of the learning disability (LD) category in 1975, there has been an exponential increase in the number of students identified as having a reading disability (Cortiella, 2009). In "Rethinking Learning Disabilities," an article published in 2001, researchers suggested that the LD category had become a catchall for low-achieving students and that, from its inception as a category, LD had served as a "sociological sponge that attempt[ed] to wipe up general education's spills and cleanse its ills" (as cited by Cortiella, 2009, p. 10).

Two mitigating factors attributed to the increase in students identified as having LD are problems with inaccurate and inconsistent identification (Macmann, Barnett, Lombard, Belton-Kocher, & Sharpe, 1989; MacMillan, Gresham, & Bocian, 1998; Vellutino et al., 1996) and problems in identification of LDs using the IQ-achievement discrepancy model (Aaron, 1997; Fletcher et al., 1994; Vellutino et al., 2000). Other concerns, such as minority overrepresentation in the special education system (Bahr, Fuchs, Stecker, & Fuchs, 1991; MacMillan, Gresham, Lopez, & Bocian, 1996; Reschly & Hosp, 2004) and a growing need to focus on student outcomes (Fuchs & Fuchs, 1998; Gresham, 2002; National Commission on Excellence in Education, 1983) brought to bear the need for a different approach for identifying students—RTI.

After years of increasing numbers, it is encouraging that, according to the National Center for Literacy Disabilities, the number of elementary students identified as having LDs has decreased (Cortiella, 2009). This decline appears to be a result of multiple factors, including a better understanding of reading acquisition, efforts to provide early intervention prior to special education referral, changes in the definitions of disability categories in special education law and regulations, and a shift in the assessment and identification process through the RTI method. However, there is much work still to be done. The percentage of students referred nationally to special education services remains high—5.6%, or 2.6 million students (Cortiella, 2009). In addition, declining referral rates indicate that fewer students are referred for special education services, but they do not guarantee that students are receiving the instruction they need to become successful readers and writers. Therefore, we remain cautious in our optimism. Although a decline of referrals to special education gives rise to hope that students are receiving appropriate instruction, we are wary of celebrating too soon.

Why Students Struggle With Literacy Learning

The IRA and the National Council of Teachers of English (1994) identify five factors contributing to literacy difficulties: (1) differences in home languages, (2) learning abilities, (3) literacy experiences, (4) learning opportunities, and (5) access to reading materials. Of the five, only poor learning abilities (LDs) are attributed to neurological miscalculations of the brain. Unfortunately, many students whose literacy difficulties are caused by environmental factors rather than neurological factors may end up in special education classrooms. This phenomenon may explain in part why students who come from impoverished homes have a higher incidence of testing into special education (Cortiella, 2009). Studies have evidenced that students entering school from advantaged homes possess a receptive vocabulary five times greater than those from less-advantaged homes (Hart & Risley, 1995). This finding is significant considering vocabulary in first grade predicts 30% of 11th grade reading comprehension and serves as a much better predictor than reading skill in first grade (Cunningham & Stanovich, 1997). Consequently, it seems reasonable to expect that those students who enter school from a rich literacy environment will readily profit from the school curriculum, becoming better readers and writers. But what about those students who do not?

In the article "Learning to Be Learning Disabled," Clay (1987) posits students with LDs and low-achieving readers were indistinguishable groups. She was one of the first researchers to address the impact of inappropriate reading instruction on students' reading development. She maintained that inappropriate reading programs might lead students to practice inappropriate processing, day after day, year after year. As a result, these students develop highly practiced inappropriate response systems, which become very resistant to intervention. Therefore, they are "learning to be learning disabled with increasing severity as long as the inappropriate responding continues" (p. 160).

Clay was an early advocate of systematic observations and responsive teaching for preventing reading failure; she claimed that there is no evidence to suggest that students with LDs should be taught any differently than students with reading difficulties (Clay, 1987). Indeed, she maintained that many of the challenges faced by struggling readers could be traced back to the quality differences among teachers and the programs they deliver to their students.

Clay's advocacy for struggling readers led to the development of the Reading Recovery training model as a design for increasing teachers' expertise in systematic observation and responsive teaching. She introduced a school-embedded professional development model grounded in the notion that the only way to change the trajectory for struggling literacy learners was to approach the problem at a systems level and focus on developing teacher expertise to make the moment-to-moment decisions necessary for accelerating individual students' literacy progress. In *Redesigning Education*, Wilson and Daviss (1994) describe Reading Recovery as "a design for combining research, teacher education, and professional development in an orchestrated system of change" (p. 76).

The Teacher as Expert

With the goals of RTI, the expectation is that teachers will develop greater expertise in assessing, identifying, and instructing the struggling learners in the classroom. If students are not responding to instruction, teachers must examine the impact of their teaching on students' learning. Many researchers have documented the relationship of teachers' knowledge and expertise to the literacy achievement of their students (Clay, 2001; Darling-Hammond & McLaughlin, 1999; Duffy, 2004; Duke & Pearson, 2002; Johnston, Allington, & Afflerbach, 1985; McCutchen et al., 2002; Pearson, 2003; Taylor, Pearson, Clark, & Walpole, 2000).

Teaching and learning are reciprocal processes, and any change within a school begins with change within the teacher. Teachers' perceptions and beliefs about low-performing students affect the methods they use to assess and instruct their students (Lipson & Wixson, 2009; Mathes et al., 2005). From this perspective, we believe that an RTI approach must focus on creating opportunities within a school where teachers can refine their craft of teaching through observing, interacting, and learning from one another (Dorn, French, & Jones, 1998; Johnston, 2009). In the process, they develop greater expertise for teaching students, including how to differentiate their instruction to meet the unique needs of each learner.

A Systems Approach to RTI

The first step in a systems approach to RTI is to take a close look at how the school perceives the struggling reader. How do classroom teachers view their responsibilities for teaching the lowest students? What programs are in place to address these students? What are the qualifications of the individuals who teach struggling readers? Are students referred to special education without an opportunity to participate in high-quality instruction? What assessments are used to make these decisions? These are just a few questions to motivate teachers to discuss potential reasons for the identification of students with LDs.

Over the past decade, researchers have found ample evidence that this problem-solving, systemic approach is required to improve student achievement. Preuss (2003) encourages schools to conduct a root cause analysis, which consists of looking beneath the surface behaviors to identify the underlying causes that may be contributing to particular problems. Bernhardt (2004) explains how schools should analyze system problems through a comprehensive lens that examines the relationship among multiple factors, including teacher perceptions, programs, instructional practices, and student outcomes. Fullan and Stiegelbauer (2001) advocate the alignment and schoolwide coordination of programs and learning goals. Crévola and Hill (1998) claim that quantum improvements can only occur within the context of a fully implemented, systemwide, comprehensive approach to early literacy.

In a recent publication by the National Staff Development Council (2001), schoolwide collaborative professional learning was identified as a critical factor in increasing student achievement in high-poverty schools. Others argue that school improvement must create optimal learning conditions for students and a similar set of working conditions for teachers (Gallimore, Ermeling, Saunders, & Goldenberg, 2009; Tharp, 1982; Tharp & Gallimore, 1988). DuFour, DuFour, Eaker, and Karhanek (2004) describe how professional learning communities can become problem-solving contexts for teacher collaboration and data-driven responses. They encourage a "multi-step system of interventions [that] arms itself with a variety of tools for meeting the needs of its students and thus is more likely to find the appropriate strategy" (p. 165). Together, these scholars provide support for implementing a systemic and comprehensive approach as an RTI method.

A Systemic and Comprehensive Approach

The CIM proffers that teachers are the catalyst for continuous school improvement and that scripted packages and kits are counterproductive to teacher and student development. The CIM framework is a combination of high-quality, differentiated classroom instruction, a portfolio of research-based interventions, seamless assessment systems at individual and systems levels, professional development provided through university partnerships, and school-embedded professional learning teams for increasing teacher efficacy and building capacity in schools.

Each school is committed to creating a problem-solving culture that enables teachers to learn from one another, along with an emphasis on building collaborative structures for promoting professional dialogue among general education teachers, intervention teachers, and special education teachers. Accountability is measured at multiple levels, including change over time in student learning as well as change over time in how the system is addressing the needs of its learners. Schoolwide leadership and data teams are central to the accountability component, including preparing and distributing school reports that compare the progress of specific subgroups (e.g., LD, second language, low progress) to their average-performing peers.

A Tiered Approach to RTI

The most common structure for implementing an RTI method is the three-tiered framework, with Tier 1 being classroom instruction and successive degrees of intensity being Tiers 2 and 3 (Fuchs & Fuchs, 2006). Typically, this model uses a standard protocol approach that includes timed assessments and scripted programs that are implemented with treatment fidelity. From this perspective, if the student does not respond to the standard treatment, the student, not the program, is the problem. In contrast, interventions, such as Reading Recovery (Clay, 2005), the CIM (Dorn & Schubert, 2008), and the Interactive Strategies Approach (ISA; Scanlon & Vellutino, 1996), use a standard lesson framework, but require teachers to make moment-to-moment decisions within this structure. It is becoming increasingly clear that teacher judgment and decision making are the cornerstones of an effective RTI method (Johnston, 2009; Lose, 2007; McEneaney, Lose, & Schwartz, 2006).

The CIM uses a layered approach within a four-tier framework for aligning classroom instruction, supplemental interventions, and special education (see Figure 4.1). The difference between the CIM structure and the typical three-tier approach is that CIM interventions are not delivered in a rigid, lockstep manner. Teachers use data, including classroom observations, to place students in the most appropriate intervention, and students may receive multiple interventions at the same time. In our opinion, the traditional tiered model is grounded in remediation theory (i.e., try this and if it does not work, do the same with more

Figure 4.1. Layers of Intervention Within a Four-Tier Framework

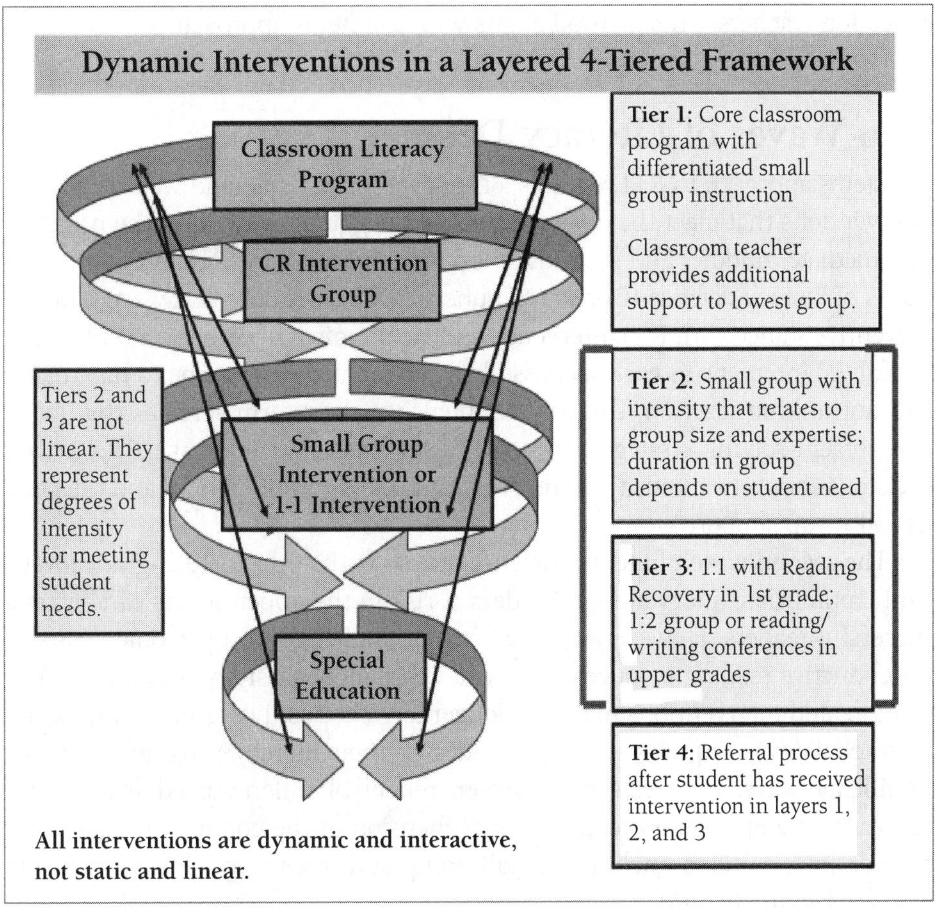

Dynamic Interventions in a Layered 4-Tiered Framework

Classroom Literacy Program

CR Intervention Group

Small Group Intervention or 1-1 Intervention

Special Education

Tiers 2 and 3 are not linear. They represent degrees of intensity for meeting student needs.

Tier 1: Core classroom program with differentiated small group instruction

Classroom teacher provides additional support to lowest group.

Tier 2: Small group with intensity that relates to group size and expertise; duration in group depends on student need

Tier 3: 1:1 with Reading Recovery in 1st grade; 1:2 group or reading/writing conferences in upper grades

Tier 4: Referral process after student has received intervention in layers 1, 2, and 3

All interventions are dynamic and interactive, not static and linear.

Note. Figure used with permission from *Journal of Reading Recovery.* CR = classroom.

intensity), whereas the layered approach is grounded in acceleration theory (i.e., assess, intervene, adjust the teaching if the student is not learning).

Within a layered approach, teachers observe how students are responding to instruction (intervention), and if the student is not learning, the problem is with the teaching, not with the student. This diagnostic model requires teachers to use data in systematic ways, including observations of how students are learning on different tasks across changing contexts (e.g., classroom, Title I, special education). The layered framework views all teachers as intervention specialists, including classroom teachers, supplemental teachers, and special education teachers. This method aligns with a systems approach.

Two Waves of Literacy Defense

A systems approach to RTI requires a framework of unique and well-developed interventions that meet the diverse needs of struggling students at the primary, intermediate, middle, and secondary levels. Our model for RTI represents two waves of literacy defense (Dorn & Schubert, 2008), with the first wave taking a preventive stance with K–3 interventions. The premises of early intervention are logical: (a) intervene as early as possible before confusion becomes a habituated and unthinking reaction, (b) provide intensive, short-term services that focus on problem-solving strategies in continuous texts, and (c) make data-driven decisions about the intensity of interventions, the duration period, and the need for follow-up support.

The second wave of literacy defense occurs at the 4th- to 12th-grade levels. With appropriate interventions, readers at risk in the upper grades can become successful readers. However, there are major challenges to overcome: Years of unproductive reading practices can create resistance, passivity, and lack of motivation, and interventions may take longer to yield positive results. Addressing these challenges requires schools to redesign their literacy programs in three significant ways: (1) create a classroom model of differentiated instruction, (2) place an emphasis on reading comprehension in the content areas, and (3) provide interventions, including small group and one-to-one, for the students who are lagging behind.

Taking a closer look at each wave, we begin with the elementary grades. The purpose of the first wave is to increase the overall literacy achievement by the end of third grade and reduce the number of students identified as having LDs within 1.5% or less of the general population. Toward this goal, struggling readers are provided with multiple layers of intervention. To illustrate, at Tier 1 the classroom teacher provides the entire class with a 90-minute literacy core of differentiated instruction: whole group (e.g., shared reading, interactive read-aloud, strategy-based minilesson), small group (e.g., guided reading, literature discussion, assisted writing), one-to-one (e.g., reading and writing conferences), and independent (e.g., easy or familiar reading, word study). For struggling readers, the teacher provides an additional classroom intervention; for example, the teacher might add a 10-minute word-study lesson prior to the guided reading lesson for those students who need tailored support in word-solving strategies. (See Figure 4.2 for an example of a Tier 1 classroom schedule that uses a workshop framework with classroom interventions within each workshop block.)

Concurrent with Tier 1, the lowest students may also receive a Tier 2 small-group intervention or a Tier 3 one-to-one intervention. In some cases, a student might receive three interventions at the same time. If a student is not progressing at the expected rate, the classroom teacher, in collaboration with the school's

Figure 4.2. Example of Tier 1 Elementary Classroom Framework for RTI Scheduling

❏ **Shared Reading Poetry** (10 minutes)
8:10–8:20

❏ **Spelling/Phonics** (20 minutes)
8:20–8:35

❏ **Reading Workshop** (90 minutes)
8:40–10:10
❖ Reading Minilesson
❖ Small-Group Instruction: Guided Reading, Literature Discussion Group
❖ Reading Conferences
❖ RTI: Word Study
❖ RTI: Writing in Response to Reading
❖ Debriefing and Closure

❏ **Math Workshop Part I** (65 minutes)
10:10–11:15
❖ Math Minilesson
❖ Small-Group Math Investigations, Teacher Conferences

❏ **Lunch/Recess** (50 minutes)
11:20–11:40, 11:40–12:10

❏ **Specials** (40 minutes) 12:10–12:50

❏ **Language Studies** (35 minutes)
12:55–1:30
❖ Language Minilesson
❖ Small-Group Language Investigations, Teacher Conferences
❖ Debriefing and Closure

❏ **Writing Workshop** (45 minutes)
1:30–2:15
❖ Writing Minilesson
❖ Independent Writing, Teacher Conferences
❖ RTI: Assisted Writing
❖ RTI: Writing Conference
❖ Debriefing and Closure

❏ **Content Workshop** (45 minutes)
2:15–3:00
❖ Content Minilesson
❖ Small-Group Investigation, Content Strategy Groups
❖ RTI: Content Strategy Group
❖ Debriefing and Closure

intervention team, may initiate the referral process for special education. In Tier 4, the special education students continue to receive Tier 1 classroom instruction to meet their literacy needs, and the classroom and special education teachers collaborate on a seamless approach across the two contexts. The expectation is that the special education students continue to make good progress, with the potential to reach literacy proficiency over time.

In the second wave of literacy defense, Tier 1 instruction uses a workshop framework for differentiating instruction, including small groups and one-to-one conferences. Interventions focus on comprehension of content area text through strategy-based instruction. In Tier 2, struggling readers receive supplemental small-group instruction from intervention specialists. Tier 3 interventions include individual or small groups of 1:3 or less and are provided to students who are reading below average levels. In schools with literacy coaches, the coaches spend up to 40% of their time providing Tier 2 and Tier 3 interventions to the students who need the most help. Special education teachers provide Tier 4 intervention in collaboration with Tier 1 classroom intervention to provide a seamless transition for students with LDs.

The CIM

In this section, we examine the research supporting a comprehensive literacy approach as an RTI method. Then, we describe how the CIM interventions are organized within a portfolio framework that enables teachers to make decisions about the best interventions for particular students. Also, we explain how teachers use assessments for screening, placement, and progress monitoring. Finally, we share how schools use an assessment wall to measure the growth of particular subgroups within and across grade levels.

Supporting Research

A critical element of RTI is that the approach must be research based; furthermore, it should be based on a well-articulated design to ensure fidelity in implementation (Denton, Vaughn, & Fletcher, 2003). Yet, at the same time, the design must be flexible enough to respect the decision-making knowledge of teachers and accommodate the variability in students' learning (Allington, 2006; Johnston, 2009; Lose, 2007; McEneaney et al., 2006; Scanlon, Gelzheiser,

Vellutino, Schatschneider, & Sweeney, 2008; Scanlon, Vellutino, Small, Fanuele, & Sweeney, 2005; Vellutino, Scanlon, Zhang, & Schatschneider, 2008).

One intervention within the CIM portfolio is Reading Recovery, which is possibly the world's most widely researched early literacy intervention. In 2007, Reading Recovery received the highest rating by What Works Clearinghouse (2008), a branch of the United States Department of Education's Institute of Education Sciences, for positive effects on general reading achievement and alphabetics and for potentially positive effects on reading comprehension and fluency. This perhaps is not surprising given that Reading Recovery has been examined by high-quality experimental and quasi-experimental studies (Pinnell, Lyons, DeFord, Bryk, & Seltzer, 1994; Rodgers, Gómez-Bellengé, Wang, & Schulz, 2005; Rodgers, Wang, & Gómez-Bellengé, 2004; Schwartz, Askew, & Gómez-Bellengé, 2007; Schwartz, Schmitt, & Lose, 2008), state and national evaluation studies (see www.ndec.us), and meta-analyses (D'Agostino & Murphy, 2004; Elbaum, Vaughn, Hughes, & Moody, 2000). The Reading Recovery framework incorporates the essential components of reading instruction, including phonemic awareness, phonics, vocabulary, fluency, and comprehension.

The CIM also includes a portfolio of small-group interventions that range from kindergarten to middle school. Numerous studies of small-group interventions have demonstrated their effectiveness with struggling readers (Fowler, Lindemann, Thacker-Gwaltney, & Invernizzi, 2002; Goldenberg, 1992; Graham & Harris, 2005; Hiebert & Taylor, 2000; Saunders & Goldenberg, 1999; Torgesen et al., 1999, 2001; Vellutino & Scanlon, 2002). Three state-level studies in Arkansas provide support for a comprehensive literacy model that includes Reading Recovery and small-group components (Dorn & Allen, 1995; Harrison, 2003; James, 2005). These studies found that Reading Recovery and small-group programs are complementary interventions that recognize the diverse needs of struggling readers and provide varying degrees of intensity.

Critical factors that increase the likelihood of success for small-group interventions have been cited in numerous research reports (Allington, 2002; Clay, 1982, 1991; Denton, Fletcher, Anthony, & Francis, 2006; Elbaum et al., 2000; Juel, 1988; Leslie & Allen, 1999; Mathes et al., 2005; Mathes & Torgesen, 1998; Pikulski, 1997; Scanlon & Vellutino, 1996; Schwartz, 2005; Snow, Burns, & Griffin, 1998; Torgesen et al., 2001; Vellutino et al., 2008). The small-group interventions in the CIM were developed by examining research on successful literacy practices and refined through partnerships with teachers in the schools

(Dorn et al., 1998; Dorn & Soffos, 2001b, 2005). Literacy components within the CIM are phoneme awareness, phonics, oral language, fluency, vocabulary, comprehension, and writing. The collaborative process with teachers to teach these components effectively is facilitated through ongoing professional development, field observations, and action research projects.

A Portfolio of K–6 Interventions

The CIM portfolio of interventions is an RTI method for diagnosing literacy difficulties, providing tailored interventions with degrees of intensity, monitoring how well students are responding to intervention, and collaborating with general education and specialty teachers on student progress across multiple contexts. All interventions within the portfolio are structured around predictable lesson components and established routines with daily instruction. Within this framework, teachers employ data-driven, decision-making processes, including selecting books, prompting for strategies, and teaching for independence and transfer.

The effectiveness of the intervention is based on the teacher's ability to do the following:

- Create a tailored environment for promoting self-monitoring behaviors
- Narrow the degrees of freedom through managed choices within the intervention
- Provide sensitive scaffolding at critical points in the problem-solving process
- Promote self-regulated activity, including the ability to generalize (transfer) knowledge, skills, and strategies from one learning context to another

The portfolio builds on the following four principles:

1. Teachers select the most appropriate intervention to meet student needs.
2. The intervention aligns with high-quality classroom instruction.
3. Student progress is closely monitored across interventions and classroom instruction.
4. Intervention teams collaborate on student learning and make data-based decisions for continued improvement.

Within the CIM portfolio, assessment and instruction are viewed as reciprocal and recursive processes—dynamic assessment (Lidz & Gindis, 2003). From an RTI perspective, this method is especially relevant because it embeds intervention within the assessment procedure. Teachers must be sensitive observers of student's literacy behaviors—specifically, how they are responding to instruction—and must be able to adjust their teaching to accommodate their students' learning. All interventions are designed to occur in the student's zone of proximal development (Vygotsky, 1978).

The CIM portfolio comprises the following evidence-based interventions:

- Reading Recovery
- Emergent language and literacy
- Guided Reading Plus
- Assisted writing/interactive writing
- Assisted writing/writing aloud
- Writing process group
- Comprehension focus/genre units of study
- Comprehension focus/strategy units of study
- Comprehension focus/content units of study

Each intervention can be implemented within or outside the classroom, with the exception of Reading Recovery, which is always taught as a pull-out intervention, and writing process group, which is always taught within the classroom writing workshop. The purpose of this section is to describe the eight small-group interventions, which can be taught by classroom teachers (Tier 1), supplemental teachers (Tiers 2 and 3), and special education teachers (Tier 4). The intensity of each intervention is determined by group size, which ranges from two to five students. Following diagnostic assessment, an intervention team meeting convenes for teachers to collaborate on the most appropriate intervention to meet the unique needs of the students.

Emergent Language and Literacy Intervention

The emergent language and literacy intervention is designed for kindergarten and beginning first graders with at-risk behaviors. The intervention emphasizes six essential elements for learning to read: oral language fluency, early concepts about print, phonemic awareness, vocabulary development, attention to print, and talking about literacy.

The intervention is organized within a predictable framework whose major components are listening to the sounds of language, attending to visual information in language, and using writing as a tool for integrating oral and written language. The first component is addressed through the shared reading of nursery rhymes and poetry, which provides students with a fluent context for listening to the sounds of language and acquiring new vocabulary. The second component begins with the shared reading of a large alphabet chart, followed by opportunities to sort magnetic letters into categories and build simple high-frequency words. The third component focuses on assisted writing with four levels of teacher support:

1. The teacher guides students to compose a group message based on a common experience.

2. The teacher uses an interactive writing technique to involve students in recording the group message while focusing their attention on concepts about print.

3. The teacher prompts each student to compose a personal message.

4. The students write their messages while the teacher conducts one-to-one conferences to meet individual needs.

A central element of the intervention is the opportunity for at-risk learners to hear and use literate language (concepts about print) and subsequently develop awareness of literacy conventions.

Guided Reading Plus Intervention

The Guided Reading Plus intervention is designed for students in grades 1–4 are reading at the early to transitional levels of reading and writing but are lagging behind their classmates in reading abilities (see Dorn & Soffos, 2009a). The intervention is designed to enable struggling readers to acquire flexible strategies for solving problems in reading and writing while maintaining a focus on comprehension. The addition of writing and word study to the traditional guided reading group is especially important for struggling readers. Writing plays a special role in lifting reading achievement, as writing slows down the reading process and increases readers' orthographic and phonological knowledge through motor production.

The lesson format spans two days, with 30 minutes of instruction per day. Day 1 includes the following components: preplanned word study activity, orientation to the new text, independent reading with teacher observations, and follow-up teaching points, including discussion of the message. On Day 2, the teacher takes a running record on two students while the other students read easy or familiar texts. Then, the focus shifts to the writing component, which includes four distinct parts: (1) students verbally respond to the previous day's guided reading text, (2) students verbally compose individual messages, (3) students write messages independently, and (4) students participate in one-to-one writing conferences with the teacher. The Guided Reading Plus intervention enables struggling readers to read for understanding, practice efficient decoding strategies, and use what they know about reading to assist with their writing, and vice versa.

Assisted Writing Intervention

The assisted writing intervention is for students in first to fourth grades who are struggling with literacy processing (Dorn et al., 1998). We believe that writing is a powerful intervention for increasing reading achievement, but only if reading and writing are taught as reciprocal processes. The physical act of writing slows down the reading process, and if the writing is meaningful, it promotes the integration of these language systems: comprehension of ideas (meaning system), expression of ideas (language system), and facility with mechanics (graphophonemic and motor systems).

Assisted writing is an umbrella term for classifying two types of writing: interactive and writing aloud. At the emergent to early levels, the interactive writing intervention enables students to do the following:

- Acquire foundational concepts about print
- Understand that writing is about communicating a message
- Apply rereading strategies to predict and monitor reading
- Articulate words slowly and hear and record letters in words
- Use simple resources as self-help tools (e.g., ABC chart, personal dictionary)
- Become fluent with correct letter formation
- Build a core of high-frequency words
- Cross-check multiple sources of information

The interactive writing intervention uses a predictable structure that is divided into three 10-minute blocks: (1) letter and word study, including recording known (high-frequency) words in a personal dictionary, (2) group interactive writing, followed by generation and rehearsal of a personal message, and (3) individual journal writing, including one-to-one conferences with the teacher.

The writing-aloud intervention is designed for students who are reading at higher levels but experiencing difficulty with the writing process. The goal is to assist students in understanding that writing is a process of generating ideas, drafting a message, revising, editing, and preparing a piece for a particular audience. The writing-aloud intervention comprises these elements: explicit teaching through writing-aloud lessons, group compositions, individual writing, teacher conferences, and student self-assessments.

Writing Process Intervention

The writing process intervention is delivered within the writers' workshop block of the classroom (Dorn & Soffos, 2001a). It is a supplemental intervention taught by a specialty teacher (e.g., CIM interventionist, Title I, Reading Recovery, special education). The interventionist comes into the classroom during writers' workshop and leads a small group of struggling writers to a table, where he or she assists them with their writing. This assistance includes composing a meaningful message, applying problem-solving strategies for working on words, revising and editing the message, and maintaining a focus for completing the writing task. The interventionist observes the writing behaviors of individual students within the group and provides tailored support that enables each student to accomplish the classroom writing goals.

Comprehension Focus Interventions

Comprehension focus group (CFG) interventions are designed for elementary and middle school students who are struggling with reading comprehension (see Dorn & Soffos, 2009b). *Comprehension focus group* is an umbrella term that consists of three types of comprehension units: genre, strategy, and content. Each intervention consists of a series of reading and writing lessons with a specific focus that occurs over a period of weeks. The intervention is organized around units of study that require readers to apply higher level comprehension strategies to analyze relationships within and across texts (Dorn & Soffos, 2005). Reading and writing are viewed as reciprocal processes; therefore, students are taught to use their knowledge from reading to support their writing and vice versa. The CFG intervention consists of four phases: (1) preparatory, (2) reading, (3) group book discussion, and (4) writing. We look at each type of CFG intervention unit, beginning with the genre unit of study.

During the preparatory phase, the teacher engages the students in group activities that scaffold them in learning about the genre, including reading aloud a mentor text that represents the genre and completing a group text map for it. Then, the teacher introduces the books within the unit of study and gives a brief talk on each. The students preview the books and rank them according to their reading preferences.

The reading phase begins with a 10-minute explicit minilesson on a comprehension strategy. Afterward, the teacher introduces the new book in the genre unit, and the students read the book independently. Then, the teacher conducts one-to-one reading conferences to assess the students' comprehension and prepare them for the group book discussion. The teacher assembles the group to discuss the strategies used during the independent reading, and the students complete a text map of the book.

During the group book discussion phase, the students participate in a discussion of the book. As they interact with one another, they apply discourse moves (see Dorn & Soffos, 2005) for building, clarifying, and sustaining the conversation. The teacher provides three or four prompts throughout the discussion to focus the talk on deeper meanings. In the final component, the teacher provides a high-level comprehension prompt, and the students respond in their reading response logs.

At the end of the reading unit, the CFG intervention moves into a sustained writing unit. During the writing phase, the students use their knowledge of text and genre structure to develop a piece of writing and carry it through the writing process. Generally, the writing phase lasts two weeks and consists of the following: minilessons, mentor texts, independent writing, one-to-one conferences, strategy checklists, and self-assessments.

The strategy unit of study follows the same four-part structure as the CFG; however, texts are not organized within genre studies. Students learn to apply comprehension strategies for regulating their reading for different purposes on varied texts. The 10 units of study are as follows: questioning, predicting, inferring, visualizing, analyzing, summarizing, critiquing, organizing, problem solving, and reciprocity. Each unit contains subunits; for example, a strategy unit on organizing might include a focus on note-taking using a variety of texts, followed by the writing phase on using notes to organize and develop a piece of writing.

A strategy unit on analysis might focus, for instance, on character analysis across multiple genres or texts, followed by writing a character study during the writing phase. For another example, a strategy unit on summarization would require students to apply summarizing strategies during the reading phase, then transfer this knowledge to crafting a summary during the writing phase. The ultimate goal of the writing phase, in contrast to the genre unit, is to help students acquire the specialized skills for academic writing.

In the CFG content unit, the intervention focuses on grade-level expectations that align with content standards; for instance, a unit of study might focus on the solar system, the water cycle, or weather. The intervention has four goals: (1) acquire self-monitoring and self-regulating strategies for reading the content materials, (2) understand how content texts are organized, (3) comprehend the content information, and (4) compose well-written expository texts.

In summary, the CIM portfolio of interventions enables school teams to make decisions about the most appropriate intervention to meet the needs of diverse learners. The interventions are based on evidence-based practices that mirror high-quality classroom instruction. Each intervention is structured within a 30-minute predictable lesson framework that emphasizes the reading and writing relationship.

Assessment in the CIM

Assessment is defined as "the act or process of gathering data in order to better understand the strengths and weaknesses of student learning, as by observation, testing, interviews, etc." (Harris & Hodges, 1995, p. 12). However, we believe that to myopically focus on individual student achievement is shortsighted at best. In the CIM, both the individual student and the system are examined.

To address the complexity that surrounds the identification and teaching of students who experience literacy difficulties, the CIM teachers engage in a process of comprehensive literacy diagnosis (Dorn & Henderson, 2010). Literacy diagnosis, in contrast to literacy assessment, is a comprehensive process, combining literacy assessment, literacy evaluation, and decision making for literacy instruction. Adopting a problem-solving process method of inquiry, literacy diagnosis requires teachers to identify needed information, obtain that information, interpret and evaluate it; determine what further information (if any) is needed, and plan instruction based on student response (adapted from Kibby, 1995, p. 2).

Universal Screener for Identification Process

To begin the literacy diagnostic process, a universal screener is administered to all students in a CIM school. Although no particular screener is compulsory, schools are given five questions to use in selecting an appropriate screener:

1. Does it accurately classify at-risk students?
2. Is it a good predictor of later reading outcomes?
3. Is it sensitive to different levels of reading development?
4. Can it be administered quickly, efficiently, and economically?
5. Does it enable at-risk students to receive timely and effective intervention?

After the universal screener is administered, those students scoring below grade-level proficiency at the beginning of the year (i.e., approximately the lowest 20%) are assessed using a literacy diagnostic to provide more detailed information on the students' strengths and needs. The literacy diagnostic includes measures such as the following: (a) running records to assess text level, strategic behaviors, and reading fluency, (b) writing samples, (c) observation checklists and rubrics, (d) word-identification or developmental spelling tests, (e) reading logs, (f) formal test results, (g) written responses to reading, and (h) selected class work. (See the case study in Chapter 5 for more details; see also Dorn & Henderson, 2010.) A text reading and writing measure is highly encouraged to assess how students are performing on authentic literacy tasks. The literacy diagnostic greatly reduces the problem of misidentification by providing intervention to students who do not need it (i.e., false positives) or denying intervention to students who do need it (i.e., false negatives).

Following the literacy diagnostic, all stakeholders (e.g., classroom teachers, specialists, administrators) meet as an intervention team to review the data. After a thorough analysis of multiple and varied assessments, the intervention team decides on the most appropriate intervention(s) for the particular student. Once the student is selected to receive an intervention, the team completes an intervention planner. (See the case study in Chapter 5 for more details.) The intervention planner serves as a chronological history for any intervention that a student receives (e.g., classroom, small group, one-to-one) and outlines the plan for instruction, how the plan is monitored, and the intensity and duration of the intervention.

Formative Assessments for Progress Monitoring

Formative assessments in the form of teacher observations, anecdotal notes, checklists, rubrics, and running records are collected to make instructional decisions on a day-by-day, student-by-student basis (visit www.arliteracymodel.com for sample assessments). Data are collected at regular intervals to systematically monitor a student's progress in a particular intervention and consists of the following: (a) systematic and periodic assessments of learning behaviors, (b) measuring and comparing growth over time, and (c) using assessment to plan next steps. These data are graphed to compare screening and baseline data to benchmark expectations for each assessment period and to grade-level end-of-year expectations.

If the intervention fails to alter the trajectory of the student's progress, the intervention team reconvenes to engage in continued and collaborative problem solving. This problem-solving process consists of the following: (a) identifying any additional information that may need to be collected, (b) identifying how to best obtain that information, (c) interpreting and evaluating the new information against previous information, and (d) adapting or designing instruction within the portfolio of interventions to ensure the student's literacy growth. Each student has an RTI portfolio that includes a chronological record with supporting documentation of the student's progress in response to the instructional interventions.

Assessment Wall for Progress Monitoring

To track progress at a systems level, an assessment wall is used (see the case study in Chapter 5 for more details; see also Dorn & Henderson, 2010). The assessment wall provides a visual representation for stakeholders to monitor progress of the school in moving all students to higher levels of literacy achievement. In comparison with computerized assessment systems, the assessment wall provides a medium for interaction, conversation, and collaboration among literacy professionals in the building.

Over the past decade, we have refined our use of the assessment wall to include a portfolio of assessments. We give special recognition to Vicki Altland, literacy coach in Conway, Arkansas, for the current format. Typically, the assessment wall is made up of four large pocket charts representing categories of students who have been determined to be at a below basic, basic, proficient, or advanced level of literacy progress in reading and writing. Each student in the school is represented by a card placed in one of these categories on the assessment wall. However, identifying information related to a particular student or teacher is coded. For example, the code 02-03-15 represents a student in grade 2, assigned to teacher 3, with a corresponding student number of 15. The use of codes ensures that conversations remain centered on how the school is performing as a system rather than identifying how a particular teacher or student is functioning.

In addition to using number codes for students and teachers, teachers and administrators use colored dots to determine which information they placed on the cards to monitor how particular factors may be influencing student performance. Frequently occurring codes include whether a student is an English-language learner, receives a free or reduced-cost lunch, has been in an intervention previously, or is a transfer student.

Two of the most powerful outcomes of using the assessment wall are that it does the following: (1) requires teachers to analyze individual student data, come to a consensus on where their students are in terms of literacy achievement, and problem solve with colleagues, and (2) enables teachers to see patterns across the system that may need to be addressed. For example, one school noticed that while many of their students had moved from the below basic category to basic, it appeared that transfer students across the grade levels were not making adequate progress. As a result, the school assembled a triage team to assess any transfer student within 48 hours of enrolling in their building. Through a problem-solving process, the intervention team implemented a plan whereby transfer students who scored below the basic level were prioritized and placed in an intervention group with frequent progress monitoring to ensure that literacy gains were achieved.

The assessment wall also serves to sharpen teachers' use of data and student observation. At the end or beginning of each academic year, stakeholders assemble to compare summative data (usually in the form of mandated state tests) to actual placement of student cards on the assessment wall. If there is a discrepancy, teachers investigate how well their formative assessments aligned with high-stakes summative assessments and evaluate their own abilities to pinpoint students' literacy achievement. In addition, pictures are taken of the assessment wall at the beginning of the year and at each monitoring period (usually each grading period). These pictures are archived and compared to assist stakeholders in (a) evaluating whether the school as a system is making progress and (b) identifying patterns of student progress that may otherwise go undetected. (See the case study in Chapter 5 for pictures of one school's assessment wall.)

Professional Development in the CIM

We are convinced that approaches to RTI that are served up "in a box" or delivered in a "one-shot workshop" format are counterproductive to designing interventions that best meet the individual needs of struggling literacy learners. Research has shown that to improve schools we must provide high-quality professional development at a systems level (Bryk, Rollow, & Pinnell, 1996; Elmore & Sykes, 1992; Evertson & Murphy, 1992; Fullan, 1993; Guskey, 1995; Hawley & Valli, 1999; Pink & Hyde, 1992). High-quality professional development focuses on academic standards and student performance (Fullan, 1993; Miller, Lord, & Dorney, 1994; Pink & Hyde, 1992). In addition, although high-quality professional development is primarily school based, it is enriched by new knowledge and skill provided by sources outside the school (Lieberman, 1995). Unfortunately, much of the professional development we observe usually falls under a category of random acts of improvement (Bernhardt, 2004) rather than a systemic approach focused on building capacity in the school.

The CIM embodies a systemic, capacity-building approach to professional development for stakeholders within the system. It reflects new ways of thinking about teacher professional development. Collinson (1996), for example, argues that professional development should be viewed as a shared, public process that promotes sustained interaction and emphasizes substantive school-related issues. In this new approach, professional development relies on internal expertise and expects teachers to be active participants, emphasizing the why as well as the how of teaching. Finally, professional development articulates a theoretical research base while anticipating that lasting change is an ongoing process.

Professional development in the CIM begins with school teams attending a weeklong intensive institute at one of the participating university training centers. The CIM institute provides declarative knowledge to include the following:

(a) RTI at the national and state level, (b) the theoretical underpinnings of the CIM, (c) instruction in the portfolio of interventions, and (d) instruction in reading diagnosis. During the CIM institute, school teams are given time to develop their procedural knowledge as well. Working as school teams, participants engage in a process of evaluating the literacy environment of their schools using Dorn and Soffos's (2007) environmental scale for assessing implementation levels (ESAIL) as well as completing a CIM needs assessment survey.

Following the CIM institute, those on the school team serving as CIM interventionists participate in yearlong clinical training with university professors, highly trained Reading Recovery teacher leaders, or literacy coach specialists. The purpose of the clinical component is not only to deepen the teachers' declarative and procedural knowledge of the CIM but also to provide multiple opportunities for interventionists to develop and refine their conditional knowledge. For example, at one of the university training centers, the CIM interventionists are provided with a flip camera to record teaching moves and student responses within an intervention on a biweekly basis. The recordings are analyzed and reflected upon collectively, with a shared purpose of building expertise when working with struggling literacy learners across multiple contexts. At points of analysis, interventionists are prompted to ask the following questions: (a) What happened? (b) What is missing that if provided would make a difference? and (c) What are the next steps based on your analysis and investigation? (adapted from Hargrove, 2003). It is expected that interventionists will internalize the language extended during professional development sessions over time. As a result, every teaching interaction (not just during scheduled progress-monitoring sessions) cycles through an internalized problem-solving process. This aspect of the CIM is paramount, as research has demonstrated that "without time for reflection and support from an expert other, teachers make very few changes in their instructional practices, however well intentioned they are" (Joyce & Showers, 1995, p. 6).

Professional Learning Teams

Professional study is another component of the CIM. First, using information collected from the ESAIL, the CIM needs assessment study, and student achievement data, intervention or grade-level teams decide on an area of professional study. Next, professional resources are surveyed and selected for weekly or biweekly study. These professional learning teams are grouped usually by grade level; however, we have seen instances in which an entire school chooses a text or teachers from different grade levels engage in a process of professional growth around a particular area. For example, in one school, we observed an entire faculty focused on deepening their understanding of the comprehension process to facilitate their students' understandings of text. After previewing multiple texts related to comprehension instruction, the teachers chose to read *Teaching for Deep Comprehension: A Reading Workshop Approach* (Dorn & Soffos, 2005) over their summer break and met biweekly to discuss the text and incorporate new understandings into the upcoming year's curriculum. When school reconvened at the beginning of the year, the teachers met in grade-level intervention teams to examine incoming student data. After careful study and collaborative problem solving and conversation, each grade-level team selected a focus area with the goal of improving their teaching to facilitate their students' learning. Once established, teachers began the process of selecting appropriate materials for study to accomplish their goals.

In contrast, in another school we worked with, we saw teachers from different grade levels come together in professional learning teams. In this school, there had been a rapid increase in student population that resulted in the hiring of many new teachers. The new teachers quickly realized that they needed to develop a focus on a classroom management system across the grade levels. For the veteran teachers who had their classroom routines established, this was not an area of need. Again, through a process of communication and collaboration, the veteran teachers decided that the newly hired teachers would engage in a professional learning team around a variety of texts that had classroom management components (with the veteran teachers' support). In contrast, the veteran teachers chose texts reflecting the academic areas they determined needed improvement (e.g., word study, writers' workshop, genre study, developmental spelling) and shared new understandings in grade-level meetings with the less experienced teachers.

The key element of the CIM professional development is that the teachers use student data to decide on an area of focus and then engage in an investigative process to determine which materials facilitate meeting those needs. It is important to note that as university professors, we serve as a support to the schools in this process but do not outline or define the process for them. Just as we want our students to regulate their own learning, we want our teachers to do the same. This is fundamental to building capacity in CIM schools. If we identify the books that teachers need to read or actively participate in the process (e.g., attend every book study group), we diminish the ability for these professional learning teams to continue when we are no longer there. Therefore, our purpose is to engage in a professional partnership with our CIM administrators, CIM intervention specialists, and literacy coach specialists to support them in their role as literacy leaders in their schools. Experience has taught us that for professional development to result in a process of continuous school improvement and growth, leadership must come from inside the school, not reside outside of it.

Using Technology to Support Teachers

An important focus of 21st-century learning is the use of technology for supporting teacher development. Earlier in this chapter, we mentioned the www .arliteracymodel.com website. The primary purpose of the website is to create an electronic context where teachers can access free materials and problem solve together on teaching and learning issues. Several of the documents referenced in our chapter are available on the website, such as writing continuums, intervention schedules, rubrics for assessing intervention groups, teaching resources (e.g., template for personal dictionary), and data collection forms. One of the most popular features of the website is the teacher discussion board. Currently, the message board has more than 7,000 postings from educators across the county, including school teams who use the board to post special topics for peer discussions.

Although the CIM involves specialized training at a university training center, we recognize the importance of supporting teachers who are unable to participate in the training. Therefore, the website serves three purposes: (1) at the classroom level, it provides resources for implementing a high-quality classroom program, (2) at the intervention level, it provides information for working with struggling readers, and (3) at the teacher level, it creates an online context for teacher collaboration and problem solving. We believe this is another component of a systems model: a mechanism for sharing information, learning from one another, and forming literacy partnerships for students.

Concluding Thoughts

In this chapter, we presented the CIM as a systems model for meeting the intentions of RTI. The heartbeat of the CIM is a responsive and knowledgeable teacher—one who understands the literacy process and is able to adjust instruction to accommodate the continuous changes in student learning. We believe that responsive teaching cannot be scripted or purchased in a box. These simplistic solutions to RTI ignore the complexity and uniqueness of the human mind and the influence of the teacher's decision making on the learning process.

From a systems perspective, the CIM is "not a model to be imposed on schools, but rather a framework to help schools identify and support students before the difficulties they encounter with language and literacy become more serious" ("RTI," 2009). This framework is grounded in a decision-making model that empowers teachers to use student data to select the best interventions for particular students. The CIM portfolio consists of nine interventions, each of which is organized within a lesson framework that consists of predictable structures, evidence-based practices, systematic observations, and frequent progress monitoring. The portfolio is housed within a four-tiered layered approach that emphasizes congruency across classroom instruction and supplemental interventions.

In essence, the CIM is grounded in the belief that to address the individual needs of all learners, we must work collaboratively across many levels—universities and schools—to increase our knowledge about what works to improve our teaching. The CIM is about expert teachers teaching students how to learn—and if students are not learning, it is about problem solving with others to improve instruction, so students do learn.

REFERENCES

Aaron, P.G. (1997). The impending demise of the discrepancy formula. *Review of Educational Research, 67*(4), 461–502.

Allington, R.L. (2002). Research on reading/learning disability interventions. In A.E. Farstrup & S.J. Samuels (Eds.), *What research has to say about reading instruction* (3rd ed., pp. 261–290). Newark, DE: International Reading Association.

Allington, R.L. (2006). Research and the Three Tier model. *Reading Today, 23*(5), 20.

Bahr, M.W., Fuchs, D., Stecker, P.M., & Fuchs, L.S. (1991). Are teachers' perceptions of difficult-to-teach students racially biased? *School Psychology Review, 20*(4), 599–608.

Bernhardt, V.L. (2004). *Data analysis for continuous school improvement* (2nd ed.). Larchmont, NY: Eye on Education.

Brown, W., Denton, E., Kelly, P., & Neal, J. (1999). Reading Recovery effectiveness: A five-year success story in San Luis Coastal Unified School District. *ERS Spectrum, 17*(1), 3–12.

Bryk, A.S., Rollow, S.G., & Pinnell, G.S. (1996). Urban school development: Literacy as a lever for change. *Educational Policy, 10*(2), 172–201. doi:10.1177/0895904896010002004

Center, Y., Wheldall, K., Freeman, L., Outhred, L., & McNaught, M. (1995). An evaluation of

Reading Recovery. *Reading Research Quarterly,* *30*(2), 240–263. doi:10.2307/748034

Clay, M.M. (1982). *Observing young readers: Selected papers.* Exeter, NH: Heinemann.

Clay, M.M. (1987). Learning to be learning disabled. *New Zealand Journal of Educational Studies, 22*(2), 155–173.

Clay, M.M. (1990). The Reading Recovery Programme, 1984–88: Coverage, outcomes and education board district figures. *New Zealand Journal of Educational Studies, 25*(1), 61–70.

Clay, M.M. (1991). *Becoming literate: The construction of inner control.* Portsmouth, NH: Heinemann.

Clay, M.M. (2001). *Change over time in children's literacy development.* Portsmouth, NH: Heinemann.

Clay, M.M. (2005). *Literacy lessons: Designed for individuals, part two: Teaching procedures.* Portsmouth, NH: Heinemann.

Collinson, V. (1996, July). *Becoming an exemplary teacher: Integrating professional, interpersonal, and intrapersonal knowledge.* Paper presented at the annual meeting of the Japan–United States Teacher Education Consortium, Naruto, Japan.

Cortiella, C. (2009). *The state of learning disabilities 2009.* New York: National Center for Learning Disabilities. Retrieved September 12, 2009, from www.ncld.org/images/stories/OnCapitolHill/PolicyRelatedPublications/stateofld/stateofld2009.pdf

Crévola, C.A., & Hill, P.W. (1998). Evaluation of a whole-school approach to prevention and intervention in early literacy. *Journal of Education for Students Placed at Risk, 3*(2), 133–157. doi:10.1207/s15327671espr0302_4

Cunningham, A.E., & Stanovich, K.E. (1997). Early reading acquisition and its relation to reading experience and ability 10 years later. *Developmental Psychology, 33*(6), 934–945. doi:10.1037/0012-1649.33.6.934

D'Agostino, J.V., & Murphy, J.A. (2004). A meta-analysis of Reading Recovery in United States schools. *Educational Evaluation and Policy Analysis, 26*(1), 23–28. doi:10.3102/01623737026001023

Darling-Hammond, L., & McLaughlin, M.W. (1999). Investing in teaching as a learning profession: Policy problems and prospects. In L. Darling-Hammond & G. Sykes (Eds.), *Teaching as the learning profession: Handbook of policy and practice* (pp. 376–411). San Francisco: Jossey-Bass.

Denton, C.A., Fletcher, J.M., Anthony, J.L., & Francis, D.J. (2006). An evaluation of intensive intervention for students with persistent reading difficulties. *Journal of Learning Disabilities, 39*(5), 447–466. doi:10.1177/00222194060390050601

Denton, C.A., Vaughn, S., & Fletcher, J.M. (2003). Bringing research-based practice in reading intervention to scale. *Learning Disabilities Research & Practice, 18*(3), 201–211. doi:10.1111/1540-5826.00075

Dorn, L.J., & Allen, A. (1995). Helping low-achieving first-grade readers: A program combining Reading Recovery tutoring and small-group instruction. *ERS Spectrum, 13*(3), 16–24.

Dorn, L.J., French, C., & Jones, T. (1998). *Apprenticeship in literacy: Transitions across reading and writing.* York, ME: Stenhouse.

Dorn, L.J., & Henderson, S.C. (2010). A comprehensive assessment system as a Response to Intervention process. In P.H. Johnston (Ed.), *RTI in Literacy—Responsive and Comprehensive* (pp. 133–153). Newark, DE: International Reading Association.

Dorn, L.J., & Schubert, B. (2008). A comprehensive intervention model for reversing reading failure: A Response to Intervention approach. *Journal of Reading Recovery, 7*(2), 29–41.

Dorn, L.J., & Soffos, C. (2001a). *Scaffolding young writers: A writers' workshop approach.* Portland, ME: Stenhouse.

Dorn, L.J., & Soffos, C. (2001b). *Shaping literate minds: Developing self-regulated learners.* Portland, ME: Stenhouse.

Dorn, L.J., & Soffos, C. (2005). *Teaching for deep comprehension: A reading workshop approach.* Portland, ME: Stenhouse.

Dorn, L.J., & Soffos, C. (2007). *Environmental scale for assessing implementation levels: Descriptions of criteria.* Little Rock: Center for Literacy, University of Arkansas at Little Rock. Retrieved March 16, 2010, from www.arliteracymodel.com/pdf/coaching/ESAIL%20Document.pdf

Dorn, L.J., & Soffos, C. (2009a). *Interventions that work: Guided Reading Plus group DVD* [Computer software]. Boston: Allyn & Bacon.

Dorn, L.J., & Soffos, C. (2009b). *Interventions that work: Comprehension focus group DVD* [Computer software]. Boston: Allyn & Bacon.

Duffy, G.G. (2004). Teachers who improve reading achievement: What research says about what they do and how to develop them. In D.S. Strickland & M.L. Kamil (Eds.), *Improving reading achievement through professional development* (pp. 3–22). Norwood, MA: Christopher-Gordon.

DuFour, R., DuFour, R., Eaker, R., & Karhanek, G. (2004). *Whatever it takes: How professional learning communities respond when kids don't learn.* Bloomington, IN: Solution Tree.

Duke, N.K., & Pearson, P.D. (2002). Effective practices for developing reading comprehension. In A.E. Farstrup & S.J. Samuels (Eds.), *What research has to say about reading instruction* (3rd ed., pp. 205–242). Newark, DE: International Reading Association.

Elbaum, B., Vaughn, S., Hughes, M.T., & Moody, S.W. (2000). How effective are one-to-one tutoring programs in reading for elementary students at risk for reading failure? A meta-analysis of the intervention research. *Journal of Educational Psychology, 92*(4), 605–619. doi:10.1037/0022-0663.92.4.605

Elmore, R., & Sykes, G. (1992). Curriculum policy. In P.W. Jackson (Ed.), *Handbook of research on curriculum: A project of the American Educational Research Association* (pp. 185–215). New York: Macmillan.

Evertson, C.M., & Murphy, J. (1992). Beginning with the classroom: Implications for redesigning schools. In H.H. Marshall (Ed.), *Redefining student learning: Roots of educational change* (pp. 293–320). Norwood, NJ: Ablex.

Farstrup, A.E. (2007). RTI: A vital concern for reading professionals. *Reading Today, 25*(3), 17.

Fletcher, J.M., Shaywitz, S.E., Shankweiler, D.P., Katz, L., Liberman, I.Y., Stuebing, K.K., et al. (1994). Cognitive profiles of reading disability: Comparisons of discrepancy and low achievement definitions. *Journal of Educational Psychology, 86*(1), 6–23. doi:10.1037/0022-0663.86.1.6

Fowler, M.C., Lindemann, L.M., Thacker-Gwaltney, S., & Invernizzi, M. (2002). *A second year of one-on-one tutoring: An intervention for second graders with learning difficulties.* Ann Arbor, MI: Center for the Improvement of Early Reading Achievement, University of Michigan School of Education.

Fuchs, D., & Fuchs, L.S. (2006). Introduction to Response to Intervention: What, why, and how valid is it? *Reading Research Quarterly, 41*(1), 93–99. doi:10.1598/RRQ.41.1.4

Fuchs, L.S., & Fuchs, D. (1998). Treatment validity: A unifying concept for reconceptualizing the identification of learning disabilities. *Learning Disabilities Research and Practice, 13*(4), 204–219.

Fullan, M.G. (1993). Why teachers must become change agents. *Educational Leadership, 50*(6), 12–17.

Fullan, M.G., & Stiegelbauer, S. (1991). *The new meaning of educational change* (2nd ed.). New York: Teachers College Press.

Gallimore, R., Ermeling, B.A., Saunders, W.M., & Goldenberg, C. (2009). Moving the learning of teaching closer to practice: Teacher education implications of school-based inquiry teams. *The Elementary School Journal, 109*(5), 537–553. doi:10.1086/597001

Goldenberg, C. (1992). Instructional conversations: Promoting comprehension through discussion. *The Reading Teacher, 46*(4), 316–326.

Graham, S., & Harris, K.R. (2005). Improving the writing performance of young struggling writers: Theoretical and programmatic research from the Center on Accelerating Student Learning. *Journal of Special Education*, 39(1), 19–33. doi:10.1177/00224669050390 010301

Gresham, F.M. (2002). Responsiveness to intervention: An alternative approach to the identification of learning disabilities. In R. Bradley, L. Danielson, & D.P. Hallahan (Eds.), *Identification of learning disabilities: Research to practice* (pp. 467–519). Mahwah, NJ: Erlbaum.

Guskey, T.R. (1995). Professional development in education: In search of the optimal mix. In T.R. Guskey & M. Huberman (Eds.), *Professional development in education: New paradigms and practices* (pp. 114–131). New York: Teachers College Press.

Hargrove, R. (2003). *Masterful coaching* (Rev. ed.). San Francisco: Jossey-Bass.

Harris, T.L., & Hodges, R.E. (Eds.). (1995). *The literacy dictionary: The vocabulary of reading and writing*. Newark, DE: International Reading Association.

Harrison, L. (2003). *A study of the complementary effects of Reading Recovery and small group literacy instruction*. Unpublished educational specialist thesis, University of Arkansas at Little Rock.

Hart, B., & Risley, T.R. (1995). *Meaningful differences in the everyday experience of young American children*. Baltimore: Paul H. Brookes.

Hawley, W.D., & Valli, L. (1999). The essentials of effective professional development: A new consensus. In L. Darling-Hammond & G. Sykes (Eds.), *Teaching as the learning profession: Handbook of policy and practice* (pp. 127–150). San Francisco: Jossey-Bass.

Hiebert, E.H., & Taylor, B.M. (2000). Beginning reading instruction: Research on early interventions. In M.L. Kamil, P.B. Mosenthal, P.D. Pearson, & R. Barr (Eds.), *Handbook of reading research* (Vol. 3, pp. 455–482). Mahwah, NJ: Erlbaum.

International Reading Association & National Council of Teachers of English. (1994). *Standards for the assessment of reading and writing*. Newark, DE; Urbana, IL: Authors. Retrieved September 12, 2009, from www .reading.org/Libraries/Reports_and_ Standards/bk674.sflb.ashx

James, K.V. (2005). *Reading Recovery and small group literacy intervention: A layered approach for comprehensive intervention*. Unpublished educational specialist thesis, University of Arkansas at Little Rock.

Johnston, P.H. (2009). *Taking Response to Intervention seriously*. Unpublished manuscript, University at Albany, State University of New York.

Johnston, P.H., Allington, R., & Afflerbach, P. (1985). The congruence of classroom and remedial reading instruction. *The Elementary School Journal*, 85(4), 465–477. doi:10.1086/ 461414

Joyce, B.R., & Showers, B. (1995). *Student achievement through staff development: Fundamentals of school renewal* (2nd ed.). White Plains, NY: Longman.

Juel, C. (1988). Learning to read and write: A longitudinal study of 54 children from first through fourth grades. *Journal of Educational Psychology*, 80(4), 437–447. doi:10.1037/0022-0663.80.4.437

Kibby, M.W. (1995). *Practical steps for informing literacy instruction: A diagnostic decision-making model*. Newark, DE: International Reading Association.

Leslie, L., & Allen, L. (1999). Factors that predict success in an early literacy intervention project. *Reading Research Quarterly*, 34(4), 404–424. doi:10.1598/RRQ.34.4.2

Lidz, C.S., & Gindis, B. (2003). Dynamic assessment of the evolving cognitive functions in children. In A. Kozulin, B. Gindis, V.S. Ageyev, & S.M. Miller (Eds.), *Vygotsky's educational theory in cultural context* (pp. 99–116). New York: Cambridge University Press.

Lieberman, A. (1995). *The work of restructuring schools: Building from the ground up*. New York: Teachers College Press.

Lipson, M.Y., & Wixson, K.K. (2009). *Assessment and instruction of reading and writing difficul-*

ties: An interactive approach (4th ed.). Boston: Pearson.

Lose, M.K. (2007). A child's response to intervention requires a responsive teacher of reading. *The Reading Teacher, 61*(3), 276–279. doi:10.1598/RT.61.3.9

Macmann, G.M., Barnett, D.W., Lombard, T.J., Belton-Kocher, E., & Sharpe, M.N. (1989). On the actuarial classification of children: Fundamental studies of classification agreement. *Journal of Special Education, 23*(2), 127–149. doi:10.1177/002246698902300202

MacMillan, D.L., Gresham, F.M., & Bocian, K.M. (1998). Discrepancy between definitions of learning disabilities and school practices: An empirical investigation. *Journal of Learning Disabilities, 31*(4), 314–326. doi:10.1177/002221949803100401

MacMillan, D.L., Gresham, F.M., Lopez, M.F., & Bocian, K.M. (1996). Comparison of students nominated for prereferral interventions by ethnicity and gender. *Journal of Special Education, 30*(2), 133–151. doi:10.1177/002246669603000202

Mathes, P.G., Denton, C.A., Fletcher, J.M., Anthony, J.L., Francis, D.J., & Schatschneider, C. (2005). The effects of theoretically different instruction and student characteristics on the skills of struggling readers. *Reading Research Quarterly, 40*(2), 148–182. doi:10.1598/RRQ.40.2.2

Mathes, P.G., & Torgesen, J.K. (1998). All children can learn to read: Critical care for the prevention of reading failure. *Peabody Journal of Education, 73*(3/4), 317–340.

McCutchen, D., Abbott, R.D., Green, L.B., Beretvas, S.N., Cox, S., Potter, N.S., et al. (2002). Beginning literacy: Links among teacher knowledge, teacher practice, and student learning. *Journal of Learning Disabilities, 35*(1), 69–86. doi:10.1177/002221940203500106

McEneaney, J.E., Lose, M.K., & Schwartz, R.M. (2006). A transactional perspective on reading difficulties and Response to Intervention. *Reading Research Quarterly, 41*(1), 117–128. doi:10.1598/RRQ.41.1.7

Miller, B., Lord, B., & Dorney, J.A. (1994). *Summary report. Staff development for teachers: A study of configurations and costs in four districts.* Newton, MA: Education Development Center.

National Commission on Excellence in Education. (1983). *A nation at risk: The imperative for educational reform.* Washington, DC: National Commission on Excellence in Education, U.S. Department of Education.

National Staff Development Council. (2001). *NSDC's standards for staff development* (Rev. ed.). Retrieved September 12, 2009, from www.nsdc.org/standards/

Pearson, P.D. (2003). The role of professional knowledge in reading reform. *Language Arts, 81*(1), 14–15.

Phillips, G., & Smith, P. (1997). *A third chance to learn: The development and evaluation of specialised interventions for young children experiencing the greatest difficulty in learning to read.* Wellington: New Zealand Council for Educational Research.

Pikulski, J.J. (1997). Preventing reading problems: Factors common to successful early intervention programs. *Reading/Language Arts Center: Preventing Reading Problems.* Retrieved March 28, 2005, from www.eduplace.com/rdg/res/prevent.html

Pink, W.T., & Hyde, A.A. (1992). Doing effective staff development. In W.T. Pink & A.A. Hyde (Eds.), *Effective staff development for school change* (pp. 259–292). Norwood, NJ: Ablex.

Pinnell, G.S., Lyons, C.A., DeFord, D.E., Bryk, A.S., & Seltzer, M. (1994). Comparing instructional models for the literacy education of high-risk first graders. *Reading Research Quarterly, 29*(1), 9–39. doi:10.2307/747736

President's Commission on Excellence in Special Education. (2002). *A new era: Revitalizing special education for children and their families.* Washington, DC: U.S. Department of Education.

Preuss, P.G. (2003). *School leader's guide to root cause analysis: Using data to dissolve problems.* Larchmont, NY: Eye on Education.

Reschly, D.J., & Hosp, J.L. (2004). State SLD identification policies and practices. *Learning Disability Quarterly, 27*(4), 197–213.

Rodgers, E., Gómez-Bellengé, F.X., Wang, C., & Schulz, M. (2005, April). *Predicting the literacy achievement of struggling readers: Does intervening early make a difference?* Paper presented at the annual meeting of the American Educational Research Association, Montreal, QC, Canada.

Rodgers, E.M., Wang, C., & Gómez-Bellengé, F.X. (2004, April). *Closing the literacy achievement gap with early intervention.* Paper presented at the annual meeting of the American Educational Research Association, San Diego, CA.

RTI: Questions reading professionals should ask. (2009). *Reading Today, 27*(1), 1, 6.

Saunders, W.M., & Goldenberg, C. (1999). *The effects of instructional conversations and literature logs on the story comprehension and thematic understanding of English proficient and limited English proficient students* (Research Report No. 6). Santa Cruz: Center for Research on Education, Diversity & Excellence, University of California, Santa Cruz.

Scanlon, D.M., Gelzheiser, L.M., Vellutino, F.R., Schatschneider, C., & Sweeney, J.M. (2008). Reducing the incidence of early reading difficulties: Professional development for classroom teachers versus direct interventions for children. *Learning and Individual Differences, 18*(3), 346–359. doi:10.1016/j.lindif.2008.05.002

Scanlon, D.M., & Vellutino, F.R. (1996). Prerequisite skills, early instruction, and success in first-grade reading: Selected results from a longitudinal study. *Mental Retardation and Developmental Disabilities Research Reviews, 2*(1), 54–63. doi:10.1002/(SICI)1098-2779(1996)2:1<54::AID-MRDD9>3.0.CO;2-X

Scanlon, D.M., Vellutino, F.R., Small, S.G., Fanuele, D.P., & Sweeney, J.M. (2005). Severe reading difficulties—can they be prevented? A comparison of prevention and intervention approaches. *Exceptionality, 13*(4), 209–227. doi:10.1207/s15327035ex1304_3

Schwartz, R.M. (2005). Literacy learning of at-risk first-grade students in the Reading Recovery early intervention. *Journal of Educational Psychology, 97*(2), 257–267. doi:10.1037/0022-0663.97.2.257

Schwartz, R.M., Askew, B.J., & Gómez-Bellengé, F.X. (2007). What works? Reading Recovery. *The Journal of Reading Recovery, 6*(2), 49–52.

Schwartz, R.M., Schmitt, M.C., & Lose, M.K. (2008, December). *The effect of teacher-student ratio on early intervention outcomes.* Paper presented at the National Reading Conference, Orlando, FL.

Snow, C.E., Burns, M.S., & Griffin P. (Eds.). (1998). *Preventing reading difficulties in young children.* Washington, DC: National Academy Press.

Spear-Swerling, L., & Sternberg, R.J. (1996). *Off track: When poor readers become "learning disabled."* Boulder, CO: Westview.

Taylor, B.M., Pearson, P.D., Clark, K., & Walpole, S. (2000). Effective schools and accomplished teachers: Lessons about primary-grade reading instruction in low-income schools. *The Elementary School Journal, 101*(2), 121–165. doi:10.1086/499662

Tharp, R.G. (1982). The effective instruction of comprehension: Results and description of the Kamehameha Early Education Program. *Reading Research Quarterly, 17*(4), 503–527. doi:10.2307/747568

Tharp, R.G., & Gallimore, R. (1988). *Rousing minds to life: Teaching, learning, and schooling in social context.* New York: Cambridge University Press.

Torgesen, J.K., Alexander, A.W., Wagner, R.K., Rashotte, C.A., Voeller, K.K.S., & Conway, T. (2001). Intensive remedial instruction for children with severe reading disabilities: Immediate and long-term outcomes from two instructional approaches. *Journal of Learning Disabilities, 34*(1), 33–58. doi:10.1177/002221940103400104

Torgesen, J.K., Wagner, R.K., Rashotte, C.A., Rose, E., Lindamood, P., Conway,

T., et al. (1999). Preventing reading failure in young children with phonological processing disabilities: Group and individual responses to instruction. *Journal of Educational Psychology, 91*(4), 579–593. doi:10.1037/0022-0663.91.4.579

Vaughn, S., & Linan-Thompson, S. (2003). Group size and time allotted to intervention: Effects for students with reading difficulties. In B.R. Foorman (Ed.), *Preventing and remediating reading difficulties: Bringing science to scale* (pp. 299–324). Baltimore: York.

Vellutino, F.R., & Scanlon, D.M. (2002). The Interactive Strategies approach to reading intervention. *Contemporary Educational Psychology, 27*(4), 573–635. doi:10.1016/S0361-476X(02)00002-4

Vellutino, F.R., Scanlon, D.M., & Lyon, G.R. (2000). Differentiating between difficult-to-remediate and readily remediated poor readers: More evidence against the IQ-achievement discrepancy definition of reading disability. *Journal of Learning Disabilities, 33*(3), 223–238. doi:10.1177/002221940003300302

Vellutino, F.R., Scanlon, D.M., Sipay, E.R., Small, S.G., Pratt, A., Chen, R., et al. (1996). Cognitive profiles of difficult-to-remediate and readily remediated poor readers: Early intervention as a vehicle for distinguishing between cognitive and experiential deficits as basic causes of specific reading disability. *Journal of Educational Psychology, 88*(4), 601–638. doi:10.1037/0022-0663.88.4.601

Vellutino, F.R., Scanlon, D.M., Zhang, H., & Schatschneider, C. (2008). Using response to kindergarten and first grade intervention to identify children at-risk for long-term reading difficulties. *Reading and Writing, 21*(4), 437–480. doi:10.1007/s11145-007-9098-2

Vygotsky, L.S. (1978). *Mind in society: The development of higher psychological processes* (M. Cole, V. John-Steiner, S. Scribner, & E. Souberman, Eds. & Trans.). Cambridge, MA: Harvard University Press.

What Works Clearinghouse. (2008). *Intervention: Reading Recovery.* Retrieved February 1, 2010, from ies.ed.gov/ncee/wwc/reports/beginning_reading/reading_recovery/

Wilson, K.G., & Daviss, B. (1994). *Redesigning education.* New York: Henry Holt.

CHAPTER 5

Spotlight on the Comprehensive Intervention Model: The Case of Washington School for Comprehensive Literacy

Kathryn E. Meyer

Washington School for Comprehensive Literacy, Wisconsin

Brian L. Reindl

Washington School for Comprehensive Literacy, Wisconsin

Although RTI is a relatively new term for the staff at the Washington School for Comprehensive Literacy, our movement toward schoolwide improvement initially began several years ago. Washington School is a K–5 elementary school of about 365 students located in Sheboygan, Wisconsin. About 85% of students receive free or reduced-cost lunch, and 41% are English-language learners (ELLs). As teachers, we were working as hard as we could, but our students were not making adequate progress. We decided to take a hard look at the way we were teaching reading and writing in our building and began a journey that would lead us to our current RTI method.

In 2004, our school trained the two of us as full-time literacy coaches to implement the partnerships in comprehensive literacy (PCL) model in grades K–5. (See www.arliteracymodel.com for a description of the PCL model.) The PCL model is a school improvement design that consists of 10 features for coordinating and monitoring school improvement: a framework for literacy, coaching and mentoring, model classrooms, high standards, accountability, the Comprehensive Intervention Model (CIM), professional learning teams, a well-designed literacy plan, technology, and spotlighting. One critical feature is the CIM, which is a system of interventions that focuses on creating structures within the school for aligning classroom instruction, supplemental interventions, and special education. In this section, we describe how we use the CIM as an RTI approach and emphasize how the CIM is both an assessment and intervention method.

Creating a Comprehensive Assessment System

The CIM emphasizes a seamless and comprehensive assessment system for monitoring progress at both the student and system levels. We use a portfolio of summative and formative assessments that allow us to triangulate multiple sources of information to measure student growth. Our formative assessments include running records, teacher observations from reading and writing conferences, writing prompts with scoring guides, and writing checklists. In addition, teachers use rubrics for independent reading behaviors, literature discussions, and reading log entries (see Dorn & Soffos, 2005).

An essential component of the assessment method is the data collection form (see Figure 5.1). This form allows the teacher to monitor student progress on multiple assessments. The teacher records students' names in the left-hand column of the data form. In the row across the top, all assessments for the quarter (both formative and summative) are listed. Then, the teacher uses proficiency categories (i.e., B = below, A = approaching, M = meeting, E = exceeding) to fill in the data sheet. Each student is given a proficiency level for each of the assessments. The form is divided into three main sections: reading, writing, and interventions. For reading, the teacher looks at how the student performed on each reading assessment, reviews classroom observation notes, and makes a decision about the student's overall proficiency. This is recorded in the "Intervention Wall Placement" column. This process is repeated for the writing section.

Often, a student will score consistently across all assessments, and the decision about overall proficiency is clear. However, a student may perform below proficiency in some assessments, while he or she is meeting or even exceeding in others. This makes the decision more difficult, and these cases are discussed among teachers during team meetings. For example, a student may be reading on grade level (indicated as "meeting" in the text-level column) but scoring below on the independent reading rubric. Based on these data, the teacher may hold additional reading conferences with the student to determine why he or she is choosing not to read independently and assist in finding books that will motivate the student. The final section of the form, interventions, allows

Figure 5.1. Data Collection Form for Student Assessment

Teacher: _____   Grade: _____

Students		Reading							Writing					Interventions This Quarter			
Last Name, First Name	Card #	Guided Reading or Literature Discussion Level and Proficiency	Benchmark Book Level and Proficiency	Reading Conference Notes	Independent Reading Rubric	Thoughtful Log Rubric	Literature Discussion Rubric	Intervention Wall Placement	Writing Portfolio Rubric	Genre Rubric Yes or No	Conference Notes	Spelling	Intervention Wall Placement	Tier 1: Classroom Intervention	Tier 2: Intervention Specialist	Tier 3: 1:1 or Reading Recovery	Tier 4: Special Education
1		/	/														
2		/	/														
3		/	/														
4		/	/														
5		/	/														
6		/	/														
7		/	/														
8		/	/														
9		/	/														
10		/	/														
11		/	/														
12		/	/														
13		/	/														
14		/	/														
15		/	/														
16		/	/														
17		/	/														
18		/	/														
19		/	/														
20		/	/														
21		/	/														
22		/	/														
23		/															
24		/															

Note. AW = assisted writing; CFG = comprehension focus group; CONF = additional conferences; EIG = emergent intervention group; GR+ = Guided Reading Plus; LD = learning disability; OR = oracy; RR = Reading Recovery; SP = speech/language; TC = task cards

Successful Approaches to RTI: Collaborative Practices for Improving K–12 Literacy edited by Marjorie Y. Lipson and Karen K. Wixson. Copyright 2010 International Reading Association. May be copied for classroom use.

teachers to document which interventions each student has received during the assessment period. The literacy coaches use this section to gather valuable information about how our implementation of the CIM is progressing.

Assessment Wall as an RTI Method

The assessment wall is a critical component of our RTI assessment method. It is based on a portfolio of assessments (largely formative) that reflect students' learning on curriculum-based tasks. The wall provides the school with a way to make the data visible and promotes problem-solving discussions about how students are responding to instruction. The wall serves three purposes as an assessment method: (1) monitoring the progress of individual students, (2) monitoring the progress of particular subgroups, and (3) monitoring the progress of the school's literacy program for increasing overall literacy achievement. Figure 5.2 provides pictures of our assessment wall at two points in time.

Our assessment wall is located in a small room in the basement level of our school. We call this room the "team room," and we use it for our weekly grade-level team meetings. The assessment wall takes up one whole wall of the room. There are five or six comfortable chairs arranged in a semicircle facing the wall, making it the focal point during all of our team meetings. We built our assessment wall using four separate full-size pocket charts, placed side by side and attached to the wall. The four pocket charts divide our wall into four sections, one for each proficiency level. Moving left to right, the pocket charts are labeled as Below, Approaching, Meeting, and Exceeding. Down the left side of the wall, we placed cards to label each row of the assessment wall, beginning with kindergarten reading. The second row is kindergarten writing, followed by first-grade reading, first-grade writing, and so forth until we have rows for reading and writing all the way through fifth grade.

Once the physical background of the wall is in place, we prepare the students' cards. Each student in our building, grades K–5, has two cards on the assessment wall. We cut index cards into thin strips to make our cards and gave each grade level a different color index card (e.g., kindergarten cards are pink, first-grade cards are white). Then, we give every student in our building an identifying number and write this number on the top of the student's reading and writing cards. The wall is designed to promote productive conversations about student achievement without feelings of competition between teachers or grade levels, so we felt that it was important to leave names off of the cards and

Figure 5.2. Intervention Assessment Wall at Two Points in Time

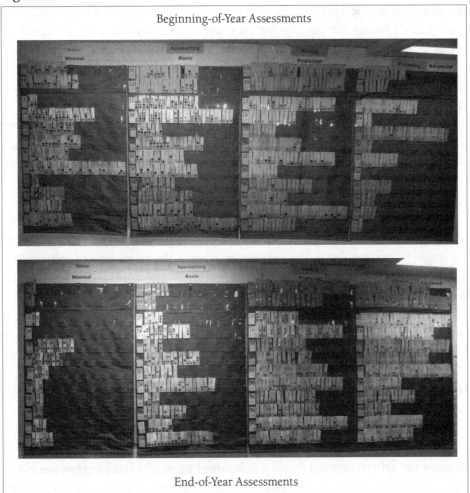

Beginning-of-Year Assessments

End-of-Year Assessments

use numbers instead. Each teacher has the numbers for her students, and as literacy coaches, we keep a master copy of the student names and numbers so that individual student cards can be quickly identified as needed. Numbering the cards also allows us to display the wall in a central area without having to worry about issues of confidentiality.

Once the wall is built and the cards are made, we place the students' cards on the wall at the beginning of the year after the initial assessment period, and move the cards on the wall at the end of each data point. This means that cards are moved four times after the initial fall placement, and we use our weekly grade-level team meeting time, which occurs during the school day, to do this. Each teacher brings her data collection sheet to the team meeting and removes his or her students' cards from the wall. Earlier we explained how teachers use multiple assessments to determine an overall proficiency level for reading and for writing, and how this proficiency is recorded in the Intervention Wall Placement section. The teachers use the proficiency recorded in that column to determine each student's new wall placement and returns each of the cards to the assessment wall. It is important to note once again that student cards are placed on the wall using information gathered from multiple assessments. We wanted to avoid the temptation of using one quick, summative assessment to determine student proficiency. We also wanted to use more than just a reading level to place students on the wall, because levels do not tell us all we need to know about students' progress. Sometimes a student's card will not move from the previous assessment period. However, when a teacher is able to move a student's card from the Below or Approaching section into the Meeting section, we are all able to celebrate!

After all of the cards have been moved, we have a powerful visual of how our students are doing. When we first started using the assessment wall on a schoolwide level, we wanted to create the feeling that these students were all of ours and that everyone in the building was responsible for the success of each and every student. We built the wall together as a staff. At the end of each year, we place pictures of the wall from the beginning of the year next to the end-of--year wall and celebrate the visible progress our students have made.

Another important feature of the wall is the ability it gives us to identify and monitor the achievement of specific subgroups as well as the layers of intervention students are receiving. Together we came up with a system for coding our assessment wall cards, which uses colored dot stickers to identify subgroups and interventions. For example, students who transfer into our building are identified by an orange dot (placed on the front of their card), and ELLs are identified by a red dot. In our building, we have four tiers of intervention, so we use a yellow dot if a student is receiving a Tier 1 classroom intervention, a green dot for Tier 2 supplemental intervention, a blue dot for Tier 3 intense intervention, and a pink dot for Tier 4, which is special education. Later, we explain more about our layered approach to interventions and how the tiers work together. Once all of the stickers are on the student cards, we can look at the wall and easily see how groups of students are performing to plan instruction and intervention appropriately. For instance, if we see a large number of cards with orange dots in the Below section, we may need to discuss ways to give more support to students who are new to our building. Sometimes we notice that there is a card in the Below or Approaching section that does not have any intervention dots on it. This would alert us that there is a student who is not meeting proficiency and not receiving the needed intervention, a screening mechanism for RTI. We can quickly identify the student and take steps to get appropriate interventions in place. In this way, the assessment system, data collection sheet, and assessment wall are all schoolwide management tools that work together to help us implement and monitor our RTI plan.

Portfolio of Interventions

Just as our assessment system is a portfolio and is as seamless as possible, so are our interventions. As we began the CIM, we developed a portfolio of interventions that is used by everyone in our school. This allows us to talk the same language and collaborate on providing interventions. Every intervention takes advantage of the reciprocity of reading and writing by including a writing component to accelerate growth. Through our training in the CIM, we have listed the interventions in our portfolio and identified the role of reading instruction and the role of writing instruction for each. Classroom teachers, intervention teachers, ELL teachers, and special education teachers collaborate at intervention meetings to choose the appropriate intervention(s) for each student. As the literacy coaches, we provide the training and support in the CIM interventions to classroom teachers. None of the interventions in the portfolio are packaged programs, but all have a consistent framework that relies on expert teacher decision making and aligns with classroom instruction. The result of using a portfolio of interventions has been a seamless approach to interventions across the school so that students do not become confused. Furthermore, the CIM as an RTI method has provided our school with opportunities for teacher collaboration and extensive professional development in literacy processing theory.

Our intervention portfolio consists of the following: Reading Recovery (our cornerstone intervention), emergent language and literacy groups, assisted writing (interactive, writing aloud, writing process, and minilessons), oracy (oral language), task cards (phonics and vocabulary), additional reading and writing conferences (highly supportive), Guided Reading Plus, and comprehension focus groups. Some interventions are geared more toward classroom interventions (e.g., task cards, additional conferences), and others are used by intervention specialists. For students who are lagging significantly behind their peers, they might receive several interventions simultaneously. This is explained further when we discuss the intervention planning sheet. Schools need to develop their own intervention portfolio starting with what is already in place. We recommend avoiding packaged programs and focusing on developing teacher expertise in working with struggling students.

Intervention Team Meetings

Collaboration is an important principle in an RTI approach and needs to be systematically planned; we learned that lesson early on in our journey. Because our teachers were so dedicated, they were meeting to discuss student progress even before we adopted the CIM. However, it was taking us a long time to schedule the meetings, and, once gathered, we sometimes met an hour or more, as our focus wandered or we got mired down in details and items. We became tired and frustrated, and we met less often than truly needed. We developed two kinds of intervention team meetings to address these issues: scheduled and as-needed. Scheduled intervention team meetings gather every intervention specialist, ELL teacher, Reading Recovery teacher, special education teacher, literacy coach, guidance counselor, and principal to collaborate and are held for one hour during the school day immediately after the classroom teachers update the assessment wall.

Our initial purpose for the meeting was to analyze and study the assessment wall. We noticed that there were student cards in the below and approaching proficiencies that did not have stickers on them. In other words, there were struggling students not receiving interventions. We wrote down the number of each student and looked up the students' names. The list was overwhelming. How were we going to make sure all those students were receiving an intervention, let alone the appropriate number of layers? As we began to go through the list as a team, we discovered that some of the students were receiving interventions, and all we had to do was add a dot to the card. For another group of students, we were able to build some Tier 2 intervention groups on the spot. For others, we felt we simply needed to talk to the classroom teacher to see if he or she was already providing a Tier 1 intervention.

If a student truly had no interventions in place, we immediately set up an as-needed intervention meeting for the student. Each time we met that first year, the list of those students not receiving needed intervention became shorter. We were able to focus on collaborating to be more efficient, sharing students among intervention groups and across specialties because we were working together. For example, a special education teacher implementing a comprehension focus group might be able to add a nonidentified student to the group. During our second year in an RTI approach, we had more time for professional development, problem solving, and data analysis. Last year we began to implement progress-monitoring documentation tools, which we describe later.

As-needed intervention team meetings are for individual students and can be called by anyone with a concern. Remember the long meetings we just described? We shortened the time to 10 minutes so that we were as focused as possible. The intervention team agreed to keep Tuesday and Thursday mornings available before school started for 30-minute meetings. We post a calendar near the intervention wall where teachers can sign up for a 10-minute slot for the meeting. Whoever signs up can invite anyone who works with the student. Everyone comes with data, which we review quickly so that we can complete the Literacy Intervention Planning Sheet. With this new format, we are meeting more often on individual students and for more students. Now we are meeting almost every Tuesday and Thursday morning.

Literacy Intervention Planning Sheet

How might a collaborative approach look in practice, and what do we mean by layers of support and expertise and degrees of intensity? We created a planning tool as a visual of these two concepts and called it the Literacy Intervention Planning Sheet (Figure 5.3; see Dorn & Schubert, 2008). Across the top of the sheet, we have two arrows that indicate changes, in degrees of intensity in a differentiated approach to classroom and intervention instruction. The most supportive and intense types of instruction are those that occur one to one, such as individual conferences, Reading Recovery, and extremely small groups. Moving to the right are small-group instructional settings with groups of 3–5 students. The "Universal" classroom row is the differentiated workshop approach with varying levels of support.

On the left side of the intervention planning sheet, the two vertical arrows indicate our layers of support and expertise. We think of our interventions as layers within tiers, which means that a student may have multiple interventions occurring simultaneously (layered) rather than in lockstep progression.

Figure 5.3. Example of a Literacy Intervention Planning Sheet

Literacy Intervention Plan for Comprehensive Intervention Model

Student Goal: Developing a Self-Regulated Learner

Student _Sabrina_ Grade _1_ Classroom Teacher _Mrs. Jones_ Date _11/19/09_

Degrees of Intensity →

Layers of Support/Expertise ↕

Classroom: Tier I — Universal

One-to-One
- ☑ Reading Conferences
- ☑ Writing Conferences

Small Group
- ☑ Guided Reading
- ☐ Literature Discussion
- ☐ Response Logs
- ☐ Language Investigations

Whole Class
- ☑ Read-Aloud
- ☑ Shared Reading
- ☑ Minilessons
- ☑ Share Time

Independent Work
- ☑ Familiar/Easy Reading
- ☑ Writing Process
- ☑ Phonics Tasks
- ☑ Literature Extensions

Plan/Monitoring/Duration

Classroom teacher will provide Guided Reading Plus intervention.

Sabrina is still sounding out every word (even known sight words).

Not flexible and fast with known sight words.

Intervention Specialist: Tier II — Intervention

One-to-One
- ☐ Additional Reading Conferences
- ☐ Additional Writing Conferences

Intervention Group
- ☑ Tailored Word Study (GRP)
- ☑ Writing About Reading (GRP)
- ☐ Oracy
- ☐ Task Card: ☐ Phonics ☐ Vocabulary
- ☐ Assisted Writing: ☐ Interactive ☐ Writing Aloud

Intervention Group (4 or more)

Small Group
- ☐ Guided Reading Plus
- ☐ Comprehension Focus
- ☐ Oracy
- ☑ Writing Process (push-in)
- ☐ Assisted Writing: ☐ Interactive ☐ Writing Aloud

Plan/Monitoring/Duration

Reading Recovery teacher will support during writing workshop.

Has gained letter knowledge. Reading Recovery teacher assessed again on the Observation Survey. Concepts about print was greatly improved. Hearing and recording sounds in words is a strength for Sabrina.

Tier III

One-to-One
- ☑ Reading Recovery

Intervention Group (2 or 3)
- ☐ Guided Reading Plus
- ☐ Comprehension Focus
- ☐ Oracy
- ☐ Writing Process (push-in)
- ☐ Assisted Writing: ☐ Interactive ☐ Writing Aloud

Plan/Monitoring/Duration

Sabrina will begin Reading Recovery the week of November 23 as a slot opens up.

Special Education — Tier IV

One-to-One
- ☐ Reading Conferences
- ☐ Writing Conferences

Small Group
- ☐ Guided Reading Plus
- ☐ Comprehension Focus
- ☐ Oracy
- ☐ Writing Process (push-in)
- ☐ Task Card: ☐ Phonics ☐ Vocabulary
- ☐ Assisted Writing: ☐ Interactive ☐ Writing Aloud

Plan/Monitoring/Duration

Team Members Present: _Classroom Teacher, Reading Recovery Teacher, Literacy Coach_

Next Meeting: _December 15, 2009, 8:00 a.m._

For example, a first-grade student in Reading Recovery (Tier 3) may be in an assisted writing group (Tier 2) with an intervention specialist and receive a Tier 1 intervention with the classroom teacher. Whenever a student has a Tier 2, Tier 3, or Tier 4 intervention, we make sure they are also receiving a Tier 1 intervention from the classroom teacher. Each layer brings a different expertise, depending on who is providing the intervention.

The Literacy Intervention Planning Sheet guides the team in scheduling intervention team meetings. First, we check the appropriate boxes in the Universal classroom row. Then, the team decides on the appropriate layers of interventions and checks the corresponding boxes. In the blank space at the end of each row, we make notes on who will provide each intervention, the short- and long-term focus of the interventions, and any data we want to collect. Finally, we set a follow-up meeting to review how the interventions are progressing. The literacy coach takes the notes and makes copies of the form for all participating teachers. We file a copy in the student's cumulative file in the office and place a copy in the student's assessment folder. With this approach of layers within tiers, we believe we are truly meeting the intention of RTI.

When describing our layers of intervention, we are often asked about when we provide the interventions. Having already established a workshop model, we have been able to provide our interventions during a 90-minute reading workshop or a 50- to 60-minute writers' workshop. Intervention and special education teachers try to provide their interventions in the classroom whenever possible to support the theory of transfer, helping students succeed in the classroom. For a student with multiple layers, we have to be careful not to have too many people working with him or her, resulting in student confusion. Sometimes we need to make a compromise and bring a student from one classroom into another for the intervention group, because there may be no other students requiring that support in his or her classroom. Either way, it takes dedicated commitment to coordinate between classroom teachers and specialists.

Progress Monitoring

The assessment wall is our primary progress-monitoring tool because it provides an up-to-date visual documentation of student progress. However, we felt we needed a system for charting and documenting individual intervention data in detail. For each of the interventions in our portfolio, we created a progress-monitoring document in the form of a file folder. Once an intervention is planned for a student, the intervention teacher begins a new folder. We believe strongly that the assessments done for progress monitoring should guide instruction (International Reading Association [IRA] & National Council of Teachers of English, 1994). With that as our guiding philosophy, we went back to our assessment system and found that we did not need to add any assessments. Instead, we conduct the assessment more frequently for intervention students, usually twice per quarter. For example, in Guided Reading Plus, the intervention teacher completes a benchmark book on a cold read and charts the level on a book graph inside the student's progress-monitoring folder. We also ask the students to respond in writing on a prompt about the story and complete a writing behavior checklist, expanded from the one in *Shaping Literate Minds: Developing Self-Regulated Learners* (Dorn & Soffos, 2001). We turned these checklists into a grid so that after each prompt we can check behaviors exhibited by the student. The end goal of the intervention is efficient and strategic problem solving. As more behaviors are observed and more boxes get checked, we are able to chart progress over time. Unobserved and unchecked behaviors help us plan our short-term instructional goals.

Concluding Thoughts

Our school's journey began with the desire to closely examine the way we were teaching reading and writing so that we could improve our instruction and positively affect student achievement. As we implement RTI, we are finding many more opportunities to reflect on our own instruction. The systems we have put in place to implement RTI are only as good as the teachers who are providing the classroom and intervention instruction. An absolutely critical part of our RTI plan is ongoing, job-embedded professional development with the goal of increasing teacher expertise. We have stated several times that teacher observation and decision making are paramount to our model. Consequently, our school has a huge responsibility to provide teachers with ongoing opportunities to collaborate and deepen their understanding of how students learn to read and write.

When we implemented the PCL model, we restructured our specialist schedule to fit weekly grade-level team meetings into the school day. Each grade-level team meets once a week to problem solve around data, read and discuss professional texts, and analyze teaching interactions. As literacy coaches, we plan the team meeting agendas with input from the teachers. During the first year of the CIM implementation, we offered a three-credit graduate-level class, which focused on interventions and literacy processing. Fourteen classroom and intervention teachers took this course. Almost all of our teachers have traveled to PCL institutes and conferences, and many have attended multiple institutes. Professional book studies occur regularly, sometimes organized by literacy coaches and sometimes by a group of teachers interested in a particular text. Cluster visits organized around particular instructional themes (e.g., interventions, conferences) provide opportunities for teachers to visit each others' classrooms, view instruction, and discuss what they saw with peers. A room with a two-way mirror was built so that we could have a place to observe and discuss teaching interactions as they occur. We still have a lot more work to do, and we certainly do not have all of the answers. We do know that we will never be done learning, and we believe that this is one of the best things about our school.

In 2008, the IRA and the Wisconsin State Reading Association (WSRA) recognized our efforts with the Exemplary Reading Program Award. The purpose of the award is to recognize outstanding reading and language arts programs at all grade levels and call the public's attention to outstanding programs in schools throughout North America. It was our comprehensive approach to literacy education, and our RTI plan in particular, that attracted the IRA's attention and has led the WSRA to invite Washington School to share our story at numerous RTI institutes across the state.

We hope that we have given you some clear, real-life examples of how the CIM might look as an RTI approach. We also hope you realize that our journey is not yet over! RTI has given us so many more things to think about and reflect on while inspiring us to keep striving for something we truly believe in: success for every student.

REFERENCES

Dorn, L.J., & Schubert, B. (2008). A comprehensive intervention model for reversing reading failure: A Response to Intervention approach. *Journal of Reading Recovery, 7*(2), 29–41.

Dorn, L.J., & Soffos, C. (2001). *Shaping literate minds: Developing self-regulated learners.* Portland, ME: Stenhouse.

Dorn, L.J., & Soffos, C. (2005). *Teaching for deep comprehension: A reading workshop approach.* Portland, ME: Stenhouse.

International Reading Association & National Council of Teachers of English. (1994). *Standards for the assessment of reading and writing.* Newark, DE; Urbana, IL: Authors. Retrieved September 12, 2009, from www.reading.org/Libraries/Reports_and_Standards/bk674.sflb.ashx

CHAPTER 6

RTI for English-Language Learners

Janette K. Klingner
University of Colorado at Boulder

Lucinda Soltero-González
University of Colorado at Boulder

Nonie Lesaux
Harvard Graduate School of Education, Massachusetts

The percentage of English-language learners (ELLs) in schools across the United States is increasing rapidly. We use the term *ELLs* to refer to those students who are in the process of acquiring English but are not yet considered fluent. They are emerging bilinguals. Between 2000 and 2005, the U.S. population of ELLs increased from 3.8 million to 4.5 million, with the largest number in urban cities across the country ("Education Week," 2009). By 2002, 43% of U.S. classrooms included at least one ELL (U.S. Department of Education, 2003). Estimates suggest that by the year 2030, about 40% of the school-age population will speak English as a second language (U.S. Department of Education, 2003). The majority of ELLs (77%) speak Spanish as their first language (Zehler et al., 2003), whereas approximately 100 other languages are represented in the remaining 23%. ELLs tend to underachieve in comparison with their non-ELL peers, especially in literacy. They also are retained more often and drop out of school in greater numbers (Zehler et al., 2003).

Many Subtypes of ELLs

ELLs reflect a diverse population that includes a wide range of languages, ethnicities, nationalities, and socioeconomic backgrounds. They vary by immigration status and generation in the United States (Garcia & Cuéllar, 2006). New students arrive in the United States each year, many with little to no knowledge of the English language. Some recent immigrants may have attended school only sporadically in their home countries or spent years in refugee camps and experienced a lot of trauma. On the other hand, recent immigrants might have attended school regularly and be well educated and ready for grade-level content in the United States. Whether ELLs are literate in their first language affects how easy it is for them to learn to read in English. Many students around the world learn English as a foreign language; thus, when they arrive in the United States, they already know some English.

Many ELLs were born in the United States. Some are "simultaneous bilinguals," meaning they speak both English and Spanish or another language in their homes and are in the process of learning two languages at once. Others are "sequential bilinguals," in which they are from homes where they and their families almost exclusively speak their first language, and they are fluent in their first language and learning English as a second or additional language. Some ELLs are from wealthy or middle class families, and others are from low socioeconomic backgrounds. Whatever their backgrounds, all ELLs have had valuable experiences that we can draw from and build on when helping them learn.

It is important to keep these differences in mind so that we do not stereotype students or make assumptions about their backgrounds and what they know and can do. If we understand the variability among ELLs, then it is more likely that we can provide appropriate, challenging instruction that is responsive to their needs. For example, students who already can read in their first language have different instructional needs than students who are not yet literate, even though they may all be at similar levels of English proficiency.

Second-Language Acquisition and Language Proficiency

ELLs vary in their English proficiency from beginning to intermediate to advanced levels. Limited proficiency in English should not be considered a sign of limited intelligence. Although this might seem obvious, in fact we know that oftentimes students' hesitancy to speak, errors, or accents are misinterpreted as signs of cognitive deficiencies (Cummins, 2000; Oller, 1991). ELLs are just as capable as their fluent English-speaking peers to engage in higher level thinking, although it might take them longer to process language, especially when a task is cognitively demanding. Even when ELLs seem fluent in oral English, they still might mentally translate to their first language when grappling with challenging content.

It is important to remember that second-language acquisition is an uneven process (Bialystok, 1991). When ELLs are taught in English in school, they can become more proficient in academic English than in their first language in specific content areas. Thus, their relative proficiency in English and their first language can fluctuate, depending on the topic.

Also, languages have many oral and written dimensions or components, and students' abilities may vary across these aspects. The dimensions of oral language include the following:

- Grammar/syntax
- Morphological skills (i.e., understanding word forms and parts)
- Semantic skills/vocabulary (i.e., understanding the meaning of words and phrases)
- Phonological skills (e.g., phonological awareness)
- Pragmatics (i.e., understanding the social rules of communication)

It is common for ELLs to be stronger in some language components than others (Solano-Flores, 2006). For example, some ELLs might have relatively strong vocabulary knowledge but struggle with grammar, and some might actually feel more confident writing than speaking in English.

When we understand students' varying levels of English proficiency and the complexities of second-language acquisition, we are in a better position to support their learning and less likely to confuse language acquisition with learning disabilities.

Features of RTI for ELLs

RTI holds promise as a way to provide ELLs with high-quality, appropriate instruction. Yet, RTI models for ELLs must take into account what we know about supporting their learning. This requires attention to various factors. The first requirement is creating a positive, responsive learning environment that views students' cultural and linguistic diversity as assets (Baca, 2002; Nieto & Bode, 2008; Ortiz, 2002). Second, teachers should know and be able to use a variety of research-based instructional approaches and assessment practices specifically designed for and validated with ELLs (McCardle, Mele-McCarthy, Cutting,

Leos, & D'Emilio, 2005). Third, teachers should be knowledgeable about the second-language process and how learning to read in English as a second or additional language is similar to and different from learning to read in English as one's first language (August & Shanahan, 2006; Teachers of English to Speakers of Other Languages, 2008).

The Foundation for RTI: Culturally and Linguistically Responsive and Appropriate Assessment and Instruction

The foundation of RTI for ELLs should be high-quality culturally and linguistically responsive assessment and instruction (see the IRA Guiding Principles on RTI in Chapter 1). This idea of being culturally and linguistically responsive is an essential one. What do we mean by "responsive"? Responsive teachers are in tune with their students and understand their strengths as well as their needs. They know how to match their ways of teaching with students' cultural ways of learning (Gutiérrez & Rogoff, 2003). What do we mean by "culture"? Culture is central to the learning process; all learning is cultural. Young children are socialized to learn in particular ways in their homes and communities. For example, in some cultures children learn by watching or apprenticing to a more expert other. In white, middle class U.S. culture, families tend to engage in more discourse and known-answer questioning. As Heath (1983) shows in her classic study, young children are more likely to excel when the teaching behaviors and norms of their schools match those in their homes. If there is a mismatch, students are less likely to achieve to their potential. Culturally and linguistically responsive instruction helps build bridges between home and school cultures.

Teachers who are culturally and linguistically responsive vary from one another in many ways. There is no set mold used to form them, but they do share certain characteristics and attributes. We know a great deal about culturally responsive teachers from observation studies in their classrooms. (For a classic example of teachers who are effective with African American students, see *The Dreamkeepers: Successful Teachers of African American Children* by Ladson-Billings [1994]. For a recent description of outstanding teachers of ELLs, see *How to Teach English Language Learners: Effective Strategies From Outstanding Educators* by Haager, Klingner, and Aceves [2010].)

Culturally responsive teachers build strong relationships with their students and their families. They convey their care and respect and show their commitment to helping each student fulfill his or her abilities, desires, and potentialities (Gay, 2000). They have high expectations for themselves as well as their students, modeling a "can do" attitude even in the face of challenges. They help students make connections across the curriculum and with their everyday lives, making sure instruction is meaningful (Gay, 2000; Ladson-Billings, 1994; Nieto & Bode, 2008). Teachers do not necessarily need to be of the same ethnicity as their students to be culturally responsive, but they should make an effort to learn what they can about their students' backgrounds, connect with their students and families, and get to know the communities in which they teach. Part of this is learning to view differences in students' literacies as strengths, not deficits (Alvermann, 2005).

Effective culturally responsive teachers are also knowledgeable about the content they teach. They are skillful instructors. They know how to differentiate instruction and provide intensive, explicit instruction (Delpit, 1995). This instruction should include numerous opportunities for students to practice reading in meaningful ways.

The Cornerstone of RTI: Assessments

We have known for decades that good instruction starts with good assessment. Assessment is the cornerstone of RTI approaches because it is through ongoing assessment that we are able to identify students' needs. Creating an appropriate assessment system is a challenge for any school or district and can be especially difficult when serving culturally and linguistically diverse students who are in need of tailored and appropriate instruction. The usefulness of any assessment depends on the extent to which it provides valid information that can be used to plan appropriate instruction for the population of interest.

When RTI is implemented well, there are two important positive consequences:

1. *Instruction is closely linked to assessment across tiers.* Assessment data help inform decisions about daily instructional content and supports at Tier 1, identify those learners who are in need of intensive interventions at Tier 2, and determine which students continue to struggle and are in need of further assessment and intervention to address their significant difficulties at Tier 3.

2. *An emphasis is placed on school contexts and the quality of instruction.* The focus is not only on individual students in need of targeted instruction

but also on the appropriateness of instruction for meeting students' needs more broadly, which creates opportunities for conversations about school-level models of prevention of difficulties to meet the needs of diverse populations of learners (see Chapters 4 and 5). This is especially important for schools with high numbers of ELLs. Given that linguistic and cultural diversity, appropriate opportunities to learn, and student success are strongly linked, RTI shows real potential for designing tailored and effective learning environments.

Several issues should be considered when designing and using an RTI assessment system for culturally and linguistically diverse students: (a) the importance of multiple measures, (b) the multidimensional nature of language and reading, (c) the role of progress monitoring in an RTI framework, and (d) the ways in which assessment information is used and with whom it is shared.

The Importance of Multiple Measures

There is no single best test or assessment strategy to use with ELLs. Rather, we need to put our efforts into selecting multiple measures and interpreting their results in appropriate ways to promote student success. It is how assessments are used, with whom, and how the results are interpreted that can be positive or negative, accurate or inaccurate.

First and foremost, not all available assessment tools and techniques are appropriate for all purposes. Any student assessment system must be comprehensive in nature, featuring multiple measures. Multiple assessments are very important in any RTI model, but especially when the model is used with linguistically and culturally diverse students.

Different assessments—even in the same language or literacy domain—capture somewhat different skills and knowledge, which is due to the assessment format, the background knowledge required for the items, and the way the skill of interest is defined. Second-language acquisition is an uneven developmental process. Some skills might develop more quickly than others; for example, some linguistically diverse students with good vocabulary knowledge might still have difficulty with grammar (or vice versa). We need to avoid thinking about students' profiles in broad terms, such as low language skills or low literacy ability, and instead generate an understanding of students' relative skills—their strengths and their weaknesses—in specific domains of language and literacy to inform instruction and intervention efforts.

Different assessments serve different functions. Taking a developmental perspective—one that focuses on the individual student—the purposes of assessment are screening, diagnosis, and progress monitoring. From an accountability perspective—one that focuses on a group, system, or institution—the purpose of assessment is primarily to assess performance against a certain set of standards, expectations, or benchmarks. Generally speaking, particularly within an RTI framework, which takes a developmental approach, an assessment that has been designed for one purpose (e.g., screening) is not suitable for another purpose (e.g., diagnosis). However, it is important to note that states and districts undoubtedly use assessments for other purposes for which they are not designed, particularly in the domain of serving linguistically diverse students. For instance, some districts routinely use an English language development test for initial placement, annual monitoring, and reclassification of students, as well as to inform decisions about interventions for struggling learners. Given the psychometric properties of the test and the complexity of the language-proficiency construct, a single assessment cannot possibly serve all of these purposes well. A test designed strictly to identify whether a learner is above or below the redesignation threshold is likely to be insensitive to fine distinctions, such as those between beginning and early intermediate students. This same test will provide little or no information on which to base interventions for individual students who are struggling. Such practices are examples of inappropriate and unethical test use (Sattler, 2001); in these instances, the benefits of tracking the academic achievement of the population are outweighed by the costs of using the tests in inappropriate ways.

The tests now being used to evaluate and monitor the English proficiency of students from linguistically diverse backgrounds have improved somewhat in recent years. However, although these assessments may tell us something about students' proficiency levels in a broad sense, they are neither fine grained nor curriculum based, and thus are not designed to inform instruction; these are assessments for classification purposes only. In addition, it is important to note that, although changing, many of these language-proficiency assessments do not adequately emphasize the complex academic language needed for reading comprehension success.

The Multidimensional Nature of Language and Reading

Assessment within an RTI framework should reflect the multidimensional nature of language and literacy learning and the diversity among students being assessed. Although typical early literacy screening batteries focus on print awareness, phonological awareness, and letter–word identification, they often do not include measures of vocabulary knowledge, oral language proficiency, or listening and reading comprehension. Therefore, classroom teachers and support personnel need training on language and literacy development in the context of an RTI framework that includes a comprehensive assessment system with measures of oral language and vocabulary. Assessment of basic skills must be complemented by assessments in the domains of language to guide tailored and appropriate instruction in these areas. These domains include grammar/syntax, morphological skills (i.e., understanding word forms and parts), language-processing skills (e.g., phonological awareness), vocabulary, oral comprehension, and reading comprehension. Whether standardized and published assessments, curriculum-based measurements (CBMs), or locally developed assessments, we recommend selecting and interpreting assessments in consultation with the ELL department or another district department with expertise in ELL assessment. We also recommend gaining detailed insight into the information provided by the standards-based language-proficiency measures.

The great majority of students from linguistically diverse backgrounds (representing many different native languages) develop word-reading skills that are equally as accurate and fluent as those of their classmates. In other words, they tend to develop foundational skills to age-appropriate levels without any notable delays. However, these same students often need significant support to develop English vocabulary knowledge and reading comprehension skills. This is an important profile to keep in mind when designing effective RTI assessment frameworks and Tier 1 instruction.

In selecting an assessment battery, particularly when the goal is to identify a student's developmental profile in language acquisition and his or her corresponding strengths and weaknesses, educators should recognize the many facets of oral language, including vocabulary. In the domain of vocabulary, linguistically diverse students often have receptive vocabularies that are much larger than their expressive (or productive) vocabularies. This also is the case with many first-language speakers. ELLs might have a broad, but not very deep, vocabulary, such as only knowing one meaning (the common one) for words that have multiple meanings. August and Shanahan (2006) state that ELLs also tend to be confused by referents (e.g., pronouns), prepositions (e.g., *on, behind*), and cohesion markers (e.g., *however, therefore*). Here, we suggest administering written or oral prompts to generate writing samples, assess oral narrative skills, and in turn, gain insight into students' grammatical skills, word knowledge, understanding, use of connectives (e.g., *however, therefore, because),* and overall language development. Many districts and schools have particular prompts to administer to all students; looking closely at students' work and comparing work across students can provide important insights about development.

Just as teachers differentiate their instruction, assessment must focus on capturing subtle shifts in English-proficiency levels and assessments that focus on providing diagnostic information. For example, running records or miscue analysis may provide needed data to capture comprehension skills and offer windows into oral reading fluency. It is important to know that recent research (Crosson & Lesaux, in press) suggests that for ELLs faced with the challenge of reading in a language in which they are not fully proficient, text-reading fluency is not a reliable indicator of reading comprehension. Across four studies conducted with ELLs or low-performing learners from diverse backgrounds, from primary grades through grade 6, text-reading fluency scores were in the average range, yet the mean score for reading comprehension was well below average (Crosson & Lesaux, in press; Kieffer & Lesaux, in press; Riedel, 2007; Schilling, Carlisle, Scott, & Zeng, 2007). These findings reinforce the need to supplement text-reading fluency measures with assessments of vocabulary for effective screening or progress monitoring in the domain of reading, particularly with ELLs.

The Role of Progress Monitoring in an RTI Framework

Progress monitoring is used to assess students' academic progress and evaluate the effectiveness of instruction. Progress monitoring is designed to do the following:

- Determine whether students are benefiting appropriately from an instructional program
- Identify students who are not demonstrating adequate progress
- Build more effective instructional programs for students who are not benefiting

- Compare the efficacy of different forms of instruction and design more effective, individualized instructional programs

Progress monitoring can be implemented with individual students or an entire class (see Chapters 2 and 4). To implement progress monitoring, the teacher determines the student's current levels of performance and identifies goals for learning. The teacher then assesses the student's academic performance on a regular basis (e.g., weekly, monthly, every 6–10 weeks). Progress toward meeting the student's goals is measured by comparing expected and actual rates of learning. Based on these measurements, teaching is adjusted as needed (see Table 6.1 for a list of questions and responses regarding progress monitoring of ELLs). The purpose of progress monitoring is to ensure that instruction is adjusted to meet the needs of individual students or classrooms of learners. Use it to find what works!

Using and Sharing Assessment Information: The Problem-Solving Team

An assessment-based system raises important questions about how data should be used. Any assessment data collected should be used expressly to support student learning, whether it be to inform constructive discussions about classroom-level instruction or student-level supplemental supports. Each assessment used may serve one purpose and function well, but it is unlikely that one assessment can serve many purposes well, especially for ELLs.

Once collected, data should be reviewed by a school-level problem-solving or RTI team with sufficient knowledge and expertise in second-language acquisition, culturally responsive instruction, and if possible, bilingual education. Everyone on the team should have some familiarity with these requisite topics. In addition, a bilingual or English as a Second Language (ESL) specialist should be involved. The ESL specialist can share valuable insights about second-language acquisition issues and how they relate to the academic performance of ELLs (Roache, Shore, Gouleta, & de Obaldia Butkevich, 2003) or model effective instructional strategies for classroom teachers (Garcia & Ortiz, 1988). At least one team member should be an expert in culturally sensitive assessment procedures. Parents should also be active members of the decision-making process.

Table 6.1. Important Questions About Progress Monitoring and ELLs

Question	Responses
Does our student assessment data show that most ELLs are making progress in general education?	• When most students are not thriving, this is a systemic issue; it is likely that general education instruction is ineffective or inappropriate. • Teachers and school leaders can use data to determine when it is necessary to adjust instruction for all ELLs.
Is the progress-monitoring element of our RTI model one component of a comprehensive evaluation for ELLs who are struggling?	• Teachers and school leaders can use CBM data to determine when it is necessary to adjust instruction for ELLs who are struggling. • For example, some use a progress-monitoring checklist (see Chapter 2), while others use multiple classroom-based measures (see Chapter 4).
Do we have a working sense of which measures are more sensitive and less sensitive to ELLs' growth?	• Because there are very few studies of progress monitoring with linguistically diverse students, it is important for districts and schools to undertake their own comparisons and analyses to determine how their ELLs are faring and what the typical patterns of growth and development are.
Do we have a working sense of how ELLs' performance is influenced on particular measures by individual and classroom characteristics? Do we examine ELLs' error patterns?	• The similarities between students' home language and English will influence their language and reading abilities, particularly in the areas of phonological awareness and phonics (e.g., ELLs may have trouble discriminating between auditory sounds not present in their language, students who learn to read in Spanish may segment at the syllable level rather than the phoneme level).
Where possible and appropriate, are we using first-language measures to assess our ELLs' skills?	• For Spanish-speakers, particularly those who have received first-language instruction, there are two progress-monitoring assessments available: AIMSweb and IDEL (a Spanish version of DIBELS). • For screening and periodic monitoring, a version of PALS (Invernizzi, Meier, & Juel, 2007; Invernizzi, Swank, & Juel, 2007) will soon be available in Spanish. NOTE: All comprehension components of any fluency measure should be administered to gain a complete picture of fluency skills. • Running records and informal reading inventories can be used in students' first language. • Another option is to take current instruments, such as the progress-monitoring checklist (in Chapter 4), and adapt it for ELLs with the guidance of experts.
Have we considered dynamic approaches to assessment within the RTI framework?	• Conduct assessments that involve preassessment, teaching, and postassessment to make sure that instruction is appropriate and tailored to students' needs and to assess ELLs' learning potential.

Classroom Literacy Instruction for ELLs

In this section, we provide guidance to general education classroom teachers, reading specialists, and ESL specialists in both English-medium and bilingual education settings on how to teach literacy to ELLs as part of good, first instruction (generally considered Tier 1). We describe specific literacy teaching strategies and activities that teachers can incorporate as part of language arts and other content areas. We want to emphasize that although the strategies and activities suggested as part of Tier 1 literacy instruction would benefit all students, they were designed or modified to address the oral language and literacy learning needs of many ELLs that are not necessarily observed in their mainstream English-speaking peers.

Instruction during the language arts block should integrate different literacy domains. In these domains, all the traditional language arts (listening, speaking, reading, and writing) are involved in a collaborative way for both social and academic purposes (see Table 6.2). Listening, speaking, reading, and writing complement one another; therefore, teachers should try to include them in every literacy lesson. For each literacy domain listed in Table 6.2, we provide examples of literacy strategies and activities that we have identified as effective for teaching ELLs within the general education classroom. These strategies stem from various research studies and research syntheses on best literacy instruction for ELLs (August & Shanahan, 2006; Avalos, Plasencia, Chavez, & Rascón, 2007; Carlo et al., 2004; Cloud, Genesee, & Hamayan, 2009; Genesee & Geva, 2006; Genesee & Riches, 2006; Gersten & Baker, 2000; Goldenberg, 2008; Jiménez, García, & Pearson, 1996; Saunders, Foorman, & Carlson, 2006) as well as descriptive studies of classrooms and out-of-school settings (González, Moll, & Amanti, 2005; Kenner, 2004; Martínez-Roldán & López-Robertson, 1999).

Oral Language

We know from research that English oral proficiency is closely related to academic achievement in English, including literacy (August & Shanahan, 2006; Saunders et al., 2006). Therefore, literacy instruction should build on and expand students' existing oral language competencies in English to support literacy learning and content knowledge. Further, all students benefit from support in building the background knowledge they need to learn a new topic, but this is especially true for ELLs. Helping students access what they already know and

Table 6.2. Domains of Literacy and Examples of Strategies and Activities

Domain	Strategies and Activities
Oral language (listening and speaking)	• Build background knowledge (i.e., preview/review) • Frontloading of vocabulary using visual cues, total physical response, and realia (i.e., real objects) • Modeling and practicing book-based sentence structures • Sentence transformations through guided dialogue • Language experience approach • Reading aloud • Storytelling using wordless picture books • Traditional songs, chants, and rhymes in the students' home languages and in English
Reading fluency	• Modeled reading • Shared reading with patterned language books • Repeated reading • Readers Theatre • Partner reading • Independent reading (e.g., silent reading, audio book)
Word work	• Phonemic awareness (i.e., segmenting, blending, syllabication, onset–rime, initial/final sound) in meaningful ways • Phonics • Sight words from books read • Dictation by the teacher or peer
Reading comprehension	• Reading aloud, modeled reading, and shared reading • Modified guided reading (select books according to stage of development) • Reciprocal teaching • Scaffolded retelling (e.g., modeling and explicit teaching of text structure, connectors) • Literature circles (select quality literature in which the students can see themselves) • Text sets (i.e., a set of books around a topic, can include different genres) • Reading responses incorporating art, music, drama, and poetry
Cross-language connections	• Word wall with cognates • Teach similarities and differences between first and second languages (e.g., syntax, spelling, text structure, punctuation) • Preview/review using students' first languages • Bilingual books (point out similarities and differences between the two languages)

(continued)

Table 6.2. Domains of Literacy and Examples of Strategies and Activities (*continued*)

Domain	Strategies and Activities
Writing	• Modeled writing (i.e., an activity using the language-experience approach) • Guided writing • Interactive writing (e.g., dialogue journal, peer editing) • Collaborative writing (e.g., story retellings, modified patterned language book, recipe book, script for Readers Theatre) • Independent writing (e.g., literature log, pen pals, self-correction) • Author's chair
Connections to home and community	• Storytelling (family and neighborhood stories) • Autobiographies and personal narratives • Books created in the home language (written, audiotaped) • Letters to family members who live far away • Research projects in students' communities/neighborhoods • Units that tap into households' funds of knowledge

make connections to what they will be learning facilitates their understanding and retrieval of the newly acquired information in the second language. When students lack sufficient prior knowledge and vocabulary about the topic being studied, it is the teacher's role to help students develop this new knowledge. This can be done by using the methodology known as preview/review, in which the students' home language can be used to build background knowledge by previewing key concepts and challenging vocabulary as well as reviewing students' understanding of important points (Ulanoff & Pucci, 1999).

For ELLs, oral language development should be promoted daily through differentiated instruction as well as instruction that is responsive to and builds on their culture, home language, and interests. Examples of such instruction include the following: modeling (e.g., read-alouds of relevant multicultural literature, chants, songs, poems), explicit instruction (e.g., frontloading of vocabulary, sentence structures, sentence transformations), scaffolding (e.g., total physical response, visual cues, realia), guided dialogue between the teacher and the students to extend and refine vocabulary and language structures, and lots of opportunities to practice in meaningful reading and writing activities (e.g., language experience, storytelling using wordless picture books).

Reading Fluency

Fluency is the ability to read quickly and accurately while maintaining meaningful phrasing. Two common ways of improving reading fluency are repeated oral reading and independent silent reading. Opportunities to hear a more expert reader model fluent, expressive reading are important for struggling readers. ELLs who are emergent readers or struggle with reading fluency can read along with a teacher or a more proficient peer or listen to and follow along with audio books. Shared reading activities, such as the reading aloud of big books, patterned language books, Readers Theatre, and partner reading can help ELLs improve their fluency (Hiebert, Pearson, Taylor, Richardson, & Paris, 1998; Peregoy & Boyle, 2005). These activities are appropriate for a wide range of students, including non-ELLs, so teachers can use them frequently to involve all students in the class. Antunez (2002) reminds us that fluency should not be confused with accent. Students can read fluently in English with a first-language accent.

Word Work

Although the main purpose of word-work activities is to build foundational literacy skills, particularly metalinguistic awareness, they should be done in meaningful and interactive ways and in the context of reading and writing activities rather than in isolation. The following are examples of word-work activities that researchers have found effective for teaching literacy to ELLs:

- Phonemic awareness, which is the ability to identify and manipulate the phonemes or sounds in spoken words, is an important component of developing decoding and encoding skills. It is important to identify what students already know in their first language and in English and then provide explicit instruction to students with low levels of phonological awareness. Many activities that work well with mainstream students should also help ELLs, such as word plays, songs, poems, language games, and word walls (Hiebert et al., 1998). It is also important to realize that enhancing ELLs' phonemic awareness and oral proficiency in their first language can facilitate the acquisition of English literacy (López & Greenfield, 2004).

- Phonics, the understanding of sound–symbol correspondence, is another literacy component that the experts recommend should be taught to facilitate English-literacy learning (August & Shanahan, 2006). When students have learned to read in another language first, the process of learning to read in English is facilitated, especially when the orthographic systems of the two languages are similar, but it can be more challenging when they are not (e.g., Farsi, Japanese).

- Sight words from books read in the classroom (Cloud et al., 2009).
- Dictation by the teacher or peer (Escamilla, Geisler, Hopewell, Sparrow, & Butvilofsky, 2009). In this method, the teacher or peer dictates words and sentences to students, and then a corrected text is constructed in collaboration between students and the teacher. A focus on spelling, grammar, conventions, and form is emphasized.

Reading Comprehension

Although literacy skills such as phonemic awareness, sight-word recognition, and fluency are important foundation blocks of reading, being able to decode words accurately has little value if comprehension is missing. Reading comprehension instruction is relevant for all students, but it is particularly critical and timely for students who are adequate word readers but lack understanding of what they read.

Some of the challenges that ELLs may face in reading comprehension are related to language proficiency, vocabulary knowledge, background knowledge, and use of comprehension strategies. Through direct instruction and interactive approaches, teachers can help students understand why, how, and when they can apply reading comprehension strategies. Examples of instructional practices developed to help students improve their reading comprehension include the following:

- Creating graphic organizers and word webs
- Thinking aloud and modeling reading comprehension strategies, such as predicting and deriving meaning from words (which should be part of reading aloud), modeled reading, and shared reading
- Modeling the use of reading skills and comprehension strategies (e.g., monitoring understanding, finding the main idea, chunking words to decode) during guided reading groups (See Avalos et al., 2007, for further details about using modified guided reading with ELLs.)
- Applying comprehension strategies during text discussions, which can be done through shared activities such as reciprocal teaching (Fung,

Wilkinson, & Moore, 2003), in which the teacher gradually reduces the temporary support as students gain control of the strategies

- Scaffolding retellings, which require explicit teaching of text structures (e.g., fiction, nonfiction) as well as challenging vocabulary and sequencing words and sentence structures using visual cues (e.g., graphic organizers, word webs). Students share and compare their retellings and provide feedback at the whole-story level, at the phrase and individual word levels, and back to the whole-story level. Incorporating different presentation modes (e.g., oral, written, role play, drawing) not only motivates students but also enhances their literacy learning (Brown & Cambourne, 1990).

- Conducting literature circles with small groups of students who read or are read the same book (or a text set related to the same theme) and meeting to discuss their understandings with others. The purpose is not to teach reading strategies but to facilitate critical thinking through meaningful and guided conversations about topics relevant to the students (see Martínez-Roldán & López-Robertson, 1999).

Cross-Language Connections

There are many skills and much knowledge that can transfer from the home language to English and thus do not need to be retaught. Some of these skills and knowledge include vocabulary (e.g., cognates, or words that look similar in two or more languages and have similar meanings, such as *democracy* and *democracia*), print awareness and concepts of print, sound–letter correspondence, comprehension strategies, and background knowledge (Genesee & Geva, 2006). ELLs draw on what they know about their home language to learn to read and write in English. In other words, a student's home language is a scaffold or "bootstrap" into English (August & Shanahan, 2006; Cloud et al., 2009). Students who capitalize on cross-language transfer learn to read and write in English more easily than students who do not use this strategy (Cloud et al., 2009; Jiménez et al., 1996). Knowledge of what literacy-related skills and experiences ELLs have in the home and school languages allows teachers to build on students' strengths and needs, promote metalinguistic awareness, and encourage this type of scaffolding. Teachers should help and encourage ELLs to identify similarities and differences between the two languages and apply them to learning to read and write in English. There is no need to reteach what students already know. Teaching for cross-language connections should be done throughout the day and across the curriculum. Some ways to promote it include identifying cognates in books read and creating a word wall; highlighting the similarities and differences between the home language and English in relation to syntax, spelling, text structure, and punctuation as part of teacher dictation; and reading bilingual books to point out parallels and contrasts between the two languages (e.g., tone, text structure, word choice), which can also be used to prepare students for new content in other content areas.

Writing

Helping students make connections between oral and written language is very important in the beginning stages of second-language literacy development. Many activities have been developed to support students' emergent writing, but one of the key criteria is that these activities are meaningful and functional. Whether students already know how to write in their home language or are in more advanced stages of writing development, instruction should be adjusted to refine and expand students' competencies and help them acquire the academic writing skills they need in the content areas. A simple rule of thumb to encourage students' interest in writing is to display different types of writing paper and writing tools in the classroom and promote different types of writing functions, genres, and formats. Next, we briefly discuss the writing strategies and activities that we included in Table 6.2.

Modeled writing activities using the language experience approach are useful for connecting oral and written language because the teacher writes down students' dictation, which they use to learn to read. This strategy has been adapted to teach ESL reading and as a way to connect English writing to students' oral competencies (Peregoy & Boyle, 2005). The text produced from students' dictation is used to emphasize aspects of reading and writing, such as sight words and words with low symbol–sound correspondence, and can serve as the basis for refining students' writing abilities.

Guided writing through poetry, rhyme, and patterned language books is especially effective in supporting early writing because of the simple structure and predictable, rhythmic, and recursive nature. Incorporating the use of literature logs as part of literature circles can be an effective way to assist students in making deeper connections to the texts. It is important for teachers to notice the strategies students use to approximate conventional writing and use this knowledge to inform the design of guided writing lessons in small groups.

Interactive writing encourages students to write authentic messages and receive responses. An example of interactive writing is dialogue journals, which are written conversations between the teacher and individual students that take place regularly. Although the purpose of dialogue journals is not to correct students' errors, it is recommended for teachers to recast them and use the correct model in their responses as a way to advance students' language proficiency (see Cloud et al., 2009 for details about the classic model of dialogue journals and suggested variations).

Collaborative writing is another useful method to support students at different stages of writing development. As in other types of differentiated instruction, it involves teacher modeling of purposefully selected language structures or patterns within specific genres. The teacher and students work collaboratively to modify the language structures and create new stories. This method can be used to generate books for the classroom library, such as modified patterned language books, stories for wordless picture books, recipe books, and scripts for Readers Theatre (see Flores, 2008, as cited in Cloud et al., 2009).

Author's chair is an effective writing activity for ELLs when it is modified to meet students' oral language and literacy learning needs. It encourages students to see themselves as writers and members of a writing community. Unlike traditional process approaches used with mainstream English-speaking students, when used for ELLs author's chair must incorporate appropriate social, cultural, and linguistic adaptations as well as support students in each stage of the writing process: developing ideas, writing them down, getting feedback, editing, producing the final draft, and publishing (see Reyes, 1991).

Independent writing strategies that involve students editing their own writing are recommended for students in intermediate and advanced stages of writing development (Cloud et al., 2009). It is important to underscore that writing instruction, from the early stages of writing, must center on communication and meaning construction over mechanics and correctness. Many ELLs may struggle with editing their own writing when correctness obscures the expression of meaning and the development of complex ideas. Cloud and her colleagues suggest the use of writing rubrics and the traits model to guide students in editing their own writing. They urge teachers to be aware that most writing rubrics do not account for bilingual strategies that ELLs use when they write; therefore, they suggest that addressing conventions be the last step in the editing process.

Connections to Homes and Community

ELLs' home and community literacy practices and funds of knowledge should be valued as resources for literacy learning at school (González et al., 2005). Devising activities and projects that are related to students' life at home or in their neighborhood increases students' motivation and involvement. The following are examples of activities that promote links between school and students' homes and communities:

- Invite students to share family and neighborhood stories, sayings, or proverbs and compile them in a book for the classroom library. They can include realistic elements like photographs and excerpts of interviews with family members.
- Create autobiographies and personal narratives. This can be done as part of a social studies unit.
- Invite students to create books in their home language (either written or audiotaped) and read them to peers with similar language backgrounds.
- Write letters to family members who live far away.
- Assign research projects in which students tap into the existing funds of knowledge in their homes and communities and report them to the class (e.g., gardening, home remedies, immigration).
- Invite parents to come to the classrooms to talk about their professions or family economic activities (e.g., making traditional foods, embroidery, knitting).

Interventions for ELLs at Tier 2 and Tier 3

If students have not made adequate progress when taught using appropriate methods at Tier 1, more intensive interventions are warranted. Tier 2 is a level of targeted support that supplements the core curriculum and is based on student needs as identified through progress monitoring, classroom observations, and other data. Interventions should be research based and instructionally, culturally, and linguistically responsive and appropriate. The duration of initial Tier 2 interventions is relatively brief (e.g., six to eight weeks). Interventions are often taught by a specialist in the target area. In other words, for reading, interventions should be provided by a reading specialist or other expert in reading instruction. Students are taught in small groups or perhaps individually.

When ELLs show growth in response to these supplemental, intensive interventions, the problem-solving team must decide whether to continue Tier 2 instruction for a short time longer, to alter Tier 2 instruction (i.e., try something new), or discontinue it. When students seem to be progressing well, presumably they no longer need Tier 2 instruction. There are some students, however, whose progress diminishes when this supplemental support is taken away. When this happens, there is no reason not to provide it again. On the other hand, when students still do not seem to be doing well, even after their teachers and support personnel have tried several different interventions, it may be appropriate to provide them with ongoing, intensive Tier 3 support.

Tier 3 is generally considered to be special education, although students might receive this level of support without an Individualized Education Program. Students should not be identified as having learning disabilities (LDs) without a full, culturally and linguistically appropriate, comprehensive evaluation (see Brown & Doolittle, 2008). Instruction at Tier 3 is tailored to the individual needs of the student, is even more focused and personalized, and has a longer duration than instruction at Tier 2. Students with LDs must also be provided with access to the general education curriculum and instructed in the least restrictive environment.

We now know much more than we used to about effective reading interventions for ELLs. In some research studies, the researchers taught interventions in students' first language, whereas in other studies, the instruction was in English.

Some researchers have focused on improving ELLs' phonological awareness. For example, Nag-Arulmani, Reddy, and Buckley (2003) worked with ELLs with reading difficulties to improve their phonological awareness. They compared a phonological intervention with an oral proficiency intervention and a control condition and found that the ELLs who received explicit phonological instruction achieved at significantly higher levels in reading than other students. This was especially true for those students who had the lowest word-reading scores at the beginning of the study.

Through an intensive professional development program, Haager and Windmueller (2001) taught first- and second-grade teachers how to improve early reading instruction for ELLs who were identified as struggling readers, including several with LDs. They found that ELLs who initially showed very little progress were able to reach benchmarks when they received supplemental, small-group instruction in phonological awareness, oral language, and ESL.

These studies suggest that intensive phonological awareness interventions are promising for ELLs at Tier 2 and Tier 3 of an RTI approach.

In several studies, Vaughn, Linan-Thompson, and their fellow researchers (Vaughn, Cirino, et al., 2006; Vaughn, Linan-Thompson, et al., 2006; Vaughn, Mathes, et al., 2006) offered intensive, small-group interventions in either Spanish or English to first-grade ELLs found to be making little progress. The language of instruction of the supplemental interventions was the same as the language of classroom reading instruction. Interventions included tasks focused on oral language and listening comprehension, as well as phonological awareness, word study, fluency, vocabulary, and comprehension. Instruction included a shared storybook reading routine in addition to enhanced language acquisition instruction (Pollard-Durodola, Mathes, Vaughn, Cardenas-Hagan, & Linan-Thompson, 2006).

In the initial Spanish studies (Vaughn, Cirino, et al., 2006; Vaughn, Linan-Thompson, et al., 2006) and a later replication study (Vaughn, Mathes, et al., 2006), the researchers found significant posttest differences in favor of the ELLs who had received the researchers' intervention. The students who received the intervention in English (Vaughn, Cirino, et al., 2006; Vaughn, Mathes, et al., 2006) also outperformed comparison students, but not to the same extent.

In a similar study, Linan-Thompson, Bryant, Dickson, and Kouzekanani (2005) provided intensive instruction in Spanish to kindergarten ELLs who seemed to be struggling. Their intervention included 12 lessons that lasted about 20 minutes each. The students who participated in the intervention made some progress toward catching up with their peers not considered at risk, but they did only slightly better than similar ELLs at a comparison school. The authors concluded that the intervention group did not achieve at higher levels in part because of the short duration of the study; they suggested that future interventions should last for a longer period of time.

These studies show the potential of early interventions that combine oral language instruction, phonological awareness, word study, vocabulary, fluency, and listening and reading comprehension to improve reading for ELLs who seem to be experiencing reading difficulties in kindergarten, first, and second grades. The duration of the interventions seems to make a difference, with longer interventions probably more effective than shorter interventions. Also, it appears to be very helpful to emphasize oral language development, English-language acquisition, and listening comprehension.

In a different line of research, Saenz, Fuchs, and Fuchs (2005) implemented peer-assisted learning strategies, a classwide peer-tutoring strategy, with native Spanish-speaking students with LDs and their low-, average-, and high-achieving classroom peers in grades 3–6. The researchers found that students who participated in peer-assisted learning strategies achieved more than comparison students in reading comprehension.

A modified version of guided reading also shows potential for helping ELLs who struggle with reading at Tier 2 or Tier 3. Avalos et al. (2007) adapted guided reading (Fountas & Pinnell, 1996) for ELLs by adding oral English language and reading activities, culturally relevant texts, word work, and a writing response to the small-group reading instruction using leveled books typical of guided reading. Before introducing the book to students, the teacher analyzes it to identify possible challenges (e.g., figurative language, key vocabulary, complex syntax) and develop teaching objectives. The teacher emphasizes two or three low-frequency words and five to nine high-frequency words unknown by the students in each lesson. Modified guided reading is promising because of its emphasis on differentiated and individualized instruction, cultural relevance, and enhanced oral language and literacy learning.

Concluding Thoughts

In closing, we offer a series of questions to consider when implementing RTI models with ELLs. These questions are intended to be for classroom teachers, reading interventionists, and other support personnel to help them reflect about their practice and make well-informed instructional and assessment decisions (adapted from Haager et al., 2010). Questions related to Tier 1 are as follows:

- Have I had sufficient preparation in teaching ELLs?

- Are all students receiving research-based reading instruction that has been found to be effective with similar students in similar contexts?

- Are students' first and second languages and cultures considered in assessment, instructional planning, and decision making?

- Does instruction take into account students' cultural, linguistic, socioeconomic, and experiential backgrounds, including English and first-language proficiency levels?

- Does the school compare students' progress and performance with that of true peers with whom educational background, culture, and language are comparable?

- Are most ELLs thriving?
- Are parents involved in instruction, planning, and decision making?
- Is instruction differentiated to meet students' needs?
- Do I value and build on the strengths of my students and their families?
- Am I knowledgeable about and skilled in accounting for differences in learning to read in students' first and second languages and those aspects of reading in English that can be confusing?
- Do I teach in students' first language or use the first language in strategic ways?

Questions related to Tier 2 are as follows:

- Do Tier 2 providers have sufficient expertise in teaching ELLs?
- Does the system for progress monitoring include multiple kinds of measures—both quantitative and qualitative—that assess what students can do as well as their learning needs?
- Are experts in students' linguistic and cultural backgrounds involved in interpreting assessment data and planning instruction?
- Is a plan in place for using assessment data to group and regroup students in small, same-ability groups and one-to-one tutoring, to plan targeted instruction, and to make adaptations?
- Are criteria for entry into and exit from Tier 2 implemented and reassessed as needed with the help of experts who are knowledgeable about the cultural and linguistic backgrounds and needs of the students involved?
- Do interventions consider students' cultural, linguistic, socioeconomic, and experiential backgrounds?
- Does the level of a student's progress match or fall behind the progress of comparable peers?
- Are interventions research based, and have they been validated with similar students in similar contexts?
- Are interventions provided in the most natural environment possible to minimize disruption and distractions?
- Do students have sufficient opportunities for feedback and response during instruction?

Questions related to Tier 3 are as follows:

- Do Tier 3 providers have sufficient expertise in teaching ELLs?
- Have multiple forms of ongoing assessment data documenting students' performance been collected?
- How does each student perform in comparison with similar peers according to level and rate of performance?
- Have all factors been considered to account for a student's performance or lack of performance, including school-level, instructional, teacher, peer, classroom, home, and student-level factors?
- Is the first language considered in instructional planning and assessment data?
- How do service providers (special education and general education teachers and English-language development specialists) collaborate at this level to ensure access to general education content, support with English-language acquisition, first-language instruction (when possible), and special education support?

Given the wide range of concerns that might be identified in this type of self-assessment, we emphasize, in particular, the final question: How do service providers collaborate to ensure access to general education content, support with English-language acquisition, first-language acquisition, and special education support? It is unlikely that any one professional possesses all of the knowledge and expertise required to create powerful and effective literacy programs for (struggling) ELLs. Collaborative problem solving and continuing professional development are essential to change the outlook for most culturally and linguistically diverse students.

In the spotlight that follows in Chapter 7, we highlight the role of collaborative problem solving as we describe one school's implementation of RTI. We also show how teachers ask, and then go about answering, questions similar to those we listed earlier. In this chapter, we have attempted to offer a broad, comprehensive description of RTI for ELLs. In the spotlight, we focus on the implementation issues faced by educators in an actual school implementing RTI for the first time and how they deal with the challenges they face, as described by a teacher in the school.

REFERENCES

Alvermann, D.E. (2005). Exemplary literacy instruction in grades 7–12: What counts and who's counting? In J. Flood & P.L. Anders (Eds.), *Literacy development of students in urban schools: Research and policy* (pp. 187–201). Newark, DE: International Reading Association.

Antunez, B. (2002). Implementing Reading First with English language learners. *Directions in Language and Education, 15.* Retrieved January 11, 2010, from www.ncela.gwu.edu/files/rcd/BE020669/Directions_Spring_2002.pdf

August, D., & Shanahan, T. (2006). *Developing literacy in second-language learners: Report of the National Literacy Panel on Language-Minority Children and Youth.* Mahwah, NJ: Erlbaum.

Avalos, M.A., Plasencia, A., Chavez, C., & Rascón, J. (2007). Modified guided reading: Gateway to English as a second language and literacy learning. *The Reading Teacher, 61*(4), 318–329. doi:10.1598/RT.61.4.4

Baca, L.M. (2002). Educating English language learners with special education needs: Trends and future directions. In A.J. Artiles & A.A. Ortiz (Eds.), *English language learners with special education needs: Identification, assessment, and instruction* (pp. 191–202). Washington, DC: Center for Applied Linguistics.

Bialystok, E. (Ed.). (1991). *Language processing in bilingual children.* New York: Cambridge University Press.

Brown, H., & Cambourne, B. (1990). *Read and retell: A strategy for the whole-language/natural learning classroom.* Portsmouth, NH: Heinemann.

Brown, J.E., & Doolittle, J. (2008). A cultural, linguistic, and ecological framework for Response to Intervention with English language learners. *Teaching Exceptional Children, 40*(5), 66–72.

Carlo, M.S., August, D., McLaughlin, B., Snow, C.E., Dressler, C., Lippman, D.N., et al. (2004). Closing the gap: Addressing the vocabulary needs of English-language learners in bilingual and mainstream classrooms.

Reading Research Quarterly, 39(2), 188–215. doi:10.1598/RRQ.39.2.3

Cloud, N., Genesee, F., & Hamayan, E. (2009). *Literacy instruction for English language learners: A teacher's guide to research-based practices.* Portsmouth, NH: Heinemann.

Crosson, A.C., & Lesaux, N.K. (in press). Revisiting assumptions about the relationship of fluent reading to comprehension: Spanish-speakers' text-reading fluency in English. *Reading and Writing.*

Cummins, J. (2000). *Language, power and pedagogy: Bilingual children in the crossfire.* Tonawanda, NY: Multilingual Matters.

Delpit, L. (1995). *Other people's children: Cultural conflict in the classroom.* New York: New Press.

Education Week. (2009). *Quality Counts, 28*(17). Bethesda, MD: Editorial Projects in Education.

Escamilla, K., Geisler, D., Hopewell, S., Sparrow, W., & Butvilofsky, S. (2009). Using writing to make cross-language connections from Spanish to English. In C. Rodríguez-Eagle (Ed.), *Achieving literacy success with English language learners: Insights, assessment, instruction* (pp. 141–156). Worthington, OH: Reading Recovery Council of North America.

Fountas, I.C., & Pinnell, G.S. (1996). *Guided reading: Good first teaching for all children.* Portsmouth, NH: Heinemann.

Fung, I.Y.Y., Wilkinson, I.A.G., & Moore, D.W. (2003). L1-assisted reciprocal teaching to improve ESL students' comprehension of English expository text. *Learning and Instruction, 13*(1), 1–31. doi:10.1016/S0959-4752(01)00033-0

Garcia, E.E., & Cuéllar, D. (2006). Who are these linguistically and culturally diverse students? *Teachers College Record, 108*(11), 2220–2246. doi:10.1111/j.1467-9620.2006.00780.x

Garcia, S.B., & Ortiz, A.A. (1988). *Preventing inappropriate referrals of language minority students to special education.* Silver Spring, MD: National Clearinghouse for Bilingual Education.

Gay, G. (2000). *Culturally responsive teaching: Theory, research, and practice.* New York: Teachers College Press.

Genesee, F., & Geva, E. (2006). Cross-linguistic relationships in working memory, phonological processes, and oral language. In D. August & T. Shanahan (Eds.), *Developing literacy in second-language learners: Report of the National Literacy Panel on Language-Minority Children and Youth* (pp. 175–184). Mahwah, NJ: Erlbaum.

Genesee, F., & Riches, C. (2006). Literacy: Instructional issues. In F. Genesee, K. Lindholm-Leary, W. Saunders, & D. Christian (Eds.), *Educating English language learners: A synthesis of research evidence* (pp. 109–175). New York: Cambridge University Press.

Gersten, R., & Baker, S. (2000). What we know about effective instructional practices for English-language learners. *Exceptional Children, 66*(4), 454–470.

Goldenberg, C. (2008). Teaching English language learners: What the research does—and does not—say. *American Educator, 32*(2), 8–11, 14–19, 22–23, 42–43.

González, N., Moll, L.C., & Amanti, C. (Eds.). (2005). *Funds of knowledge: Theorizing practices in households, communities, and classrooms.* Mahwah, NJ: Erlbaum.

Gutiérrez, K.D., & Rogoff, B. (2003). Cultural ways of learning: Individual traits or repertoires of practice. *Educational Researcher, 32*(5), 19–25. doi:10.3102/0013189X032005019

Haager, D., Klingner, J.K., & Aceves, T.C. (2010). *How to teach English language learners: Effective strategies from outstanding educators.* San Francisco: Jossey-Bass.

Haager, D., & Windmueller, M.P. (2001). Early reading intervention for English language learners at-risk for learning disabilities: Student and teacher outcomes in an urban school. *Learning Disability Quarterly, 24*(4), 235–250.

Heath, S.B. (1983). *Ways with words: Language, life, and work in communities and classrooms.* New York: Cambridge University Press.

Hiebert, E.H., Pearson, P.D., Taylor, B.M., Richardson, V., & Paris, S.G. (1998). *Every child a reader: Applying reading research in the classroom.* Ann Arbor: Center for the Improvement of Early Reading Achievement, University of Michigan School of Education.

Invernizzi, M., Meier, J., & Juel, C. (2007). *PALS 1–3: Phonological awareness literacy screening 1–3* (6th ed.). Charlottesville: University Printing Services.

Invernizzi, M., Swank, L., & Juel, C. (2007). *PALS-K: Phonological awareness literacy screening—kindergarten* (6th ed.). Charlottesville: University of Virginia.

Jiménez, R.T., García, G.E., & Pearson, P.D. (1996). The reading strategies of bilingual Latina/o students who are successful English readers: Opportunities and obstacles. *Reading Research Quarterly, 31*(1), 90–112. doi:10.1598/RRQ.31.1.5

Kenner, C. (2004). Living in simultaneous worlds: Difference and integration in bilingual script-learning. *International Journal of Bilingual Education and Bilingualism, 7*(1), 43–61.

Kieffer, M.J., & Lesaux, N.K. (in press). Exploring sources of reading difficulties for language minority learners and their classmates in early adolescence. *American Educational Research Journal.*

Ladson-Billings, G. (1994). *The dreamkeepers: Successful teachers of African American children.* San Francisco: Jossey-Bass.

Linan-Thompson, S., Bryant, D.P., Dickson, S.V., & Kouzekanani, K. (2005). Spanish literacy instruction for at-risk kindergarten students. *Remedial and Special Education, 26*(4), 236–244.

López, L.M., & Greenfield, D.B. (2004). The cross-language transfer of phonological skills of Hispanic Head Start children. *Bilingual Research Journal, 28*(1), 1–18.

Martínez-Roldán, C.M., & López-Robertson, J.M. (1999). Initiating literature circles in a first-grade bilingual classroom. *The Reading Teacher, 53*(4), 270–281.

McCardle, P., Mele-McCarthy, J., Cutting, L., Leos, K., & D'Emilio, T. (2005). Learning disabilities in English language learners: Identifying the issues. *Learning Disabilities Research & Practice, 20*(1), 1–5. doi:10.1111/j.1540-5826.2005.00114.x

Nag-Arulmani, S., Reddy, V., & Buckley, S. (2003). Targeting phonological representations can help in the early stages of reading in a non-dominant language. *Journal of Research in Reading, 26*(1), 49–68. doi:10.1111/1467-9817.261005

Nieto, S., & Bode, P. (2008). *Affirming diversity: The sociopolitical context of multicultural education* (5th ed.). Boston: Allyn & Bacon.

Oller, J.W., Jr. (1991). Language testing research: Lessons applied to LEP students and programs. In *Proceedings of the National Research Symposium on LEP Student Issues: Focus on Evaluation and Measurement* (Vol. 1, pp. 42–123). Washington, DC: Office of Bilingual Education and Minority Language Affairs, U.S. Department of Education.

Ortiz, A.A. (2002). Prevention of school failure and early intervention for English language learners. In A.J. Artiles & A.A. Ortiz (Eds.), *English language learners with special education needs: Identification, assessment, and instruction* (pp. 31–48). Washington, DC: Center for Applied Linguistics.

Peregoy, S.F., & Boyle, O.F. (2005). *Reading, writing and learning in ESL: A resource book for K–12 teachers* (4th ed.). Boston: Allyn & Bacon.

Pollard-Durodola, S.D., Mathes, P.G., Vaughn, S., Cardenas-Hagan, E., & Linan-Thompson, S. (2006). The role of oracy in developing comprehension in Spanish-speaking English language learners. *Topics in Language Disorders, 26*(4), 365–384.

Reyes, M.L. (1991). A process approach to literacy using dialogue journals and literature logs with second language learners. *Research in the Teaching of English, 25*(3), 291–313.

Riedel, B.W. (2007). The relation between DIBELS, reading comprehension, and vocabulary in urban, first-grade students. *Reading Research Quarterly, 42*(4), 546–567. doi:10.1598/RRQ.42.4.5

Roache, M., Shore, J., Gouleta, E., & de Obaldia Butkevich, E. (2003). An investigation of collaboration among school professionals in serving culturally and linguistically diverse students with exceptionalities. *Bilingual Research Journal, 27*(1), 117–136.

Saenz, L.M., Fuchs, L.S., & Fuchs, D. (2005). Peer-assisted learning strategies for English language learners with learning disabilities. *Exceptional Children, 71*(3), 231–247.

Sattler, J.M. (2001). *Assessment of children: Cognitive applications* (4th ed). San Diego, CA: Author.

Saunders, W.M., Foorman, B.R., & Carlson, C.D. (2006). Is a separate block of time for oral English language development in programs for English learners needed? *The Elementary School Journal, 107*(2), 181–198. doi:10.1086/510654

Schilling, S.G., Carlisle, J.F., Scott, S.E., & Zeng, J. (2007). Are fluency measures accurate predictors of reading achievement? *The Elementary School Journal, 107*(5), 429–448. doi:10.1086/518622

Solano-Flores, G. (2006). Language, dialect, and register: Sociolinguistics and the estimation of measurement error in the testing of English language learners. *Teachers College Record, 108*(11), 2354–2379. doi:10.1111/j.1467-9620.2006.00785.x

Teachers of English to Speakers of Other Languages. (2008, August). *TESOL/NCATE standards for P–12 ESL teacher education programs* (Rev. draft). Alexandria, VA: Author. Retrieved June 2, 2009, from www.tesol.org/s_tesol/sec_document.asp?CID=219&DID=10698

Ulanoff, S.H., & Pucci, S.L. (1999). Learning words from books: The effects of read-aloud on second language vocabulary acquisition. *Bilingual Research Journal, 23*(4), 409–422.

U.S. Department of Education. (2003). *National Symposium on Learning Disabilities in English Language Learners, October 14–15, 2003: Symposium summary.* Washington, DC: Office of Special Education and Rehabilitative Services, U.S. Department of Education.

Vaughn, S., Cirino, P.T., Linan-Thompson, S., Mathes, P.G., Carlson, C.D., Hagan, E.C., et al. (2006). Effectiveness of a Spanish intervention and an English intervention for English-language learners at risk for reading problems. *American Educational Research Journal, 43*(3), 449–487. doi:10.3102/00028312043003449

Vaughn, S., Linan-Thompson, S., Mathes, P.G., Cirino, P.T., Carlson, C.D., Pollard-Durodola, S.D., et al. (2006). Effectiveness of Spanish intervention for first-grade English language learners at risk for reading difficulties. *Journal of Learning Disabilities, 39*(1), 56–73.

Vaughn, S., Mathes, P., Linan-Thompson, S., Cirino, P., Carlson, C., Pollard-Durodola, S., et al. (2006). Effectiveness of an English intervention for first-grade English language learners at risk for reading problems. *The Elementary School Journal, 107*(2), 153–180. doi:10.1086/510653

Zehler, A.M., Fleischman, H.L., Hopstock, P.J., Stephenson, T.G., Pendzick, M.L., & Sapru, S. (2003). *Policy report: Summary of findings related to LEP and SPED-LEP students.* Unpublished document submitted by Development Associates to the Office of English Language Acquisition, Language Enhancement, and Academic Achievement of Limited English Proficient Students, U.S. Department of Education.

CHAPTER 7

Spotlight on RTI for English-Language Learners: The Case of Mountain Creek Elementary

Alysia Hayas

Boulder Valley School District, Colorado

Janette K. Klingner

University of Colorado at Boulder

Mountain Creek Elementary (pseudonym) is in its first year of implementing RTI. The school has approximately 500 K–5 students, of whom about 25% speak a language other than English in their homes and are considered to be English-language learners (ELLs). Mountain Creek is located in a large, metropolitan area of Colorado, which has mandated that all schools must make the transition to using the RTI process to qualify students for special education. Mountain Creek's school district is now requiring all schools to have a problem-solving team and to move toward adopting the RTI model.

Mountain Creek employs one half-time ELL teacher, Alysia Hayas. Alysia has been a bilingual teacher for years, but this is only her second year working in her role as an ELL teacher. Alysia's role is a complicated one. She is expected to coach teachers about how best to teach ELLs. She participates on her school's leadership team as well as its intervention team, leads problem-solving teams, and is a member of a professional learning community. She also must plan for, provide, and monitor interventions for the 100 ELL students in her caseload and plan for and monitor interventions provided by the paraprofessional who assists her. In addition, she is expected to monitor these students through the years, even after they are considered to be fully proficient in English. In this case example, we describe Mountain Creek's RTI model from her perspective, in her voice. Alysia shares the following:

Our school was one of the first to begin to implement RTI in our district because we were excited about its potential and aware of the impending change in requirements stemming from the Individuals With Disabilities Education Improvement Act of 2004. States and districts are mandating the use of RTI but are not giving much guidance about what it actually looks like in schools (Klingner, Barletta, & Hoover, 2008; Orosco and Klingner, in press). Schools are mucking through the process of how to actualize it, and I spend a lot of time thinking about how best to help my students.

The number of questions that go through my head each day is intense. I am always thinking. For example, I worry about Carmen (all student names are pseudonyms), a third-grade ELL who is receiving Tier 2 interventions. I wonder how she is doing in Jill's (pseudonym) third-grade classroom. Carmen seems to still be struggling with reading and has been at our school for two years now. Questions such as the following flood my mind:

- Is the classroom instruction she is getting culturally and linguistically responsive?

- How can I support her teacher, Jill, to better meet Carmen's needs?

- What about the 20 minutes per day that she is spending with the ELL paraprofessional—is this intervention helping?

- Do we have the data to show if it is or is not helping?

- Do the assessments we use monitor the skills and strategies being taught, and are they truly "predictive"?

- Is the intervention even targeted at her specific needs? Have we taken the time to understand what her specific needs are?

- What data did we use in the first place to put her into this intervention?

- What about the intervention is she also getting from the reading intervention teacher? Is this second intervention contextualized enough to meet her linguistic needs?

- Should we test her for special education? Does she actually have a learning disability?

- Do two interventions pull her from the general classroom more than is appropriate? Do they make her instruction disjointed?

- Are we, her interventionist teachers, communicating with one another and with Jill enough to build on and support one another's efforts?

- What about her family? Have we effectively communicated with them about how to support her? Have we considered the strengths Carmen and her family bring and built upon them?

- Are we creating an atmosphere where Carmen feels valued, is held to high expectations, and is led to believe in her own abilities?

And Carmen is just one student in one classroom! With so many challenges, we need a system in which we are truly working collaboratively in the school to ask these questions together and answer them with increasing confidence, because they drive our instruction and our professional development. This is why I have been so excited about the potential of the new RTI model we are implementing at Mountain Creek.

Professional Learning Communities

At our school we have started a process called "professional learning communities." We meet as teams to discuss three guiding questions: (1) What do we want our students to know? (2) How will we know they have learned it? (3) What will we do for those who did not learn and also for those who did learn? Then, we begin the process again (DuFour & Eaker, 1998). RTI works in tandem with professional learning communities because it gives us a way to structure our thinking about what instruction/intervention we should be providing. In collaboration, team members look at all the differentiation strategies and intervention resources that are available to determine which are appropriate for which students.

This is a change from previous years when ELL teachers and special education teachers made their own decisions about what and how to teach the students designated as needing their assistance and taught their own interventions in isolation. Although it is important to have people with different specialties, we must remember that our students are not compartmentalized beings. Problems often overlap, and we are usually not the only ones working with particular students. When you have only one specialty, you may assume that this is the source of the problem and overlook other possible contributing factors or causes.

Rather than throw together a bunch of interventions as quickly as possible at the beginning of the school year, we spent time collaboratively looking at data and talking with teachers to develop appropriate Tier 2 and Tier 3 interventions. The challenge was, and continues to be, how to coordinate these with everyone's schedules. Teachers' schedules are not coordinated by the school and may not be consistent by grade level. Also, many of the interventionists work part time, and we want to be very intentional about when we pull our groups so that students are not missing that universal first best instruction. It was beneficial to take this time to be more intentional, but more work needs to be done schoolwide to coordinate the schedules so that we can all be as effective as possible.

We have early release days for specialized professional development based on our Colorado Student Assessment Program test data and other district tests, along with the areas in which teachers feel they need the most support.

Multitiered Instruction

Mountain Creek is implementing a three-tiered RTI model. Tier 1 provides support to all students in the general education classroom, or, as the state refers to it, "universal first best instruction." Our state's department of education manual on RTI stipulates that this instruction should be research based and of high quality and support the district's curriculum guidelines. Tier 1 instruction includes flexible grouping as well as all types of teacher-directed differentiation. Given the large percentage of ELLs, we believe that it is imperative to include culturally responsive teaching techniques at this level and throughout all of the tiers.

Tier 2 provides supplemental interventions to those students who are not making expected progress in Tier 1. These interventions are provided for a limited time with frequent progress monitoring and are usually delivered in small groups. At Mountain Creek, Tier 2 interventions include any instruction that supplements universal first best instruction. That is, in addition to the differentiation strategies implemented by classroom teachers, there is additional support provided outside of the general classroom for some students.

Tier 3 has more explicit, individualized interventions that may go on for an extended period of time. This level is often associated with students who have been identified as having learning disabilities (LDs), although some students might receive Tier 3 interventions without having qualified for special education.

At Mountain Creek, we are focusing on refining the three tiers and determining how best to make decisions about which students to support, what types of interventions to provide, and how to assess learning. The school put together an intervention team that consists of reading specialists, the ELL teacher, special education teachers, the speech-language pathologist, and the counselor. As an intervention team, we decided not to start most of our Tier 2 groups until late in September.

Problem-Solving Approach

Mountain Creek implements a problem-solving approach to make decisions about movement across the three tiers. We chose to use the problem-solving approach over a standard treatment protocol approach because it appealed to us more as professionals and is the model supported by our district. Drawing on our state's department of education directives on RTI, we see the purpose of the problem-solving process as assisting classroom teachers and parents in selecting and implementing intervention strategies that have a high probability of success for improving a student's academic or behavioral performance.

Prior to RTI, Mountain Creek experimented with various forms of the prereferral child study team model. For years, the child study team comprised a group of professionals that included the psychologist, a special education teacher, a school administrator, the speech-language pathologist, the social worker, and perhaps a classroom teacher. The team met regularly to decide whether to test a student referred by a teacher for special education. Occasionally, teachers tried some interventions before testing, but this was not the priority. Then, we modified our approach by expanding the team to increase the expertise, in an attempt to focus more on prereferral interventions. The new team included the principal, the reading coach, the student achievement coach, the ELL teacher, the reading interventionist, the special education teacher, the speech-language pathologist, the social worker, a representative from every grade level, the referring teacher, and the parent of the student. Although it was powerful to have so many people to draw from, it also was a bit overwhelming. As well, we were able to discuss only a handful of students throughout the year because of challenges with scheduling and the need to have six-week follow-ups. Many of us felt it was not the most efficient or best use of our time.

Now that RTI is in place, Mountain Creek is implementing a flexible problem-solving approach. We create teams of five or six people, depending on the needs of the student. Teachers choose one member of the core team of interventionists to facilitate the meeting, and other people are selected as deemed appropriate. The team might include one of the student's previous teachers, another teacher who specializes in the difficulties the student is facing, a paraprofessional who works with this student, a specialist (e.g., music, physical education, art) who works with this student in a different setting, or other members of the interventionist team. This allows us to have multiple meetings at once, increasing the number of students we can focus on and allowing us to have a relevant focused group to discuss the particular concerns related to one student. In addition, we are *all* seen as experts in the building who may be called on at any time to contribute to a problem-solving team.

The purpose of these meetings has shifted from a special education preevaluation to a true problem-solving model. Questions that are addressed include the following:

- With what exactly does this student struggle?
- What are the student's strengths on which we can build?
- What kind of instruction/interventions (both Tier 1 and Tier 2) has this student already received, and what were the results?
- How can we support the teacher with some new ideas for Tier 1?
- How can we readjust the Tier 2 interventions?
- Are there other factors we can influence, such as motivation?
- How can we involve the family?

The problem-solving team then chooses one or more interventions to implement and decides on a way to monitor progress. They meet six to eight weeks later to evaluate how well the student is doing and revise their plan, if necessary. If after several readjustments the student is still not responding, then they look at evaluating him or her for special education. The quest to find an intervention that works never stops until we succeed. At our school, this is the area where perhaps we have been most successful. Students are now moved flexibly between interventions without the previous heavy concern on their identification and with much more attention on how they are responding. By the time students are identified as having LDs, the school already has many supports in place.

Another difference in the RTI model is that problem-solving teams sometimes talk about students who are already in special education but are still not making expected progress, even with several Tier 2 or Tier 3 interventions. Before RTI, teachers would not have revisited these students' cases. Now we meet to clarify and adjust instruction for whichever students we feel need this focused approach, even those with LDs.

Collaboration

The RTI model at Mountain Creek involves much more collaboration than in the past. There has really been a shift in teachers' thinking about this. As we have progressed, teachers have been increasingly open to collaborating with the interventionists to try new ideas. Also, interventionists are collaborating much more closely with one another to make sure their interventions are appropriate. For example, I have been working extensively with the speech-language pathologist to make sure any interventions she does for the ELLs are context embedded, and we have had many discussions and traded articles about what phonemic awareness issues might come up for Spanish speakers learning English. This collaboration is just beginning and is not as extensive as we would yet like, so we are looking to create a structure that builds these discussions into our planning time rather than having incidental discussions.

As interventionists, we also discuss students' needs informally, outside of problem-solving meetings, among ourselves, and also with classroom teachers. I meet regularly with classroom teachers with large numbers of ELLs to collaborate, model lessons, and share ideas, and I meet on an as-needed basis with those teachers who have smaller numbers. The reading interventionist and other interventionists also meet regularly with teachers and provide support. This helps the interventionists stay connected with the instruction in the classrooms and vice versa.

This level of collaboration with teachers also helps us identify students who are not making expected growth. We meet as interventionists to discuss our work collaborating with teachers and our work as facilitators of the problem-solving teams and how well these are progressing. We also share ideas about how to structure and monitor interventions and about how this looks from a whole-school perspective. We create charts of all interventions happening in the building and discuss how they break into tiers. These charts are used to help us prioritize where we need to focus our efforts.

Assessments

The professional learning communities at Mountain Creek engage in data-based problem solving. We rely on different types of assessment data to inform instructional decisions. Some of the assessments are the large summative kind, such as state-mandated tests and the district beginning-of-year and end-of-year tests, but we also are trying to implement a number of smaller progress-monitoring assessments such as curriculum-based measurements. Classroom teachers use Everyday Mathematics curriculum checklists and biweekly running records for reading, but interventionists are still developing assessments to monitor how well interventions are working. As an ELL teacher, I have struggled to find a series of assessments that can quickly monitor students' progress with the skills I am teaching in my groups. For some students, a running record may suffice, but for others we are experimenting with using checklists from the district, adopted from the state's ELL standards, and other methods, such as collecting natural language samples and evaluating them using oral language rubrics.

The team of interventionists and problem-solving teams tends to focus on student-level data. But the school also has a leadership team that examines schoolwide trends. This team puts together the accountability workbook (i.e., school improvement plan) and includes many interventionists, coaches, and a representative from each grade level. After the team members complete the workbook in late September, they begin six-week cycles of data collection and analysis. Teachers at each grade level get a full day every six weeks to examine data, design a series of lessons to teach for the six-week block, collect assessment data, and report results at a leadership team meeting. This way they keep a dialogue going about what teachers at each grade level are doing in their classrooms, how well it is working, and any support they might need.

Culturally Responsive Teaching

In a linguistically diverse school such as Mountain Creek, it is important to focus on the sociocultural contexts in which teaching and learning take place and take steps to ensure that instruction is responsive to the cultural and linguistic needs of ELLs. There have been some attempts at Mountain Creek to work at deeper contextual levels, but little has been done in an explicit attempt to examine teachers' deeper beliefs about teaching culturally and linguistically diverse students, or how their beliefs affect their teaching practices. What is done is mostly on a teacher-by-teacher basis and not as an organized schoolwide effort. For example, I have put up informative bulletin boards in the staff room that encourage teachers to build on the cultural backgrounds of their students and from there give them the opportunities to explore new points of view. I have also hosted a series of Spanish-speaking parent workshops, during which we talk with parents about the expectations and procedures in our school system and how they can support their children in their homes. But sometimes I wonder how effective a bulletin board can be and how we can strengthen the bridge to culturally and linguistically diverse families as an entire school.

These cultural issues are not exclusive to the teaching of ELLs. There are other cultural issues that come up with families that may be economically impoverished or with teachers who are culturally not accustomed to the new collaborative approaches or instructional techniques we are trying. These have surfaced as problems with fidelity in the interventions proposed, and with complaints about a lack of motivation from the students and their families. The reality is that change, especially from within, is a slow process and that much more needs to be examined and explored before the deeper changes that RTI proposes will be realized.

Professional Development

School administrators recognize that ongoing professional development is an important component of RTI. At Mountain Creek, they have set up early release days for students so that teachers can attend specialized professional development sessions based on their state and district test data and on other topics deemed important. Some professional development sessions have focused on teaching ELLs and understanding the second-language acquisition process. The school's leadership team works with teachers to identify priorities for professional development and details these in their accountability workbook (school improvement plan).

Concluding Thoughts

Our RTI model is not perfect. We probably still focus too much on finding problems with the students rather than problems with the instruction. And we can do a better job being culturally and linguistically responsive. But we have already come a long way in improving how we support students. We are encouraged by the potential of RTI. Some may comment that we can control only so much as ELL teachers, interventionists, classroom teachers, administrators, or a school, but RTI provides a framework for us to begin to work together with one another and with the larger community, to provide students with appropriate instruction, and to meet their needs responsively, at every level.

REFERENCES

DuFour, R., & Eaker, R.E. (1998). Professional learning communities at work: Best practices for *enhancing student achievement*. Bloomington, IN: Solution Tree.

Klingner, J.K., Barletta, L.M., & Hoover, J.J. (2008). Response to Intervention models and English language learners. In J.K. Klingner, J.J. Hoover, & L.M. Baca (Eds.), *Why do English language learners struggle with reading? Distinguishing language acquisition from learning disabilities* (pp. 37–56). Thousand Oaks, CA: Corwin.

Orosco, M., & Klingner, J.K. (in press). One school's implementation of RTI with English language learners: "Referring into RTI." *Journal of Learning Disabilities*.

CHAPTER 8

RTI for Secondary School Literacy

Sandra K. Goetze

Oklahoma State University

Barbara Laster

Towson University, Maryland

Barbara J. Ehren

University of Central Florida

As RTI efforts have expanded across the country, secondary educators have realized that RTI can provide a valuable framework within which to structure educational opportunities for students in secondary schools. There are several important and interwoven reasons for considering RTI approaches at the secondary level: (a) the status of adolescent literacy is of major concern nationally (Greenleaf & Hinchman, 2009; Kamil et al., 2008); (b) federal legislation in the United States requires secondary schools, as well as elementary schools, to be accountable for academic achievement in reading of all students as indicated by adequate yearly progress measures; (c) educators in secondary schools can still prevent school failure and its negative consequences for adolescents; and (d) schools need options to address learning needs outside of special education (Ehren & Whitmire, 2009). The last two are especially important for our discussion in this chapter.

Because RTI rests on an assumption that early prevention and intervention will largely reduce or eliminate the problems of students struggling with literacy, the role of RTI in secondary school teaching and learning is still evolving. Let us consider, for example, the idea of "prevention." What might that mean in the context of adolescents? There are a large number of students who appear to have progressed normally through the early years of schooling but begin to struggle at middle or high school. They may have adequate reading and writing skills to perform well in elementary school, but they are not prepared to address the increased demands of the texts and tasks in secondary school (Leach, Scarborough, & Rescorla, 2003). They may struggle to understand informational texts or texts with many more challenging concepts, or they may lack the strategies to sustain their attention and comprehension of demanding and lengthy texts. For many of these students, a major contributor to their difficulties is limited vocabulary development that hinders their performance on various reading and writing tasks (Farstrup & Samuels, 2008; Lipson & Wixson, 2009).

Another group of adolescent students may have received support in earlier years but continue to struggle because earlier interventions were ineffective. There are also students whose needs have been neglected who have only experienced failure in reading and writing. It is clear from these examples that the assumption that literacy difficulties can be prevented may mean something different at the secondary level than it does at the elementary level. Nevertheless, RTI at the secondary level is an opportunity to create better learning environments for struggling or striving adolescents. As challenging as it is to meet the needs of adolescents struggling with literacy, educators should be encouraged by the results of the meta-analysis reported by Scammacca et al. (2007) on interventions for adolescent struggling readers that clearly indicate that intervention during adolescence is not too late.

Despite the clear indications that RTI has promise for adolescent students and their teachers, it is important to note that RTI approaches cannot simply be imported from elementary schools. Defining what it means to be literate as an adolescent has become particularly important to educators and researchers during the past 15 years (Fisher & Ivey, 2006; Irvin, Meltzer, Mickler, Phillips, & Dean, 2009; Kamil et al., 2008; Langer, 2001). The trajectory of student learning moves readers from understanding simple narrative text and easy content area text into more complex texts requiring higher order thinking, and it expands to include multiple literacies across the disciplines along with the ability to read and use multiple texts such as digital text. Today's adolescent readers must also be literate with other symbol systems such as video, moving text, audio clips, and instant messaging (Flood & Lapp, 1995). These types of reading acts are considered part of the new literacies that make adolescent literacy more complex than before (Alvermann, 2004).

The nature of adolescent literacy, the organizational structure of secondary settings, the challenges that adolescents face, and the unique features of curriculum, instruction, and assessment in these settings require specific attention in developing and implementing approaches to RTI in middle, junior, and high schools (Ehren & Deshler, 2009). Successful implementation of RTI at the secondary level is likely to involve a systemic approach that addresses literacy across the curriculum with research-based literacy practices taught by all teachers and specialists. The purpose of this chapter is to offer teachers and other educators guidance in planning and implementing RTI approaches for adolescents. We begin with a section on how core instruction in content classrooms can address literacy. We continue to a discussion of intervention beyond the content classroom and conclude with a section on the systemic issues involved in employing RTI in secondary schools.

Core Instruction in Content Classrooms

As schools contemplate or actively engage in RTI implementation, success depends on the effectiveness of instruction/intervention. The focus of RTI must first be on high-quality, differentiated, core instruction before consideration is given to more intensive options. We begin this section with a discussion of core literacy instruction within the context of the secondary school, including issues of integrating English language arts, student engagement, and classroom texts that need to be addressed at all levels of RTI. We also briefly describe instructional strategies focused on vocabulary and comprehension that are appropriate for use in the content classroom. The final portion of this section provides suggestions for differentiating instruction in science, English language arts, mathematics, and social studies classrooms.

Core Instruction

When secondary educators think of core instruction, they are likely to focus on core subjects such as mathematics, science, social studies, and language arts or English, with high school English more about literature than literacy. Literacy may not always be considered part of core instruction. Yet, given the importance of language and literacy to the mastery of academic subjects, it is essential for secondary educators to conceptualize listening, speaking, reading, and writing as part of their core content instruction (Biancarosa & Snow, 2006; Vacca & Vacca, 2005).

Many secondary content teachers protest that they are not reading or writing teachers, so they need encouragement to see that students' ability to acquire domain knowledge is dependent on their ability to access that content through reading, writing, listening, and speaking. For example, a biology teacher might note that students must be able to read, write, and discuss ideas, or they will not learn the concepts associated with the reproduction of seed plants and related curriculum standards in sufficient depth. In this view, literacy is not an add-on to content instruction; rather, it is an integral part of it.

Good first instruction, or "core" teaching (called Tier 1 in many RTI approaches), at the middle and high school levels requires content teachers to highlight the nature of discourse in their respective disciplines for all students. Every academic discipline, or content area, has its own set of characteristic literacy practices (Heller & Greenleaf, 2007). Because students have to learn specific types of discourse for each academic subject, teachers should include in their instruction specific attention to how professionals in their fields communicate. "Most students need explicit teaching of sophisticated genres, specialized language conventions, disciplinary norms of precision and accuracy, and higher-level interpretive processes" (Shanahan & Shanahan, 2008, p. 43).

For example, history teachers pay considerable attention to the circumstances in which text material was produced, because understanding the context of the historical document is essential for deep understanding of the text (Heller & Greenleaf, 2007; Schleppegrell, Achugar, & Oteiza, 2004). Therefore, when introducing text about the race into outer space, for example, a teacher would work with students to define the context of the primary or secondary sources that they are reading. Together, they might ask, Is the author an American or from another country? Was the document written before or after astronauts landed on the moon? Who published this text, whom did they expect to read it, and what was their purpose? Answers to these questions and others would provide perspective and support students in becoming critical readers of historical texts.

All content teachers can facilitate content acquisition and the required literacy access skills and strategies by providing instructional supports for all students in their classes.

Integrating Language and Literacy Processes. An important but often neglected principle in adolescent literacy instruction is the integration of listening, speaking, reading, and writing. These language processes are reciprocally related and need to be addressed in relation to each other for all students (Ehren, Lenz,

& Deshler, 2004); this approach is especially important for English-language learners (ELL; Genesee, Lindholm-Leary, Saunders, & Christian, 2006).

In practical terms, teachers and specialists should weave work together across spoken and written language domains as well as within written language processes. Several authors have highlighted the importance of interactive dialogue (i.e., listening and speaking) around content knowledge. In describing text-based collaborative learning, Biancarosa and Snow (2006) clarify that when students work in small groups, they should not just discuss a topic but rather interact around a text. They report that this approach is effective in improving not only reading skills but also writing skills. Short and Fitzsimmons (2007), in emphasizing the interaction of all four language processes with ELLs, caution that oral language practice should not be sacrificed for more instructional time on reading and writing.

In the same vein, recommendations by Kamil et al. (2008), with regard to providing opportunities for extended discussion of text meaning and interpretation, incorporate spoken and written language experiences. Specific suggestions include the following:

- Prepare carefully for the discussion by selecting engaging materials and developing stimulating questions.
- Ask follow-up questions that help provide continuity and extend the discussion.
- Provide a task or discussion format that students can follow when they discuss text in small groups.
- Develop and practice the use of a specific discussion protocol.

It is not a new concept that reading and writing are reciprocal processes or that integrating reading and writing instruction enhances both (Seidenberg, 1989; Taylor & Beach, 1984). When teachers integrate reading and writing into classroom activities, they can highlight the relationships among understanding and using words and structures. For example, we know that students who are familiar with the way texts are typically organized can use that knowledge to understand and remember information (Pearson & Camperell, 1994; Williams, Brown, Silverstein, & deCani, 1994). Therefore, engaging students in writing activities using the genre they are working to understand is an appropriate instructional practice (Dickson, Simmons, & Kame'enui, 1998; Seidenberg, 1989). To implement this practice, a science teacher trying to help students understand cause and effect in earth science might work with students to construct cause-and-effect essays.

Student Engagement. Engagement is an important issue in learning for students of any age. However, educators working with adolescents can attest to the futility of any instruction/intervention in which teens are not actively involved. Motivating adolescents to read, especially when they have difficulties in this area, is a major component in instruction and intervention (Torgesen et al., 2007). Experts cast motivation as a metacognitive component because they believe it may be the force that propels students to develop, use, and control, or self-regulate, their literacy knowledge and skills (Borkowski, 1992; Johnston & Winograd, 1985).

As part of core instruction, student motivation and engagement in literacy learning needs to be highlighted. Kamil et al. (2008) recommend that teachers do the following:

- Establish meaningful and engaging content-learning goals around the essential ideas of a discipline as well as around the specific learning processes used to access those ideas.

- Provide a positive learning environment that promotes student autonomy in learning.

- Make literacy experiences more relevant to student interests, everyday life, or important current events.

- Build classroom conditions to promote higher reading engagement and conceptual learning through such strategies as goal setting, self-directed learning, and collaborative learning.

- Involve adolescents in goal setting and progress monitoring to be successful.

Within the context of RTI initiatives, it is important to engage all adolescents as part of the process. They should participate in goal setting and the monitoring of their progress, regardless of their literacy levels.

Classroom Texts. Students need opportunities to engage with text at their reading level. Therefore, teachers need to make available to students a wide variety of materials at various reading levels to facilitate student engagement in learning activities in their content courses. The use of books and materials that have been rated using the Lexile system (Lennon & Burdick, 2004) is one tool that can be used by teachers and students alike to guide selection of reading materials for different purposes and at different challenge levels.

Adolescents also need experience with complex texts that are appropriate for their age and grade levels. Content specialists have argued that domain knowledge may be compromised by attempts to reduce the level of reading difficulty, that it is not possible to convey complex information with simplified text (Otero, León, & Graesser, 2002). Students need opportunities to engage with more complicated text along with support in how to use background knowledge and text structure to determine relationships among ideas and draw conclusions (Peterson, Caverly, Nicholson, O'Neal, & Cusenbary, 2000). So, in addition to making leveled texts available, it is important to support students in processing text at their grade placement level so that they can interact with complex vocabulary and language structures and become familiar with the discourse of the domain. Use of technology can help in this regard with text-to-speech tools that permit students access to text while it is being read for them.

Professionals working specifically with struggling students to improve their language and literacy also need to be concerned about the difficulty of the text that students encounter. Well-structured or considerate text can help build fluency but does not help struggling readers move beyond literal levels of understanding (McNamara & Kintsch, 1996; McNamara, Kintsch, Songer, & Kintsch, 1996; Peterson et al., 2000). Work with leveled text may focus on word recognition and mastery of basic comprehension strategies, whereas work with grade-level text would focus on manipulating complex language involved in higher level thinking skills within a content area and expansion of such cognitive skills as inferential reasoning.

A Focus on Vocabulary. One of the most important areas in which content teachers can make an impact is in teaching vocabulary. Specific vocabulary techniques that can be used in core instruction in content classrooms include repeated exposure to conceptual vocabulary, interactive classroom talk, scaffolded read-alouds with decontextualized book language, specific word instruction aimed at usefulness and frequency, and semantic maps (Beck, McKeown, & Kucan, 2002). Each of these techniques is described in the following sections with specific examples.

Conceptual vocabulary is the teaching and use of key technical terms (Anders & Bos, 1986), which is known to correlate with reading fluency and is strongly related to comprehension. Awareness by a content teacher to actively highlight and directly teach conceptual vocabulary can support all students.

Interactive classroom talk is also helpful for acquiring new vocabulary, particularly for ELLs. When students are involved in specific learning or inquiry tasks, teachers should model the language of what they are doing. The teacher has a specific role in scaffolding the language, so students experience a demonstration of what a new concept or word means. For example, an art teacher might spotlight the word *shading* while he or she is shading a geometric figure in a painting, or a science teacher might highlight the phrase *balancing a chemical equation* while the students are doing the activity of balancing a chemical reaction.

Scaffolded read-alouds present teachers with the opportunity to read short sections of technical text to students while helping them connect what they already know to the new vocabulary. The teacher's role during the read-aloud is to read, stop, and reflect aloud, helping students situate the new learning in their understanding of the broader concepts. Very difficult pieces of text can be broken down in this manner to study specific words (Penno, Wilkinson, & Moore, 2002). English teachers often help students access Shakespearean plays using this method. Similarly, health teachers may use scaffolded read-alouds to assist students with understanding difficult sections of a text about disease prevention.

Finally, semantic maps are useful in extending students' knowledge of words they already know. These are graphic organizers ordered around a specific word and used to generate other words (Finesilver, 1994; Pittelman, Levin, & Johnson, 1985). Related words are clustered around the keyword. Features of the words, which are similar or dissimilar, and other meanings with shared linguistic components can be used. The identification of critical attributes can also be used to map words. Mapping software is a technology tool that allows students to delve into many layers of word meaning as they create their own semantic maps. A similar visual representation is a concept of definition map (MacKinnon, 1993; Schwartz & Raphael, 1985) that helps students define a concept and determine its essential facets. Content enhancement routines also employ visual devices as anchors for dialogue around vocabulary and concept development in content areas; see, for example, the concept mastery routine (Bulgren, Deshler, & Schumaker, 1993), the concept comparison routine (Bulgren, Lenz, Deshler, & Schumaker, 2005), and the clarifying routine (Ellis, 1997).

A Focus on Comprehension. Content teachers can also incorporate comprehension strategies to assist all students in constructing meaning from text. Adler (2004) notes that strategies to improve comprehension are plans that are put into practice for reading to be understood, including metacognition, graphic and semantic organizers, and answering questions. The explicit teaching of cognitive comprehension strategies to be used by students is also broadly supported by research (Edmonds et al., 2009).

There is considerable research to suggest that teachers' use of think-alouds is an effective way to improve students' comprehension. Block and Israel (2004) define a think-aloud as "a metacognitive technique or strategy in which a teacher verbalizes thoughts aloud while reading a selection orally, thus modeling the process of comprehension" (p. 154). The process is not a smooth one; rather, it is marked with frequent pausing, questioning, and connection making (Block & Israel, 2004). The goal of the think-aloud strategy is the verbal process of thinking through a piece of text (Block & Israel, 2004). Teachers can model a think-aloud and then have all students practice in pairs or small groups. During a think-aloud, both good and poor readers are asked to verbally work through a text. The process is documented and questioned during the process for better understanding, thus developing a think-aloud protocol (Edmonds et al., 2009).

Another example of a strategy to promote comprehension is question–answer relationship (QAR), which facilitates the use of questioning to understand (Adler, 2004). Raphael and Au (2005) assert, "QAR first and foremost provides teachers and students with a much-needed common language" (p. 208). In addition, the teacher models the QAR strategy for the students; thus, the students are able to "see" the connection process. Raphael and Au (2005) further state,

> The vocabulary of QAR—In the Book, In My Head, Right There, Think & Search, Author & Me, and On My Own—gives teachers and students a language for talking about the largely invisible processes that constitute listening and reading comprehension across grades and subject areas. (p. 208)

A relatively small set of cognitive strategies are linked to effective comprehension (Duke & Pearson, 2002; Paris, Cross, & Lipson, 1984). These include monitoring and regulating reading behaviors, identifying important information, summarizing, self-questioning, predicting and inferring, and evaluating. Content teachers engaging in comprehension strategy instruction should take note of the following specific recommendations from Kamil and colleagues (2008):

- Select carefully the text to use when beginning to teach a given strategy.
- Show students how to apply the strategies they are learning to different texts.
- Make sure that the text is appropriate for the reading level of students.
- Use a direct and explicit instruction lesson plan for teaching students how to use comprehension strategies.
- Provide the appropriate amount of guided practice depending on the difficulty level of the strategies that students are learning.
- Talk about comprehension strategies while teaching them.

Differentiating Instruction Within Core Content Instruction

An important feature of core instruction in an RTI framework is differentiation of instruction ("IRA Commission on RTI," 2009); that is, teachers have to vary their instructional approaches to meet the needs of the diverse students in today's classrooms. The content teacher can accomplish some of this differentiation as part of core, or Tier 1, instruction by means such as grouping students for different learning activities and providing assignment options. However, some types of differentiation require support from an educational specialist (e.g., special educator, reading specialist, speech-language pathologist) who joins the classroom teacher in helping students gain access to content curriculum through language and literacy. This type of support is commonly referred to as Tier 2 instruction. At the root of differentiated instruction is the principle that one size does not fit all.

Implementing differentiated instruction in secondary schools is more difficult than at the elementary level for a variety of reasons. As curricular demands escalate in secondary schools, teachers feel increased pressure to have students meet standards, earn credits, and pass high-stakes standardized tests. They have a great deal of content to teach as well as a large number of students. Also, they do not have the structure of an entire day within which to work with students; typically they have a class period, or, at best, a block of two periods within which to organize instruction.

Educators must creatively apply differentiation principles and practices in secondary settings, not merely import practices that work in elementary grades.

For example, a high school chemistry teacher may not be able to spend a lot of time giving individual assistance to a small number of students, but he or she could apply research-based techniques with the entire class and provide opportunities for smaller groups of students to work on different tasks to reinforce or expand their understanding of a topic. Biancarosa & Snow (2006) state,

> The use of such tools as graphic organizers, prompted outlines, structured reviews, guided discussions, and other instructional tactics that will modify and enhance the curriculum content in ways that promote its understanding and mastery have been shown to greatly enhance student performance—for all students in academically diverse classes, not just students who are struggling. (p. 15)

With specific regard to literacy, differentiation should involve provision of materials (print and multimedia) at appropriate instructional levels so that students who are struggling can learn the content.

The following discussion provides examples of what differentiation might look like in each of the following content areas: science, English language arts, mathematics, and social studies.

The Science Classroom. Literature circles with content area text (Wilfong, 2009) and comprehension strategies, as suggested by Shanahan (2004), are two approaches that fit well with science content to differentiate student learning. Several times per week the teacher uses small groups within the regular classroom period to hold a literature circle related to close reading of the text. Students are given the roles of discussion director, summarizer, vocabulary enricher, and webmaster. Each "text masters" session has a set routine. The students read silently for 20 minutes, fill out their role sheet for 20 minutes, then share roles to end in a culminating activity. The discussion director develops a list of questions, and the summarizer drafts a brief summary of the day's reading. The vocabulary enricher is on the lookout for key vocabulary. Last, the webmaster takes all of the information from the session and incorporates it into a graphic organizer. As students become more adept in their roles, they should be able to engage in these types of discussions without the formal assignment of roles.

This type of differentiation can be tailored to student needs by grouping specific students for more intensive, scaffolded instruction by the teacher. While scaffolding, the teacher might teach specific comprehension strategies such as teaching students to write and answer their own questions. Other types of scaffolding might involve the use of writing frames for summarizing support or the creation of idea maps for organizing work (Shanahan, 2004). The teacher can model each idea and provide a scaffold for understanding the new content in the text, while other students who do not need this level of differentiation work independently in their text masters group.

The English Language Arts Classroom. Opportunities abound in the English language arts classroom for differentiation. Using texts written at levels the students can read independently with at least 95% accuracy is recommended. Houge and Geier (2009) suggest using young adult literature, which often is marked with a reading level and is usually appealing to adolescents; this provides the teacher with the opportunity to offer a choice of texts at different levels aligned to the theme of the instructional unit.

Specific instructional techniques to consider include talk posters and writing workshop interventions. Talk posters (Fisher, Frey, & Rothenberg, 2008) are tools to manage classroom talk while enhancing student learning. For example, Fisher, Frey, and Rothenberg suggest using a poster on cause-and-effect linguistic frames. The poster contains signal words, such as *so, because, therefore*, and *since*. On the other side of the poster are sample sentence frames to practice these ideas by adding in one's own words. Talk posters can encompass any idea in language arts with which students are struggling. Students use them as a reference in the classroom and refer to them often. Other ideas are language and learning posters that provide examples of key academic phrases, such as *to inquire, to describe, to explain, to hypothesize, to deduce*, and *to evaluate*. Each idea is followed by three sentences to spur talk and scaffold learning (e.g., "to instruct—The first step is.... Next.... The last part is...."). This technique allows the teacher to focus a small group of students on developing their own poster or using a completed one to scaffold learning.

Another approach is writers' workshop, which provides much needed time for teachers to work individually with students on their writing. Some students may see the teacher more frequently to move their progress along. This extra feedback can also provide some time for minilessons on a specific writing goal. Atwell's (1998) classic study of middle school students in a reading–writing workshop classroom focuses on authentic reading and writing and maps students' progress using pre- and postsurveys and multiple artifacts of student work. Roller (1996) uses a workshop approach to assist older students who have severe lags in their reading and writing; the motivating support of literature discussion groups, personal writing projects, and choice of materials have resulted in significant gains for these students.

The Mathematics Classroom. There are multiple features, including uncommon syntax, that are unique to mathematics text materials. This makes it important for the mathematics teacher to provide specific language and literacy instruction about equations, geometric theorems, charts, and graphs with which students often have difficulty. Graphic literacy tasks typical of a mathematics classroom provide distinctive challenges with language and literacy. Breaking down or chunking a chart or a graph into overlays of information may help: Talk about a visual that has the simplest form first, and then, as the graph becomes more complex, new information can be added and discussed. Students can develop a strategy for this and later apply it to new charts or graphs that they encounter. Differentiation groups could meet once per week to work directly with the teacher or alongside the reading specialist in a coteaching situation.

Learning-centered approaches are another way to support students in mathematics classes through the use of scaffolding instruction and frontloaded exercises (Johannessen & McCann, 2009). Frontloading exercises include scenarios, opinionnaires, and role-play. The goal is to connect what students already know from prior experiences to the new reading. Consequently, a new lesson on determining tax on a new car could include a role-play on a car purchase. These authors suggest that role-play and scenarios prepare students by having them focus on simulation activities that, in turn, lead to reading more difficult text.

The Social Studies Classroom. Differentiation in social studies classrooms might focus on vocabulary and concept development. Vaughn et al. (2008) suggest that "mnemonics and word association embedded in content lessons is the most effective way for increasing vocabulary and maintaining the use of newly learned words" (p. 339). Two techniques to support these ideas are historiography and concept-oriented reading instruction (CORI; Guthrie, Anderson, Alao, & Rinehart, 1999).

Historiography is considered process teaching in the social sciences. Stahl and Shanahan (2004) describe it as "teaching the process of history, focusing on the critical analysis of the various narratives that exist about any particular event or cluster of events" (p. 96). Historiography involves the reading of text as a strategy to interpret what the author meant to convey—the general message. Then, students use other sources to refute the ideas and attempt to make a critical analysis case for a differing viewpoint. The second set of readings can be correlated with students' reading levels so that they may access the text with success. Critical reading is the key part of the technique, because students develop these skills only by engaging in them. One caveat is that students should not see historiography as seeking relative truth, but, rather, other positions or points of view.

The CORI model builds deep conceptual knowledge, while also promoting strategic reading. CORI combines explicit strategy instruction with hands-on experiences, individual student learning, and the use of multiple texts. Although the seminal research was with science texts, later adaptations for social studies and other content areas have more recently been published (e.g., Swan, 2003, 2004). For more specific information about the CORI model, see www.cori.umd.edu/.

Comprehensive Core Literacy Instruction

It is perhaps most desirable to adopt a comprehensive approach to core instruction that embodies as many of the features of the quality, secondary literacy instruction highlighted previously as possible. An example of such an approach is reading apprenticeship (Schoenbach, Greenleaf, Cziko, & Hurwitz, 1999), which is intended to help adolescents develop the knowledge, strategies, and dispositions they need to become more powerful readers. We characterize this approach as comprehensive because it is designed to address the needs of all students and teachers involved in secondary students' content area and literacy learning.

Teachers are the content area experts, and students are apprenticed into the ways reading and writing are used within a content area. The strategies and thinking that are particularly useful in that content area and the use of a reading apprenticeship help develop better readers through a variety of practices, including making teachers' discipline-based reading processes and knowledge visible to students and making students' reading processes, motivations, strategies, knowledge, and understandings visible to the teacher and to one another. It also engages students in more reading—for recreation as well as for content area learning and self-challenge—and helps them gain insight into their own reading processes. Finally, as teachers scaffold students, they develop a repertoire of problem-solving strategies for overcoming obstacles and deepening comprehension of texts from various academic disciplines.

To accomplish these goals, content teachers are encouraged to plan along four interacting dimensions of classroom life that support reading development:

- The social dimension draws on adolescents' interests in peer interaction by building a reading inquiry community. Through ongoing conversations rooted in text, students learn to ask critical questions about content, purpose, and perspective.

- The personal dimension draws on strategic skills used by students in out-of-school settings. Teachers help students recognize and work with these skills and support them as they strive to become more strategic and purposeful about their reading.

- The cognitive dimension involves developing students' repertoire of specific comprehension and problem-solving strategies, with an emphasis on group discussion of when and why particular cognitive strategies are useful.

- The knowledge-building dimension includes identifying and expanding the knowledge readers bring to a text, including knowledge about word construction, vocabulary, text structure, genre, language, topics, and embedded content.

These dimensions are woven into content area teaching through metacognitive conversations as teachers and students work collaboratively to make sense of texts while engaging in a conversation about what constitutes reading and the thinking processes they engage in as they read.

Systemic approaches to core instruction such as reading apprenticeship provide a solid foundation for adopting RTI as a means of working with secondary students who are struggling with literacy. These approaches must, however, be expanded to include more intensive interventions for the students who continue to struggle beyond high-quality core instruction. This is the topic of the next section and of the case study in Chapter 9. Later sections of this chapter also consider the various issues related to infrastructure that must be addressed if a systemic approach is to be successful.

Instruction for Students Who Need Support Beyond the Content Classroom

RTI approaches involve increasingly intensive instruction/intervention to meet students' needs. For adolescents who struggle with literacy, supports must be available in a variety of configurations. Special educators, reading teachers and specialists, speech-language pathologists, ELL teachers, and others may join a team—along with the content teachers—that monitors the progress of students who need intensive interventions. For adolescents struggling with literacy, Kamil et al. (2008) recommend that educators should make available intensive, individualized interventions (frequently referred to as Tier 3 instruction) that can be provided by qualified specialists according to the following guidelines:

- Use reliable screening assessments to identify students with literacy difficulties and follow up with formal and informal assessments to pinpoint each student's instructional needs.

- Select an intervention that provides an explicit instructional focus to meet each student's identified learning needs.

- Provide interventions in which intensiveness matches student needs—the greater the instructional need, the more intensive the intervention.

Results from the National Assessment of Educational Progress indicate that only 29% of eighth graders in the United States are at or above proficient reading levels, with 43% only at basic levels and 27% below basic (Lee, Grigg, & Donahue, 2007). Clearly we have reason to be concerned about struggling adolescent readers. What kind of problems are involved? Biancarosa and Snow (2006) indicate that the bulk of older struggling readers can read (i.e., recognize words) but cannot understand what they read, although Hock et al. (2009) have found a significant number of adolescents struggling with word recognition. It is clear that adolescent literacy involves complex processes and students who are struggling may exhibit any number of problems. Therefore, an important component of RTI is to identify the specific nature of students' problems.

Identifying Struggling Students

Identification is not a simple matter. It is not sufficient to identify adolescents whose language and literacy skills are not up to par to meet complex curricular demands. Educators must have information that is specific enough to provide a direction for instruction/intervention. The reality is that identifying literacy difficulties is a complex process that cannot be reduced to performance on a single measure. We need to pinpoint whether decoding, fluency, or comprehension problems are an issue and determine beyond that the kinds of problems students may be having in these areas. It is equally important to ascertain students' abilities across multiple literacies as well as their specific strengths and interests across literacy tasks.

In the area of reading, Torgesen et al. (2007) identify six factors underlying proficiency at the late elementary, middle, and high school levels that can provide guidance to educators in planning assessment systems: (1) fluency of text reading, (2) vocabulary, or the breadth and depth of knowledge about the meaning of words, (3) active and flexible use of reading strategies to enhance comprehension, (4) background, or prior knowledge related to the content of the text being read, (5) higher level reasoning and thinking skills, and (6) motivation and engagement for understanding and learning from text.

To address the range of information needed to plan literacy instruction, educators should consider different layers of assessment. A global screening measure might be used to identify students who are struggling. These screening measures can help guide core instruction and help identify a subset of students who may be challenged by the curriculum. Even when group-assessment instruments provide more detailed information by reporting subtest results or item analysis, they may not provide enough information to guide instruction.

Formative or diagnostic assessments, then, are necessary to guide instruction/interventions. Educators need to investigate the underlying factors of students' less-than-adequate reading or writing. The importance of assessment to the instructional process, as well as its complexity, calls for a collaborative approach among secondary educators. This kind of work is beyond the scope of many secondary content teachers to address by themselves, although they certainly are valuable participants in the assessment process. They will not have the time or likely the expertise to engage in the kind of formative assessment that provides specific targets for instruction/intervention. The work of reading specialists, ELL teachers, speech-language pathologists, and other professionals whose expertise is focused in language and literacy is an important part of this process.

Some questions that might guide the investigation of particular areas of strength and weakness are as follows:

- Is the student struggling with comprehension because of word-level is-sues, either with identifying words or with meaning?

- Is the student a fluent reader with difficulty manipulating meaning?

- Does the student have syntax-level issues in which he or she gets lost in complex structures?

- How is background knowledge used in constructing meaning?

- What comprehension strategies (e.g., predicting, questioning, monitoring) are used?

- Is higher level reasoning such as critical evaluation evident?

- Are some discipline literacies easier for the student than others (e.g., deter-mining author's tone or style, geometrical syllogisms, algebraic equations)?

- How does the student fare with literacies outside the context of school (e.g., functional literacy skills such as reading medicine labels, lease agree-ments, tables, and charts)?

- How proficient is the student with nonprint literacy such as navigating the Internet?

- Which writing tasks—descriptive, persuasive, or narrative—are strengths, and which are areas in need of improvement?

Useful tools include informal reading inventories, spelling inventories, writing samples, metacognitive interviews, motivation to read and write sur-veys, textbook use and note-taking assessments, retellings, and observations to determine students' purposes for reading and writing, what they already do, and where they could use some help (Braunger & Lewis, 2006; Fisher & Ivey, 2006). For ELLs, Short and Fitzsimmons (2007) recommend multiple measures that might assess first-language content knowledge and literacy skills as well as English vocabulary and content knowledge in formats that might include port-folios and formative classroom assessments.

As noted above, multiple assessment measures assist the specialists—in collaboration with the content teachers—in discovering how best to address the needs of specific students. Assessment may include error analysis, miscue anal-ysis, and retrospective miscue analysis (Goodman & Marek, 1996; Goodman, Watson, & Burke, 2005), which can address these questions: What kinds of deviations from the text (miscues) does the reader make, and how do these miscues affect comprehension? What do the miscues reveal about the strategies and cues the reader uses? (Braunger & Lewis, 2006). The more extensive the student's language and literacy difficulties, the more likely it will be that he or she will require further intervention.

Intensive Intervention for Students Struggling With Literacy (Tier 2 and Tier 3)

As we have maintained throughout this chapter, there is no one pattern of difficulty in adolescent language and literacy. Data suggest that older students present very diverse profiles of reading difficulty, and teachers need to be aware that a single approach does not meet the needs of all students. Packaged programs focused on one aspect of literacy may be appropriate for only a small portion of struggling students (Valencia & Buly, 2004). As well, teachers must remember that interventions appropriate for younger students may not be effective with older students. For example, the meta-analysis of research studies conducted by Edmonds and colleagues (2009) demonstrates that instruction in reading fluency is not associated with increased comprehension for older students. They suggest that for students whose word-reading skills are exceedingly low, it makes sense to build these word-level skills while teaching comprehension so that expectations are not reduced for these students. Basic reading and writing instruction should be coupled with practice using the language, content, and reasoning found in all of the distinct content disciplines. In this way, students are not left out of thoughtful reading, writing, and discussion about content when they attend their regular classes.

Because students who struggle have different patterns of performance, educators need to try different mixes of instruction/intervention elements to find the ones that work best for individual students (Biancarosa & Snow, 2006; see Figure 8.1 for two sample student profiles). Despite the diversity of student profiles at middle and high schools, educators should select techniques with a track record of effectiveness and stay alert to common patterns of reading difficulty in their settings. For example, in a research synthesis, Gajria, Jitendra, Sood, and Sacks (2007) summarize findings of studies with middle school students, plus some high school students, related to comprehension of expository text by students with learning disabilities. They found effective single interventions, including text structure, cognitive mapping, identifying main idea, paraphrasing, summarization, and self-questioning. Combined strategies include summarization

Figure 8.1. Two Sample Profiles of Adolescent Literacy Development

An is a student who has large gaps in literacy and who needs intensive interventions/ instruction. He was assessed by a specialist at the suggestion of many of his content teachers. The reading specialist conferred with the ELL teacher, who confirmed that An had progressed well and been dismissed from her class; he was no longer considered a student with limited English proficiency. However, an assessment using an analysis of oral reading showed that he is still having major difficulty with language at the word, sentence, and conceptual levels.

The intensive intervention that is initially planned for An has three major parts:

1. The reading specialist or his assistant will work with An before school each day. Using visual and kinesthetic methods, the reading specialist or assistant will reteach a few key vocabulary/conceptual words currently central to each content discipline.

2. The textbooks in all of An's classes are too hard for him to read independently, so the reading specialist will introduce print-to-voice technology that An can use to hear some of the central passages of the assigned readings in English, social studies, and science.

3. The speech-language pathologist will do some diagnostic teaching with An to investigate the nature of his problems using English syntax. This information will be shared with other professionals working with An. An's progress will be monitored by a specialist, in collaboration with the classroom teacher, using multiple measures of An's oral and silent reading.

Dell is a ninth-grade student who benefited from collaboration among her content teachers, the reading specialist, and the speech-language pathologist. Dell seems to have major challenges with comprehension, as assessed via an informal reading inventory. The reading specialist examined the retellings on that assessment as well as summaries from Dell's English, science, and social studies textbooks and found that Dell tried to remember everything in a text. She did not focus on the most important or salient ideas and did not organize information in her mind.

In earlier grades, this approach likely worked quite well, but now that the volume of content material has increased, Dell needs a new way to keep up with all of the novel concepts, vocabulary, and key ideas. The reading specialist, in consultation with the speech-language pathologist, and all of Dell's content teachers, devised a plan of instruction. Each of them consistently highlighted the important points from a text or lecture using graphic organizers within their regular teaching. The reading specialist reinforced these visual representations of the content material in small-group or individual work sessions with Dell three times per week.

During these sessions, the reading specialist modeled the use of sticky notes to write only one summarizing sentence from each paragraph in the history textbook. Then, Dell practiced the same strategy using the science textbook under the direction of the reading specialist.

This collaborative support for Dell from all of her teachers and one specialist continued for many months. By the end of the ninth grade, Dell independently used all of the strategies for identifying and remembering important information.

with self-monitoring, identifying main ideas with self-monitoring, reciprocal teaching with other strategies, and collaborative strategic reading.

Similarly, Edmonds et al. (2009) identify strong support for explicit instruction in comprehension practices for students with reading difficulties and disabilities, including practices that engage students in thinking about text, learning from text, and discussing what they know. These findings support conclusions by Torgesen et al. (2007), Scammacca et al. (2007), and Kamil et al. (2008).

More comprehensive approaches to comprehension instruction have also been shown to be effective in improving reading comprehension (Liang & Dole, 2006). One well-known comprehension instructional framework—reciprocal teaching (Palincsar & Brown, 1984)—focuses on the importance of students becoming independent in their use of four key strategies: predicting, summarizing, questioning, and clarifying. Other intensive options include the reading and writing strategies developed by the University of Kansas Center for Research on Learning after more than 30 years of research with adolescents (Schumaker & Deshler, 1992; Schumaker et al., 2006).

Systemic Issues

In this section, we look at the opportunities for RTI to reinvigorate a school's climate and the practical constraints that all educators in secondary schools must address for RTI to succeed. RTI is focused on adolescents' learning, and although the credit-driven system in schools is a reality and a driving force in conceptualizing what curriculum is needed for graduation, student achievement must be the primary consideration for student outcomes. Stakeholders should not only take into consideration the focus on credit orientation but also use RTI as a way to spotlight the emerging competencies of adolescents in language, literacies, and content discipline knowledge.

Underlying Principles and Structures

There are some underlying principles and structures that pertain to all secondary schools in relation to an RTI framework. Previously, we discussed the need to have very strong core instruction that includes differentiation to meet students' needs, to provide supports at increasing levels of intensity for students with special needs, and to use assessments appropriately and productively.

Collaboration among all stakeholders is also a centerpiece of RTI. In order for all those involved in a school to grow an organic RTI model that fits their specific needs, educators must continually grow as professionals and as part of an educational community. Finally, to be successful, RTI also requires educational leadership that is effective in involving faculty in school transformation.

Collaboration. Genuine collaboration among all stakeholders, including teachers, specialists, administrators, students, and parents, is an important feature of RTI. All educators in a secondary school—along with the students and their parents—should articulate a shared vision and common goals for the adolescent students.

It is essential for educators to build into the school day adequate time for communication and coordinated planning. Because RTI is neither a general education initiative nor a special education initiative, but rather a total-school initiative that includes all teachers and specialists, there must be time and supports for getting these professionals to talk in the "same language" and jointly plan and teach. Without shared meaning, educators may not be able to engage successfully in problem solving and decision making. For more ideas about how to get teachers and other specialists out of their "silos" and better able to communicate with one another, see Ehren, Laster, and Watts-Taffe (2009).

With the goal of optimizing instruction for all students, including those who are struggling with language and literacy, general education teachers in an RTI framework cannot shift responsibility solely to special educators. Further, specialists (including special educators, reading specialists, speech-language pathologists, and school psychologists) must integrate their specialized knowledge of how to support atypical students into the content discipline classroom activities. As RTI is carried out within a context of true collaboration and shared expertise, it is a very different way of conceptualizing general and special education, the link between the two, and the roles of all of the educators in a building. RTI calls for deliberate, intentional, ongoing collaboration—a joining of forces, pooling of resources, and sharing of expertise—to meet shared goals for instruction and assessment.

Professional Development. A key element of RTI is professional development. At the secondary school level, teachers often come to teaching through a passion for a particular content discipline. Each teacher is typically an expert in content knowledge. They may, however, lack some knowledge and skill about teaching language and literacy. As described earlier in this chapter, adolescents need complex language and literacy skills to succeed in the 21st century; as a consequence, their teachers—whatever their content specialty—need pedagogical knowledge and skills to help young people develop in reading, writing, listening, and speaking. One of the tenets of RTI is to ensure that every student has a teacher who can assist with developing language and literacy skills. Thus, targeted professional development is essential for building capacity for teaching all students in all disciplines. According to Kamil (2003), many content area teachers believe they should be teaching their content, not literacy. Yet, in a school committed to assisting all of its students, teachers should think, What can I do to scaffold this student's learning? rather than, They should already have basic reading and writing skills.

We are not arguing that content teachers should teach basic reading and writing skills. However, the professionalism of secondary teachers includes knowledge of, among other topics, ways of appropriately matching students to texts and methods of scaffolding instruction for students who struggle with writing or comprehending. The goal is for teachers to be experts who engage students in their content and guide students who need to progress in reading, writing, listening, and conversing. This implies that ongoing professional development is crucial to support teachers as they assist low literate or aliterate (i.e., those who can read but choose not to read) students.

Professional development must be built into the structure of the school systemically and in a comprehensive way. One approach is for a school improvement team, faculty advisory committee, or forum of department chairs, along with the building administrators, to do a needs assessment regarding what faculty say they need to learn to serve all students in their building. Based on this needs assessment, the leadership team of administrators and faculty plans a series of readings, conversations, workshops, and feedback. This should be a multiyear process of planning and implementation. Professional development that is organic and school based, rather than imposed from outside the school, is most effective.

Teachers will need ongoing, ecologically based professional development (see Chapter 10). To implement an RTI framework, teachers may need to increase their comfort level of working with a variety of students and increase their own level of skills. They may invite specialists in their school or district to offer workshops on a variety of topics, such as vocabulary development, accommodating less-than-fluent readers, and how best to provide reading scaffolding.

They may also, with the assistance of a strong administrator, create professional learning communities in which they choose professional articles or books to read and discuss.

For the sake of the students, there needs to be a long-term commitment to teachers' growth. And, just as youthful students continually develop their literacy, teachers must continually learn new ways of teaching their students. Dozier (2006) states, "Continuous inquiry leads to substantive rather than superficial changes, but we need to remain mindful that change occurs at different times, in different ways for different people. Teachers, like students, move on different paths as learners" (p. 141).

Schoolwide and Comprehensive. We view RTI as a framework that is infused into all aspects of academic planning, instructional delivery, and evaluation. When a principal of one public high school in the mid-Atlantic region observes his teachers, he does not spend time scripting what the teacher says. Rather, he walks into a classroom and asks students, at random, "What are you doing? What are you learning?" If the students are not engaged in the learning process and not able to articulate what they are learning, then the principal wonders whether the teacher is doing his or her job. The premise of RTI is that all students should be engaged in the learning process in all of their classes.

Central to the success of RTI is that this focus on the holistic development of the adolescent is systemic and comprehensive in a secondary school. The whole adolescent—physical, social-emotional, curricular and cocurricular, and behavioral—must be addressed within a school structure that values the natural changes of adolescence. Systemic means that the entire school community—all faculty, administrators, staff, and parents—is focused on guiding youths to be active readers and writers, good listeners, and appropriate conversers. Rather than relying on informal conversations among teachers or occasional after-school tutoring sessions, having a systemic and comprehensive approach means that the focus is built into the school day in significant ways.

Systemic also refers to a way of collecting data about student progress that is consistent and regular. Student data, then, becomes the foundation for sound decision making about instruction. For example, if a student already receives special education services and has an Individualized Education Program (IEP), or if he or she is just struggling and does not have one), he or she, along with his or her parents or guardians and all of his or her teachers from all of the content disciplines, are involved in making plans—including differentiated instruction and the best evaluation of learning—for the development of the young person. In a school that uses RTI, the responsibility for this student is not transferred to the special education teacher; rather, all teachers and other staff take responsibility for collecting data, finding and trying out alternative instructional approaches, and regularly monitoring the student's progress.

To sustain a school focus on a holistic view of students, Irvin et al. (2009) spotlight the development of literacy leaders in a school and how teachers can mentor each other. Many secondary schools have formed professional learning communities to fill the need for ongoing, teacher-generated professional development (see Chapter 10). As Tharp and Gallimore (1988) emphasize, "The instructional conversation can only occur in a community of learners, and it is by means of that conversation that the community is created" (p. 34).

One illustration of an approach to a systemic and comprehensive RTI integration is the content literacy continuum (CLC) developed by the University of Kansas Center for Research in Learning (Lenz & Ehren, 1999; Lenz, Ehren, & Deshler, 2005). The CLC is a schoolwide literacy effort organized around five levels of instruction/intervention that increase in intensity to be responsive to diverse student needs. Both Level 1, Enhanced Content Instruction, and Level 2, Embedded Strategy Instruction, take place within the regular content classroom and focus on high-quality core instruction, integrating content mastery and literacy skills. Levels 3–5 provide more intensive options for students who need them, and they can occur within the regular classroom or other settings, such as after-school programs, before-school programs, summer programs, labs, or in specially designed courses. In Level 3, Intensive Strategy Instruction, specific learning strategies (Schumaker & Deshler, 2006) are taught within an explicit eight-stage instructional model (Ellis, Deshler, Lenz, Schumaker, & Clark, 1991) designed for and validated with struggling students. Someone other than a content teacher usually provides this intensive instruction. At Level 4, Intensive Basic Skill Instruction, specialists provide instruction that targets foundational language and literacy skills. In Level 5, Therapeutic Intervention, a speech-language pathologist works on language underpinnings for students with language impairments.

Middle Schools

The transition from elementary school to secondary school is often difficult, but it need not be if the focus is on the variable and developmental nature of learning for young adolescents. Tomlinson (2004) says,

Despite what we know about human variability in learning—particularly in adolescence (National Middle School Association, 1995)—we seem to pursue a path that suggests we jettison decades of accumulated knowledge about learner variance in favor of pedagogy that ignores rather than plans proactively for student differences. (p. 228)

Over the past 30 years, middle school educators made great strides in working in teams across disciplines (Flowers, Mertens, & Mulhall, 1999; Mertens & Flowers, 2004), integrating curriculum beyond the boundaries of content areas, and giving young adolescents choices and links to real-life experiences. RTI gives us the opportunity to extend student-centered approaches of the middle school movement.

The structure of many large middle schools revolves around grouping students into teams. Teachers on one team collaborate on assignments and procedures to help ensure student success. Interdisciplinary instruction, through which concepts taught in one discipline are applied in another, is stressed. In one illustrative school (Middle School A), there are five teams, each with approximately 120 students. The faculty for each team includes one teacher from each of the core disciplines of English, mathematics, social studies, and science, and those four teachers have conjoined planning time every day. The students participate in physical education and their chosen elective classes—music, theater, visual arts, foreign language, career explorations, and so forth—during the teachers' joint planning time. Elective teachers meet with the core teachers at least once per month, either before or after school. These academic-plus-elective meetings are focused on either the progress of specific students or on collaborative curriculum activities. Specialists, such as guidance counselors, reading specialists, speech-language pathologists, and special educators, meet with each team at least twice per month. Preferably there is a special educator and a reading specialist assigned to each team so that they meet daily with their colleagues.

RTI can be easily integrated into the structure of a team-based middle school. Addressing the needs of students who have a range of aptitudes is the goal of middle schools, and through RTI, there can be a positive frame around a variety of activities aimed at enhancing students' performance and developing academic, social, emotional, and physical competence. In fact, at Middle School B, there is a melding of intervention and enrichment planning and activities. These involve all stakeholders in focusing on the strengths and needs of students. Students may be gifted in one area, such as mathematics, but need support for advancing literacy. By using a comprehensive and systemic framework, this school aims for an optimal match of instruction/curriculum with the individual needs of each student. An inverted pyramid illustrates the intervention model, and a rectangle captures the enrichment scenarios at Middle School B (see Figure 8.2 and Figure 8.3).

At Middle School B, parent support for academic and extracurricular activities is central. This is indicated by the first box in the intervention pyramid "Classroom Interventions" and the "Administrative Level" in the enrichment rectangle. At this heterogeneous school, all stakeholders want to see the continuum of services offered to all students. The intervention pyramid complements the enrichment rectangle, and by linking the two, there is more acceptance of students' strengths and needs—and less stigma for students who need additional academic assistance.

At Middle School B, which focuses heavily on students with special needs, classroom and report card grades are used to indicate student progress, not just mastery of a content area. For students not functioning on grade level, for example, grading reflects not only content achievement but also progress toward personal academic goals or special education (i.e., IEP) objectives. If students have not successfully passed their benchmark tests, which are given after each unit at a minimum of once per month, they are required to attend a benchmark remediation class during one of their elective periods. As a result, intensive academic assistance is readily available all year long.

What is significant in Middle School B is the schoolwide systemic and comprehensive framework. This framework was not imposed by a school or district administrator. Like other RTI frameworks, this one was developed by the faculty community. The particular population of the school was the driving force for how and what would be included in the framework.

High Schools

Three elements of high schools are particularly challenging: (1) how the school day is organized in terms of time, (2) how struggling students are given space to advance, and (3) how consistent data management systems support decision making. High schools are often the focus of community traditions, with generations of parents who are alumni sending their children to the same high school that they attended. As a consequence, change is neither easy nor quick in high schools.

Figure 8.2. The Intervention Pyramid: Involving All Stakeholders

Classroom Interventions (teacher and specialists)

- Preferential seating
- Peer/partner tutoring
- Reteaching/reassessing
- Modified classwork/assignments
- Extended time
- Time to Soar assistance
- Immediate, detailed feedback
- Readability of text materials
- Agenda check for homework
- Modeled behavior and expectations
- Altered format
- E-mail/phone parent or guardian
- Preprinted/modified notes
- Student conference
- Contract for learning

Parent Involvement

- Parent-with-student conferences
- Agenda check for homework
- Team coffee
- Parent/team plan
- Chalkboard check (daily online communication)
- Miniconferences
- Progress report to parents by individual teachers/team

Team Interventions

- Team meeting discussions
- Time to Soar modifications
- Instruction/intervention provided by specialists (reading, SLP, ESOL)
- Student conference with team
- Counselor input
- Goal-setting conference

School Interventions

- Referral to "Soaring Eagles"
- Team for special assistance (Tier 3)
- Adult mentors
- Peer tutoring
- ESOL/LD assistance
- Placement in Power Literacy/Power Math (with SLP or reading specialist)

Administration Intervention

- Team referral to SST committee to review previous interventions and implement new interventions prior to local screening referral

Note. ESOL = English for Speakers of Other Languages; LD = learning disabilities; SLP = speech-language pathologist, SST = student study team.

Figure 8.3. The Enrichment Rectangle: Moving All Students Forward

Student Level

- Problem-based learning activities
- Choice of multiple genres for reading and writing
- Independent reading contracts

- Higher level thinking assessments and activities
- Interdisciplinary projects
- Choice of creative performances to express mastery of content

Teacher Level

- Alternative assignments
- Tiered/differentiated assignments

- Flexible grouping within the classroom
- Resident expert/peer tutor

Administrative Level

- Team meeting with counselor to discuss student assessment data
- Meeting of administrators and teachers with curriculum specialists

- to plan new approaches and instructional strategies
- Meeting with parents

School Level

- Moving student to higher level class

Reorganizing Time. Some students, parents, or teachers are heard to say, "We can't do any tutoring sessions after school because of sports," or "We can't do any tutoring sessions after school because there is no late bus transportation." Instead of adhering to the traditional structures when it comes to making significant student gains in language and literacy, there has to be a commitment by all of the stakeholders and a decision—often as part of the school improvement plan—that the status quo is untenable. The commitment to change the school day or change the venue and approach of instruction is monumental.

A major challenge is staff expectation that there is a set process for how to do RTI. With the help of skilled administrators, faculty members discover and accept that RTI is a collaborative process that must be developed as a professional learning community. There are no easy answers, and answers are unique to each school. For example, in a system using three tiers of instruction/ intervention, rules for moving across the tiers or how student monitoring is going to be achieved must be decided on by a whole faculty. In the process, the faculty comes to own the attitude that all teachers are responsible for all students.

It is difficult to teach in consistent, in-depth ways when the students are not in school, so many administrators have found creative new structures for keeping adolescents in school. For those students who are struggling academically, extra time in school is needed. Extending the hours of the school day can include integrating the arts into reading, writing, listening, and speaking. These cross-curricular endeavors are also avenues for improved self-esteem and career explorations. Possibilities include creating video documentaries, audiovisual displays on community issues, performance pieces that involve reading and writing on the content and skills of broadcasting, marketing, or public speaking. Furthermore, summer school can be proactive by preparing for the course work that will be addressed in the forthcoming school year.

In order for struggling readers to develop background knowledge and connections to the real world through books, adolescents need to be surrounded by high-quality texts and given ample time to read without the interference of test preparation and skill-and-drill approaches. School administrators must make provision for the fact that the amount of text read by a struggling adolescent reader needs to be far greater than the amount of text read by the average adolescent reader. Extra time for the acceleration of students who are academically behind their peers must be built into the school day, month, and year. For some students, extra time in school means extra years of schooling. Administrators and others (e.g., general educators, special educators, school psychologists, social workers, guidance counselors) need to map ways of destigmatizing the need for extra time to accomplish graduation.

Reorganizing Space. Homogeneous grouping for specific literacy instruction is sometimes needed for short periods of time. Instead of old-fashioned tracking, we can create a "school-within-a-school" or "academy." In this scenario, students spend a short time in this coaching setting and, when they are ready, move back to their regular classes. A corps of teachers or specialists—skilled in diagnostic assessment and excellent instruction of striving readers and writers—is the backbone. In some cases, this school-within-a-school is one wing or just one classroom in the school. The school-within-a-school functions year round; there may be a fairly large number of ninth graders, but as students gain the literacy skills they need, fewer and fewer older students need this offering. These students must stay integrated into the whole school for most curricular and extracurricular activities, such as sports, band, choral music, and theater. Most important is the watchful eyes of all educators that the socioemotional development of these teenagers is aligned with the general school population. For example, these students should be included in all extracurricular and social events.

Collaborative, Data-Based Decision Making. A strong instructional leader is essential to envisioning transformation in a school. Equally important for any significant change, including RTI, is the involvement of the entire faculty in all stages of the transformation. Together, the team—involving at least administrators and representative faculty, but may also include student representatives and parents—examines the aggregate data of student performance and pinpoints areas of focus (see Chapter 10). Then, the team helps create new structures for addressing students' needs, and finally they regularly evaluate the impact of the change.

At James Madison High School, school principal Mr. Merrell and his faculty realized that change would mean changing the entire school culture. They decided to take four minutes off of each class period to establish a daily 35-minute student assistance period (SAP). The SAP is a schoolwide initiative for students to pursue extra assistance or enrichment activities each day. For ninth graders, there are specific assigned mentors during the first grading period. After that, students take the initiative to seek out assistance from whichever teacher is best suited to help them. Merrell notes, "faculty, students, and parents were skeptical when we instituted the student assistance period. Now, they would all rebel if we tried to get rid of it" (personal communication, July 2009). After five years, the data show that all students are benefiting. The team has noted that the SAP has offered extra time for reteaching, alternative explanations, and more practice for students across the spectrum:

> We are raising the bar insofar as students who were getting B pluses are now getting As. But, more importantly, we are raising the floor. Keeping the faculty and the

curriculum basically constant, we had 53 students who failed one academic subject, whereas four years ago we had 73 students who failed one subject. It is really heartening to see the students who were too busy to stay afterschool really use SAP (the Student Assistance Period)—the middle ground students; they are the ones we can show used to have C plusses and now have Bs in their core academic subjects. (M. Merrell, personal communication, July 2009)

A focus on students rather than course content is a change of worldview for many high school teachers. Yet, once it is established within a school culture, it continues to affect the students who are most at risk for failure and leaving school. The use of student data for collaborative decision making becomes part of the school structure, and there is a climate of positive momentum rather than blame and negativity.

"At our school, a Latino male is five times more likely to fail than a white male student. These are the kids that we are focused on this next year!" remarked Mr. Merrell. He and his team have consequently designed a peer-mentoring program that pairs academically successful Latino male seniors with incoming ninth-grade Latino males. The supports for these mentoring teams are evolving but will likely include special meeting times for the mentor pairs, support from the guidance department, field trips to explore careers and colleges, and peer tutoring. The systemic focus is on all teachers collaborating to teach all students. That is the promise of RTI.

Concluding Thoughts

Theoretically and practically, becoming a literate adolescent is a complex process that occurs both within secondary schools and beyond. Young people define who they are and the ways they respond to texts, which includes digital media and discipline-specific literacy. Secondary schools can support all adolescents who are developing deeper understandings of multiple texts, and advancing facility to read, write, speak, and listen. When schools focus on RTI at the secondary level, they use an integrated focus of literacy across the curriculum with research-based literacy practices taught by all teachers and specialists. In this chapter, we described different kinds of assessment and instruction for three levels of service to students: core instruction with differentiation, collaborative instruction/intervention, and increasingly intensive interventions/instruction.

Any RTI framework is based on consistent and ongoing collaboration among educators. Globally, the RTI framework takes into account the teachers' perspective on their roles in content area instruction along with the specialists' perspective on their roles in working with students. Continuous professional development, which is ecological in nature, supports teachers in understanding language and literacy differences, differentiating instruction, and becoming more effective in teaching their content discipline to all students. For RTI to work, it needs to be conceptualized as a schoolwide approach to meeting the literacy needs of all students. The organizational structures (e.g., time, space) have to be viewed differently to create facilitative infrastructures. An essential element in creating a systemic and comprehensive approach to RTI at the school level is strong administrative leadership.

The point of view that secondary school is and has always been a credit-driven system is something that schools can wrestle with and even change with RTI structures. Rather than a credit-driven system, a learning-driven system such as RTI—in which students demonstrate their growth—may be more aligned with the goals of helping all adolescents acquire 21st-century literacy.

NOTE

All authors contributed equally to the writing of this chapter.

REFERENCES

Adler, C.R. (2004). Seven strategies to teach students text comprehension. Retrieved June 20, 2009, from www.readingrockets.org/article/3479

Alvermann, D.E. (Ed.). (2004). *New literacies and digital epistemologies: Vol. 7. Adolescents and literacies in a digital world.* New York: Peter Lang.

Anders, P., & Bos, C.S. (1986). Semantic features analysis: An interactive strategy for vocabulary development and text comprehension. *Journal of Reading, 29*, 610–616.

Atwell, N. (1998). *In the middle: New understandings about writing, reading, and learning* (2nd ed.). Portsmouth, NH: Boynton/Cook.

Beck, I.L., McKeown, M.G., & Kucan, L. (2002). *Bringing words to life: Robust vocabulary instruction.* New York: Guilford.

Biancarosa, G., & Snow, C.E. (2006). *Reading next: A vision for action and research in middle and high school literacy. A report to Carnegie Corporation of New York* (2nd ed.). Washington, DC: Alliance for Excellent Education.

Block, C.C., & Israel, S.E. (2004). The ABCs of performing highly effective think-alouds. *The Reading Teacher, 58*(2), 154–167. doi:10.1598/RT.58.2.4

Borkowski, J.G. (1992). Metacognitive theory: A framework for teaching literacy, writing, and math skills. *Journal of Learning Disabilities, 25*(4), 253–257. doi:10.1177/002221949202500406

Braunger, J., & Lewis, J.P. (2006). *Building a knowledge base in reading* (2nd ed.). Newark, DE: International Reading Association; Urbana, IL: National Council of Teachers of English.

Bulgren, J.A., Deshler, D.D., & Schumaker, J.B. (1993). *The concept mastery routine.* Lawrence, KS: Edge Enterprises.

Bulgren, J.A., Lenz, B.K., Deshler, D.D., & Schumaker, J.B. (2005). *The concept comparison routine*. Lawrence, KS: Edge Enterprises.

Dickson, S.V., Simmons, D.C., & Kame'enui, E. J. (1998). Text organization: Instructional and curricular basics and implications. In D.C. Simmons & E.J. Kame'enui (Eds.), *What reading research tells us about children with diverse learning needs* (pp. 279–294). Mahwah, NJ: Erlbaum.

Dozier, C. (2006). *Responsive literacy coaching: Tools for creating and sustaining purposeful change*. Portland, ME: Stenhouse.

Duke, N.K., & Pearson, P.D. (2002). Effective practices for developing reading comprehension. In A.E. Farstrup & S.J. Samuels (Eds.), *What research has to say about reading instruction* (3rd ed., pp. 205–242). Newark, DE: International Reading Association.

Edmonds, M.S., Vaughn, S., Wexler, J., Reutebuch, C., Cable, A., Tackett, K.K., et al. (2009). A synthesis of reading interventions and effects on reading comprehension outcomes for older struggling readers. *Review of Educational Research, 79*(1), 262–300. doi:10.3102/0034654308325998

Ehren, B.J., & Deshler, D.D. (2009). *Using the Content Literacy Continuum as a framework for implementing RTI in secondary schools*. Lawrence: University of Kansas Center for Research on Learning.

Ehren, B.J., Laster, B., & Watts-Taffe, S. (2009). *Creating shared language for collaboration in RTI*. Retrieved July 21, 2009, from www.rtinetwork.org/GetStarted/BuildSupport/ar/Creating-Shared-Language-for-Collaboration-in-RTI

Ehren, B.J., Lenz, B.K., & Deshler, D.D. (2004). Enhancing literacy proficiency with adolescents and young adults. In C.A. Stone, E.R. Silliman, B.J. Ehren, & K. Apel (Eds.), *Handbook of language and literacy: Development and disorders* (pp. 681–701). New York: Guilford.

Ehren, B.J., & Whitmire, K. (2009). Speech-language pathologists as primary contributors to Response to Intervention at the secondary level. *Seminars in Speech and Language, 30*(2), 90–104. doi:10.1055/s-0029-1215717

Ellis, E.S. (1997). *The clarifying routine*. Lawrence, KS: Edge Enterprises.

Ellis, E.S., Deshler, D.D., Lenz, B.K., Schumaker, J.B., & Clark, F.L. (1991). An instructional model for teaching learning strategies. *Focus on Exceptional Children, 23*(6), 1–24.

Farstrup, A.E., & Samuels, S.J. (Eds.). (2008). *What research has to say about vocabulary instruction*. Newark, DE: International Reading Association.

Finesilver, M. (1994). *An investigation of three methods to improve vocabulary learning at the middle school level*. Unpublished doctoral dissertation, National-Louis University, Evanston, IL.

Fisher, D., Frey, N., & Rothenberg, C. (2008). *Content-area conversations: How to plan discussion-based lessons for diverse language learners*. Alexandria, VA: Association for Supervision and Curriculum Development.

Fisher, D., & Ivey, G. (2006). Evaluating the interventions for struggling adolescent readers. *Journal of Adolescent & Adult Literacy, 50*(3), 180–189. doi:10.1598/JAAL.50.3.2

Flood, J., & Lapp, D. (1995). Broadening the lens: Toward an expanded conceptualization of literacy. In K.A. Hinchman, D.J. Leu, Jr., & C.K. Kinzer (Eds.), *Perspectives on literacy research and practice: The 44th yearbook of the National Reading Conference* (pp. 1–16). Chicago: National Reading Conference.

Flowers, N., Mertens, S.B., & Mulhall, P.F. (1999). The impact of teaming: Five research-based outcomes. *Middle School Journal, 31*(2), 57–60.

Gajria, M., Jitendra, A.K., Sood, S., & Sacks, G. (2007). Improving comprehension of expository text in students with LD: A research synthesis. *Journal of Learning Disabilities, 40*(3), 210–225. doi:10.1177/00222194070400030301

Genesee, F., Lindholm-Leary, K., Saunders, W.M., & Christian, D. (Eds). (2006). *Educating English language learners: A synthesis of research evidence.* New York: Cambridge University Press.

Goodman, Y.M., & Marek, A.M. (1996). *Retrospective miscue analysis: Revaluing readers and reading.* Katonah, NY: Richard C. Owen.

Goodman, Y.M., Watson, D.J., & Burke, C.L. (2005). *Reading miscue inventory: From evaluation to instruction* (2nd ed.). Katonah, NY: Richard C. Owen.

Greenleaf, C.L., & Hinchman, K. (2009). Reimagining our inexperienced adolescent readers: From struggling, striving, marginalized, and reluctant to thriving. *Journal of Adolescent & Adult Literacy, 53*(1), 4–13. doi:10.1598/JAAL.53.1.1

Guthrie, J.T., Anderson, E., Alao, S., & Rinehart, J. (1999). Influences of concept-oriented reading instruction on strategy use and conceptual learning from text. *The Elementary School Journal, 99*(4), 343–366. doi:10.1086/461929

Heller, R., & Greenleaf, C.L. (2007). *Literacy instruction in the content areas: Getting to the core of middle and high school improvement.* Washington, DC: Alliance for Excellent Education.

Hock, M.F., Brasseur, I.F., Deshler, D.D., Catts, H.W., Marquis, J.G., Mark, C.A., et al. (2009). What is the reading component skill profile of adolescent struggling readers in urban schools? *Learning Disability Quarterly, 32*(1), 21–38.

Houge, T.T., & Geier, C. (2009). Delivering one-to-one tutoring in literacy via videoconferencing. *Journal of Adolescent & Adult Literacy, 53*(2), 154–163. doi:10.1598/JAAL.53.2.6

IRA Commission on RTI: Working draft of guiding principles. (2009). *Reading Today, 26*(4), 1, 4–6.

Irvin, J.L., Meltzer, J., Mickler, M.J., Phillips, M., & Dean, N. (2009). *Meeting the challenge of adolescent literacy: Practical ideas for literacy leaders.* Newark, DE: International Reading Association.

Johannessen, L.R., & McCann, T.M. (2009). Adolescents who struggle with literacy. In L. Christenbury, R. Bomer, & P. Smagorinsky (Eds.), *Handbook of adolescent literacy research* (pp. 65–79). New York: Guilford.

Johnston, P.H., & Winograd, P.N. (1985). Passive failure in reading. *Journal of Reading Behavior, 17*(4), 279–301.

Kamil, M.L. (2003). *Adolescents and literacy: Reading for the 21st century.* Washington, DC: Alliance for Excellent Education.

Kamil, M.L., Borman, G.D., Dole, J., Kral, C.C., Salinger, T., & Torgesen, J. (2008). *Improving adolescent literacy: Effective classroom and intervention practices: A practice guide* (NCEE No. 2008-4027). Washington, DC: National Center for Education Evaluation and Regional Assistance, Institute of Education Sciences, U.S. Department of Education. Retrieved July 15, 2009, from ies.ed.gov/ncee/wwc/pdf/practiceguides/adlit_pg_082608.pdf

Langer, J.A. (2001). Beating the odds: Teaching middle and high school students to read and write well. *American Educational Research Journal, 38*(4), 837–880. doi:10.3102/00028312038004837

Leach, J.M., Scarborough, H.S., & Rescorla, L. (2003). Late-emerging reading disabilities. *Journal of Educational Psychology, 95*(2), 211–224. doi:10.1037/0022-0663.95.2.211

Lee, J., Grigg, W., & Donahue, P. (2007). *The nation's report card: Reading 2007* (NCES No. 2007-496). Washington, DC: National Center for Education Statistics, Institute of Education Sciences, U.S. Department of Education.

Lennon, C., & Burdick, H. (2004). *The Lexile Framework as an approach for reading measurement and success.* Retrieved January 11, 2010, from www.ade.state.az.us/azreads/Lexile/FrameworkOverview/Lexile-Reading-Measurement-and-Success-0504.pdf

Lenz, B.K., & Ehren, B.J. (1999). Strategic content literacy initiative: Focusing on reading in secondary schools. *Stratenotes, 8*(1), 1–6.

Lenz, B.K., Ehren, B.J., & Deshler, D.D. (2005). The content literacy continuum: A school reform framework for improving adolescent literacy for all students. *Teaching Exceptional Children, 37*(6), 60–63.

Liang, L.A., & Dole, J.A. (2006). Help with teaching reading comprehension: Comprehension instructional frameworks. *The Reading Teacher, 59*(8), 742–753. doi:10.1598/RT.59.8.2

Lipson, M.Y., & Wixson, K.K. (2009). *Assessment and instruction of reading and writing difficulties: An interactive approach* (4th ed.). Boston: Allyn & Bacon.

MacKinnon, J. (1993). *A comparison of three schema-based methods of vocabulary instruction.* Unpublished doctoral dissertation, Florida State University, Tallahassee.

McNamara, D.S., Kintsch, E., Songer, N.B., & Kintsch, W. (1996). Are good texts always better? Interactions of text coherence, background knowledge, and levels of understanding in learning from text. *Cognition and Instruction, 14*(1), 1–43. doi:10.1207/s1532690xci1401_1

McNamara, D.S., & Kintsch, W. (1996). Learning from texts: Effects of prior knowledge and text coherence. *Discourse Processes, 22*(3), 247–288. doi:10.1080/01638539609544975

Mertens, S.B., & Flowers, N. (2004). *NMSA research summary #21: Interdisciplinary teaming.* Retrieved July 12, 2009, from www.nmsa.org/portals/0/pdf/publications/On_Target/teaming/teaming_6_research21.pdf

Otero, J., León, J.A., & Graesser A.C. (Eds.). (2002). *The psychology of science text comprehension.* Mahwah, NJ: Erlbaum.

Palincsar, A.S., & Brown, A.L. (1984). Reciprocal teaching of comprehension-fostering and comprehension-monitoring activities. *Cognition and Instruction, 1*(2), 117–175. doi:10.1207/s1532690xci0102_1

Paris, S.G., Cross, D.R., & Lipson, M.Y. (1984). Informed strategies for learning: A program to improve children's reading awareness and comprehension. *Journal of Educational Psychology, 76*(6), 1239–1252. doi:10.1037/0022-0663.76.6.1239

Pearson, P.D., & Camperell, K. (1994). Comprehension of text structures. In R.B. Ruddell, M.R. Ruddell, & H. Singer (Eds.), *Theoretical models and processes of reading* (4th ed., pp. 448–468). Newark, DE: International Reading Association.

Penno, J.F., Wilkinson, I.A.G., & Moore, D.W. (2002). Vocabulary acquisition from teacher explanation and repeated listening to stories: Do they overcome the Matthew effect? *Journal of Educational Psychology, 94*(1), 23–33.

Peterson, C.L., Caverly, D.C., Nicholson, S.A., O'Neal, S., & Cusenbary, S. (2000). *Building reading proficiency at the secondary level: A guide to resources.* Austin, TX: Southwest Educational Development Laboratory.

Pittelman, S.D., Levin, K.M., & Johnson, D.D. (1985). *An investigation of two instructional settings in the use of semantic mapping with poor readers* (Program Report No. 85-4). Madison: Wisconsin Center for Education Research, University of Wisconsin.

Raphael, T.E., & Au, K.H. (2005). QAR: Enhancing comprehension and test taking across grades and content areas. *The Reading Teacher, 59*(3), 206–221. doi:10.1598/RT.59.3.1

Roller, C.M. (1996). *Variability not disability: Struggling readers in a workshop classroom.* Newark, DE: International Reading Association.

Scammacca, N., Roberts, G., Vaughn, S., Edmonds, M., Wexler, J., Reutebuch, C.K., et al. (2007). *Interventions for adolescent struggling readers: A meta-analysis with implications for practice.* Portsmouth, NH: RMC Research Corporation, Center on Instruction.

Schleppegrell, M.J., Achugar, M., & Oteiza, T. (2004). The grammar of history: Enhancing content-based instruction through a functional focus on language. *TESOL Quarterly, 38*(1), 67–93.

Schoenbach, R., Greenleaf, C., Cziko, C., & Hurwitz, L. (1999). *Reading for understanding: A guide to improving reading in middle and high school classrooms*. San Francisco: Jossey-Bass.

Schumaker, J.B., & Deshler, D.D. (1992). Validation of learning strategy interventions for students with learning disabilities: Results of a programmatic research effort. In B.Y.L. Wong (Ed.), *Contemporary intervention research in learning disabilities: An international perspective* (pp. 22–46). New York: Springer-Verlag.

Schumaker, J.B., & Deshler, D.D. (2006). Teaching adolescents to be strategic learners. In D.D. Deshler & J.B. Schumaker (Eds.), *Teaching adolescents with disabilities: Accessing the general education curriculum* (pp. 121–156). Thousand Oaks, CA: Corwin.

Schumaker, J.B., Deshler, D.D., Woodruff, S.K., Hock, M.F., Bulgren, J.A., & Lenz, B.K. (2006). Reading strategy interventions: Can literacy outcomes be enhanced for at-risk adolescents? *Teaching Exceptional Children, 38*(3), 64–68.

Schwartz, R.M., & Raphael, T.E. (1985). Concept of definition: A key to improving students' vocabulary. *The Reading Teacher, 39*(2), 198–205.

Seidenberg, P.L. (1989). Relating text-processing research to reading and writing instruction for learning disabled students. *Learning Disabilities Focus, 5*(1), 4–12.

Shanahan, C. (2004). Teaching science through literacy. In T.L. Jetton & J.A. Dole (Eds.), *Adolescent literacy research and practice* (pp. 75–93). New York: Guilford.

Shanahan, T., & Shanahan, C. (2008). Teaching disciplinary literacy to adolescents: Rethinking content-area literacy. *Harvard Educational Review, 78*(1), 40–59.

Short, D., & Fitzsimmons, S. (2007). *Double the work: Challenges and solutions to acquiring language and academic literacy for adolescent English language learners: A report to Carnegie Corporation of New York*. Washington, DC: Alliance for Excellent Education.

Stahl, S.A., & Shanahan, C. (2004). Learning to think like a historian: Disciplinary knowledge through critical analysis of multiple documents. In T.L. Jetton & J.A. Dole (Eds.), *Adolescent literacy research and practice* (pp. 94–115). New York: Guilford.

Swan, E.A. (2003). *Concept-oriented reading instruction: Engaging classrooms, lifelong learners*. New York: Guilford.

Swan, E.A. (2004). Motivating adolescent readers through concept-oriented reading instruction. In T.L. Jetton & J.A. Dole (Eds.), *Adolescent literacy research and practice* (pp. 283–303). New York: Guilford.

Taylor, B.M., & Beach, R.W. (1984). The effects of text structure instruction on middle-grade students' comprehension and production of expository text. *Reading Research Quarterly, 19*(2), 134–146. doi:10.2307/747358

Tharp, R.G., & Gallimore, R. (1988). *Rousing minds to life: Teaching, learning, and schooling in social context*. New York: Cambridge University Press.

Tomlinson, C.A. (2004). Differentiating instruction: A synthesis of key research and guidelines. In T.L. Jetton & J.A. Dole (Eds.), *Adolescent literacy research and practice* (pp. 228–248). New York: Guilford.

Torgesen, J.K., Houston, D.D., Rissman, L.M., Decker, S.M., Roberts, G., Vaughn, S., et al. (2007). *Academic literacy instruction for adolescents: A guidance document from the Center on Instruction*. Portsmouth, NH: RMC Research Corporation, Center on Instruction.

Vacca, R.T., & Vacca, J.A.L. (2005). *Content area reading: Literacy and learning across the curriculum* (8th ed.). Boston: Allyn & Bacon.

Valencia, S.W., & Buly, M.R. (2004). Behind test scores: What struggling readers *really* need. *The Reading Teacher, 57*(6), 520–531.

Vaughn, S., Fletcher, J.M., Francis, D.J., Denton, C.A., Wanzek, J., Wexler, J., et al. (2008). Response to Intervention with older students with reading difficulties. *Learning and Individual Differences, 18*(3), 338–345. doi:10.1016/j.lindif.2008.05.001

Wilfong, L.G. (2009). Textmasters: Bringing literature circles to textbook reading across the curriculum. *Journal of Adolescent & Adult Literacy, 53*(2), 164–171. doi:10.1598/JAAL.53.2.7

Williams, J.P., Brown, L.G., Silverstein, A.K., & deCani, J.S. (1994). An instructional program in comprehension of narrative themes for adolescents with learning disabilities. *Learning Disability Quarterly, 17*(3), 205–221.

CHAPTER 9

Spotlight on RTI for Adolescents: An Example of Intensive Middle School Intervention Using the Interactive Strategies Approach-Extended

Lynn M. Gelzheiser

University at Albany, State University of New York

Donna M. Scanlon

Michigan State University

Laura Hallgren-Flynn

University at Albany, State University of New York

The previous chapter (Chapter 8, "RTI for Secondary School Literacy") emphasizes the importance of adopting a systemic approach to RTI at the secondary level. This spotlight chapter, however, provides an example of an intensive intervention, which many approaches to RTI would consider appropriate for Tier 3. We chose to highlight this intervention because a comprehensive approach to RTI at the secondary level needs to include such interventions, and there are very few interventions available of this type that are developmentally appropriate for older students. Although this intervention has its origins in an approach for elementary students, it has been adapted in ways that make it entirely appropriate for students at the middle and high school levels who need assistance beyond differentiated content area instruction.

Context

Efforts to improve literacy for middle and high school students are critically important (see Chapter 8). Even with a strong focus on excellent content teaching and a systemic approach to RTI in middle and high schools, there are many students who require additional support and intervention. Although there is a good deal of research on reading interventions for young children who struggle with literacy learning, there is remarkably little research on interventions for older struggling readers. Most of the research on these readers has shown that teachers have little influence on students' reading comprehension (Scammacca et al., 2007). We report on a promising intervention for middle school struggling readers, the Interactive Strategies Approach-Extended (ISA-X), which we are in the process of evaluating. The ISA-X evolved from the Interactive Strategies Approach (ISA; described in Chapter 2), which has been found to be effective in accelerating the progress of struggling learners in kindergarten and first grade (Scanlon, Gelzheiser, Vellutino, Schatschneider, & Sweeney, 2008; Scanlon, Vellutino, Small, Fanuele, & Sweeney, 2005; Vellutino et al., 1996) and in a volunteer tutoring program for fourth-grade struggling readers (Gelzheiser, Scanlon, & D'Angelo, 2001). The two approaches were initially integrated and used to successfully accelerate the reading development of many of the struggling fourth-grade readers who participated in a study evaluating the intervention's effectiveness (Gelzheiser, Scanlon, Hallgren-Flynn, & Vellutino, 2008).

We are currently evaluating the effectiveness of the ISA-X in accelerating the reading progress of seventh-grade struggling readers who receive special education services. Because early results for the ISA-X are promising, it is presented in this chapter as an example of intensive services for middle-grade students. We begin with a brief description of the research that is currently underway. The primary focus of this chapter is a description of the intervention' content and the professional development conducted with the reading and special education teachers who provided the intervention. We conclude by discussing some of the implications of this work for middle schools implementing RTI.

This research on ISA-X was conducted in two relatively small middle schools (500–600 students) in which the average class size for English language arts (ELA) was roughly 18 students, with few students (1%) identified as English-language learners. One school was urban, serving a student body that was 51% white and in which 60% of students were eligible for free or reduced-cost lunch. The other was rural, serving a population that was predominantly white (91%) and in which 25% of students were eligible for free or reduced-cost lunch. While the rural school was successful in meeting adequate yearly progress goals in ELA, the urban school was undergoing restructuring for failing to meet adequate yearly progress goals in ELA for students identified as minority, disadvantaged, or disabled.

At these schools, one special education teacher and one reading teacher were released from their traditional teaching assignments to provide the ISA-X intervention. Teachers worked with five students each semester, providing daily 40-minute sessions (roughly 60 in all). Eight to 10 additional sessions were used for students' pre- and postassessment. All of these intervention sessions were one to one.

Intervention was treated as a "class" and built into students' schedules. All sessions were planned and individualized. Sessions followed a routine of a five-to seven-minute minilesson, 25–30 minutes of reading and discussion, and five minutes of writing or reflection. In the first 20–30 sessions, all reading was done orally. In later sessions, teachers also included silent reading. Explicit connections to the general education curriculum were built into the intervention, using texts that aligned with students' classroom social studies instruction. Intervention teachers were also encouraged to share with the students' ELA instructors the reading strategies being used during intervention so that these could be reinforced in the general education setting.

The students who participated in the intervention were receiving special education services and had reading goals on their Individualized Education Programs (IEPs). In a situation characteristic of struggling readers in the middle grades, there were widely varying student profiles. Some students had comprehension that was limited primarily by their very narrow decoding skills and could be described as having a word-learning emphasis reader profile. Other students could accurately identify words but had quite limited comprehension, so they were described as having a meaning-emphasis reader profile. The majority of the students had both word and comprehension instructional goals and could be described as having a dual-emphasis reader profile.

At the start of the school year, teachers participated in four days of professional development in a workshop format. Discussions were guided by PowerPoint slideshows and augmented with video examples of ISA-X instruction to illustrate the major instructional activities and approaches. Teachers were provided with a teacher handbook that elaborated on the approaches introduced in the ISA-X professional development as well as a curriculum guide that provided suggestions regarding the student texts. Ongoing support was provided through group meetings held once every two weeks and individual coaching sessions that focused primarily on modeling and instructional planning for individual students.

Over the course of the intervention, students gained an average of three guided reading levels for both accuracy and comprehension on the Fountas and Pinnell (2007) Benchmark Assessment System. Moderate effects were also observed on measures of reading fluency, social studies knowledge, and strategy knowledge.

Rationale and Key Components of the ISA-X

The ISA-X intervention reflects six premises about reading intervention for older struggling readers (see Chapter 8). In the sections that follow, we detail each premise and how it was enacted in the ISA-X intervention.

Premise 1: Responsive Instruction Is Critical for Students With Disabilities

Although some interpretations of RTI suggest that packaged interventions should be delivered with integrity, it is hard to imagine one intervention that would have worked with all of the middle school students in our project. As described earlier, some students had severe word-learning needs, while the majority had needs in both comprehension and word learning.

A responsive approach to intervention requires that teachers have access to high-quality assessment information. The students with IEPs had already passed through several levels of screening and progress monitoring. Thus, we began intervention for such heterogeneous students with formal and informal assessments focused on providing useful diagnostic and instructional information. The nonfiction passages from the Fountas and Pinnell (2007) Benchmark Assessment System allowed us to compare students' word-reading and comprehension levels and estimate texts that would be at a student's instructional level. For students with word-learning needs, more detailed information about their phonics knowledge was gathered.

For each student, teachers identified and prioritized goals and then planned a program of instruction. For a typical student with a word-learning emphasis profile, the primary goal was to increase sight vocabulary through the development of alphabetic knowledge and use of word-identification strategies. Another goal was to foster motivation for reading; comprehension was focused on the major ideas in a text. For a student with a dual-emphasis profile, instruction typically addressed some word-level goals as well as literal, inferential, and critical comprehension. Student goals such as the ones in the following list were regularly reviewed and updated.

- *Motivation*—The student will develop the belief that reading is an enjoyable and informative activity that is not beyond his or her capability.

- *Comprehension*—The student will use information and ideas in the text and background knowledge to actively construct an understanding of the text and independently solve comprehension problems.

- *Alphabetics*—The student will effectively use alphabetic information in word solving.

- *Word learning*—The student will build his or her sight vocabulary using word-identification strategies to puzzle through unfamiliar words encountered while reading.

- *High-frequency words*—The student will effortlessly read high-frequency words in all contexts.

- *Vocabulary and language*—The student will learn the meanings of new words encountered in instructional interactions and be able to use the words both in conversation and in reading and comprehending social studies content. The student will become more proficient at understanding the syntax of literary English.

The approach to progress monitoring used in the ISA-X was structured teacher observation, which helped support instructional planning. Teacher observation of students was guided by a checklist (see Figure 9.1) that provided more detailed information about the instructional goals. Based on what they observed during oral reading and in discussion, teachers completed the checklist roughly once every 12 sessions.

Premise 2: Independence Is Critical for Students With Disabilities

Teaching for independence was a novel practice for the teachers with whom we worked. Like many teachers who work with struggling readers, they had developed the habit of providing word-specific prompts when students struggled to identify a word and providing feedback that confirmed that the student had

Figure 9.1. Teacher Observation Checklist for Use With the ISA-X

Student: _____ Teacher: _____

Motivation to Read and Write			
	Rarely	Sometimes	Regularly
Demonstrates motivation to read			
• Is eager to begin reading			
• Remains engaged while reading			
Demonstrates stamina for reading; able to read for long periods without needing a break			
Demonstrates interest in the content			
• Initiates conversations about content			
• Indicates that he or she thinks about the texts beyond the context of the lesson			
• Expresses interest in reading beyond the context of the lesson; asks to read the book at home			
Expresses book preferences (e.g., author, genre)			
Demonstrates interest in learning new words			

Strategic Word Identification			
	Support/Prompting Needed		
	Specific	Open-ended	Without
Uses code-based strategies to identify unfamiliar words			
• Thinks about the sounds in the word			
• Looks for parts he or she knows			
• Tries different pronunciations			
• Breaks the word into smaller parts			
Uses meaning-based strategies to identify unfamiliar words			
• Checks the pictures			
• Thinks of words that might make sense			
• Reads past the puzzling word			
• Goes back to the beginning and starts again			
Demonstrates appropriate use of 1- or 2-syllable words			
Demonstrates appropriate use of 3–5-syllable words			
Integrates sources of information to cross-check identification of unfamiliar words			

(continued)

Figure 9.1. Teacher Observation Checklist for Use With the ISA-X (*continued*)

Fluency			
	Rarely	Sometimes	Regularly
Reads text with fluency			
• Accuracy			
• Appropriate phrasing			
• Appropriate speed			
• Appropriate expression			
Active Comprehension			
Within the Text			
	Support/Prompting Needed		
	Specific	Open-ended	Without
Notices, comments, and reacts to text			
• Details			
• Critical events, major ideas			
Monitors that what was read makes sense			
• Sentence level			
• Paragraph/page level			
• Chapter/text level			
Applies fix-up strategies			
• Rereads for accuracy, and information			
• Checks the illustrations			
• Checks the punctuation			
• Reads ahead for more information			
• Asks for assistance			
• Asks specific clarifying questions			
Uses story structure to support comprehension			
• Looks for character and setting at beginning			
• Attends to character motive and development over time			
• Attends to the problem and its resolution			
• Attends to point of view			
Uses text features to support comprehension			
• Illustrations			
• Headings			
• Captions and text inserts			

(continued)

Figure 9.1. Teacher Observation Checklist for Use With the ISA-X (*continued*)

• Charts and maps			
• Timelines			
Beyond the Text			
Uses knowledge to support comprehension			
Sets purposes; asks questions for reading			
Seeks text information that addresses purposes and questions			
Makes personal connections with text			
Integrates text clues to make appropriate inferences			
Uses information in the text as the basis for predictions about what will happen next			
Attends to and reads with comprehension highly descriptive or inferential language			
Synthesizes information and attends to the big ideas and messages in the text			

About the Text			
	Support/Prompting Needed		
	Specific	Open-ended	Without
Reads strategically, using the major features of genre to support comprehension			
• Informational text			
• Folk tale			
• Historical fiction			
• Biography			
• Realistic fiction			
Considers the author's purpose and decision making while reading			

Vocabulary			
	Rarely	Sometimes	Regularly
Monitors whether he or she knows a word's meaning			
Uses resources to help determine meaning of unknown words			
• Context			
• Glossary			
• Teacher assistance			

(continued)

Figure 9.1. Teacher Observation Checklist for Use With the ISA-X (*continued*)

Alphabetics			
	Knows Few	Knows Some	Knows All
Consonants			
• Consonant digraphs			
• Consonants that require flexibility			
Vowels			
• Long vowels			
• Short vowels			
• Combinations that make unique sounds			
• R-controlled vowels			
Common prefixes and suffixes			
	Rarely	Sometimes	Regularly
Applies knowledge when decoding			
• 1- or 2-syllable words			
• 3–5-syllable words			

Note. Knows Few = most exemplars are not automatic; Knows Some = some exemplars are automatic; Knows All = consistent and automatic with all exemplars.

Successful Approaches to RTI: Collaborative Practices for Improving K–12 Literacy edited by Marjorie Y. Lipson and Karen K. Wixson. Copyright 2010 International Reading Association. May be copied for classroom use.

identified the word correctly. In addition, teachers had been in the habit of telling students when they misread a word, rather than expecting students to monitor whether what they had read made sense.

The limitation of this teacher-controlled style of interaction is that it encouraged students to see themselves as dependent on teacher expertise, rather than as competent individuals who could independently puzzle through words. Thus, the ISA-X emphasized teaching for independence in several different ways. Three approaches to teaching for independence were (1) teaching word-identification strategies, (2) teaching students to use those strategies interactively to independently confirm the words they were identifying, and (3) encouraging students to reflect on how strategies enabled them to identify unfamiliar words.

The ISA-X intervention taught students to use strategies for word identification, as summarized in Chapter 2 (see Figure 2.3). As described more fully in

Chapter 2, the purpose of strategy instruction was to increase sight vocabulary by encouraging students to develop a "self-teaching mechanism" (Share, 1995, p. 151). Share posits that if students learn to puzzle through unfamiliar words and then encounter those words again in subsequent reading, they will learn to recognize the words on sight.

In the studies using ISA and the ISA-X, readers were taught to use both meaning-based and code-based strategies for identifying unfamiliar words in text (Vellutino & Scanlon, 2002). Meaning-based strategies (e.g., look at the pictures, think about what makes sense, reread, read ahead to find more information) were taught because they actively engaged the reader with the meaning of the text and allowed students to identify irregularly spelled and multisyllable words. If students relied exclusively on code-based strategies, they would encounter words that they could not identify. Code-based strategies (e.g., think about the sounds of the letters, break the word into parts, look for parts you know, and try a different sound for the letters) were taught because they encouraged students to fully analyze the orthographic and phonological features of printed words and thereby increased the likelihood that students would recognize those words on future encounters.

During professional development, teachers were encouraged to begin intervention by observing students to determine which of the code-based and meaning-based strategies the students were already using. Thereafter, teachers used explicit instruction to introduce students to the remaining strategies and the idea of interactive strategy use. At first, teachers prompted students to use specific strategies, then students were encouraged to select strategies from the word-identification strategy list. Teachers learned to wait and listen during students' productive "word solving" with an eye toward building independence in word learning. Initially, teachers provided feedback about strategy use (not word-identification accuracy), naming the strategies that the student had used to identify and confirm the word. As the students began to demonstrate competence, they were prompted to reflect on the strategies they had used and how these promoted productive word identification. The purpose of this reflection was to increase students' sense that they were effective problem solvers—that is, increase students' sense of self-efficacy.

One particularly powerful strategy for middle school readers was to be flexible with letter sounds or try different pronunciations for some of the letters (Scanlon, Anderson, & Sweeney, 2010). Rather than learning rules that will be helpful only some of the time (Clymer, 1963), students were encouraged to systematically try the long and short sounds for the vowels and, for vowel combinations, try both sounds for each of the vowels until their efforts resulted in a word that fit the context of the sentence they were reading. This approach allowed students to independently identify words such as *great* and *field*, which would otherwise be taught as irregular words. As students developed more knowledge of the sounds that letters make, this strategy was also used with letter groups (e.g., "oo") and silent letters. Students were encouraged to use the strategies interactively, that is, to use multiple strategies to both hypothesize and confirm a word's identity. For example, a student might break a word into parts to identify a word and confirm that the word made sense.

Independence was also in the forefront of the ISA-X approach to fostering comprehension. In the past, the intervention teachers had learned to employ an approach to discussion in which the teacher controlled the topics and opportunities for discussion by asking questions to which students responded. Often these were questions with a single correct answer. Teachers then provided feedback and elaboration. This pattern of interaction is one that teachers might have used in helping students understand the information contained in texts that were required by their content area courses but were too challenging for students to read. Unfortunately, this pattern of interaction does little to provide students with tools they can use to construct meaning from text (Almasi & Garas-York, 2009). Further, questions with one correct answer and the possibility of being incorrect may alienate some students.

The ISA-X professional development detailed a view of comprehension in which the reader constructs an understanding of the text by integrating the author's words with the reader's knowledge (Perfetti, Landi, & Oakhill, 2005). In this view, because of their knowledge differences, two readers may differ in their interpretation of a text. Of course, not all interpretations are equally logical and acceptable, as the meaning constructed must rely on the author's words. The ISA-X professional development was designed to help teachers understand that different interpretations are to be expected. It was stressed that the goal of instruction was not understanding of "this text" but the ability to construct meaning from texts.

In the ISA-X, teachers were encouraged to adopt a different pattern of interaction—a more responsive approach to discussion—with the goal of fostering comprehension. Professional development guided teachers to structure discussion with students by commenting on the text and asking questions that are open ended and do not have "correct" answers. Examples include comments and questions such as "I bet Hannah is upset about her father and brother arguing," "I wonder what Hannah is feeling right now," and "How might Hannah's brother and father work out their differences?"

Another tactic teachers used was to establish routines in which the student was expected to initiate the topics for discussion. For example, students were taught that after they read a portion of the text silently, they should comment on what they had read. Also, in a manner similar to reciprocal teaching, teachers might engage students in asking questions about the text (Palincsar & Brown, 1986). Both of these approaches allow students to lead the discussion and provide teachers with insight as to what students found interesting or important in the text.

When a student's comments suggested confusion, teachers were encouraged to ask the student to share the information, both in the text and from their knowledge, that the student was relying on to make the comment. This helped teachers discern whether students had made reasonable inferences based on their reading and their existing knowledge. Teachers were encouraged to show students how to return to the text to check or expand on their own ideas so that they could learn to develop and support their own process of constructing meaning from text.

Premise 3: Content Is Important for Students With Disabilities

It is a well-established fact that knowledge influences comprehension; it is also the case that students in special education may have knowledge and vocabulary inadequacies as a result of their limited reading experience or because they have missed general education instruction to receive pull-out services.

Acknowledging the importance of content, in the ISA-X students read trade books that were organized into thematic units that aligned with their social studies curriculum. To accomplish this alignment, intervention and social studies teachers shared information about students and curricula. The use of social studies themes encouraged students to value the intervention, because it developed their background knowledge so that they were better able to learn and participate in social studies classes. The importance of this approach is apparent in the example of a student who thought the Underground Railroad was a subway. Reading with her intervention teacher allowed her to correct that misunderstanding so that she could better profit from the instruction offered in the classroom setting. The emphasis on content in the ISA-X helped students see themselves as individuals who could learn valued content by reading.

Thematically organized units also allowed students to compare texts in a variety of ways. Comparing how George Washington was presented in a biography and in historical fiction helped students discern the central characteristics of each genre. Comparing how Christopher Columbus was portrayed in texts written from the European or Native American perspective and comparing the information included in different biographies of Pocahontas helped students understand that authors have biases and that there is no "true" history. This focus on the development of critical literacy for struggling learners appeared to be novel for both the students and their intervention teachers.

Premise 4: Readers Need to Set a High Standard for Coherence to Comprehend

Many older struggling readers do not realize that in text every word must make sense. They lack this understanding because for many years what they have read has not made sense. This is due to their word-identification errors, limited vocabulary, lack of relevant background knowledge, and inability to interpret literary syntax (Perfetti et al., 2005). The confusion they have experienced while reading has encouraged struggling readers to skip over words and ignore inconsistencies, that is, to set a low standard for coherence as they read. A critical feature of the ISA-X is teaching students that every word makes sense and providing a reading experience in which struggling readers can set a high standard for coherence.

For many middle school students with learning disabilities, special education services have focused on supporting students as they read content area texts that are too difficult for them to read independently. In the ISA-X, all students spent some time reading short, controlled-vocabulary fiction and nonfiction texts related to their social studies curriculum. These texts had multiple purposes, including developing background knowledge and fluency with content vocabulary. But they also provided a context in which students could read and make sense of every word and develop the expectation that they construct meaning when they read.

Professional development stressed the need for instruction to ensure that students had the background knowledge and vocabulary needed to understand each word in the text. Knowledge could be developed through reading simple texts in the thematic unit and supplemented as needed by teacher instruction. Teachers were encouraged to use minilessons to introduce or revisit a few key vocabulary words; other words were explained as they were encountered in the text. Professional development also emphasized the large number of words in texts that students might not understand and the importance of teaching students to ask about word meanings. Teachers were surprised to learn that students did not know the meaning of the words *dawn* and *sew* and the name of the river (the Hudson River) a few blocks from their school.

To support this focus on coherence and the importance of meaning making, comprehension monitoring was a common goal for many students. During professional development, teachers were encouraged to employ a simple tactic: They asked "Did that make sense?" when the student made a meaning-changing error or sounded confused and when students read correctly. The purpose of this tactic was to convey to students that they, not the teacher, had responsibility for monitoring meaning.

Students were taught strategies they could use if monitoring indicated a breakdown in meaning. These "Mixed Up? Fix Up!" strategies in the comprehension-monitoring list (see Figure 9.2) were similar to those taught in other research interventions (Almasi, 1991; Klingner & Vaughn, 1999). Again, emphasis was placed on students using the strategies independently and on encouraging students to reflect on how using the strategies helped them understand what they read.

Premise 5: Struggling Readers Benefit From Reading Texts of Different Difficulty Levels and Genres

Texts at an optimal level of challenge promote perceived competence (Ryan & Deci, 2000). To foster independent strategy use, the majority of texts read by struggling readers in the ISA-X research project were at the students' instructional level. But if struggling readers read only texts at their instructional level, they are not exposed to grade-appropriate vocabulary, and their limitations in reading, language, and knowledge grow even larger (Cunningham & Stanovich, 1998). Background knowledge and vocabulary development are especially important for students from backgrounds of poverty (Neuman, 2006). Thus, reading challenging texts is critical for effecting reading growth (Stahl, Kuhn, & Pickle, 1999) and preparing students for increasing content-knowledge expectations (Hirsch, 2006). Students who read a balance of instructional and

Figure 9.2. Comprehension-Monitoring List

Mixed Up? Fix Up!

Think: Does it make sense to me?

Do I know what all the **words mean** here?

Does the **sentence** sound okay?

Does it all **fit** together?

Fix up: What can I do to make sense of this?

Reread the words.

Check the illustrations.

Pay attention to the punctuation.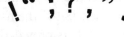

Slowly read ahead for more ideas.

Ask for clarification.

Confirm: Does it make sense now?

challenging texts within a theme have made greater reading gains (Gelzheiser, 2005). For this reason, the ISA-X encourages teachers to move from easier to more challenging texts.

A text's difficulty level is influenced by numerous factors, including the vocabulary it contains and the content knowledge needed to interpret the text. More challenging texts can be made accessible to struggling readers by developing their knowledge and vocabulary, and thematic units are one way to develop this knowledge. As students read related texts, they learn the theme's critical vocabulary and develop background knowledge. A text that would be at a student's frustration level if read in isolation can be made instructional by using thematically related readings to increase students' knowledge and vocabulary before the student encounters the comparatively challenging text.

Thus, the thematic units in the ISA-X included texts of a variety of difficulty levels. Students were encouraged to read several closely related texts to develop knowledge and to move from easier texts to harder texts. Similarly, students often began a unit or topic by choosing the culminating text they would like to read. They then read easier texts that developed the knowledge needed for the more challenging text.

Similarly, familiarity with a genre can support students as they read more challenging texts. Readers who attend to a genre's unique text structure can use that knowledge to support comprehension (Meyer, 1984). Text structure instruction has been found to improve the comprehension of students with learning disabilities (Williams, 2005).

Within each ISA-X thematic unit, one or two genres were identified as a focal genre. Teachers provided students with instruction regarding the key features to expect when reading a genre, and students read multiple examples of the genre. As students read a series of biographies, they acquired knowledge about the genre that helped them know what to expect in subsequent biographies. Students also discussed the extent to which different biographies include typical biography features.

The ISA-X professional development provided teachers with information about the importance of easier and more challenging text and about text feature instruction. Each thematic unit was supported by a curriculum guide that described each text, provided suggestions as to how the text might be used, and identified important vocabulary that might need to be addressed before or while reading the book. The curriculum guide also provided information about the distinctive features of the focal genre.

Premise 6: Motivation Is Important

Reading proficiency improves with practice. The more students read, the better able they are to read with accuracy and understanding. Yet, for most struggling readers, reading is not an enjoyable task, so they avoid it. For some struggling readers, reading induces an anxiety cycle in which errors lead to anxiety and an increased rate of error. The ISA-X has several features designed to increase students' engagement in reading and reduce anxiety.

The simplest of these was to engage students in as much reading of interesting texts as possible. Teachers were encouraged to choose moments for discussion carefully so that most of the session was spent on reading, because reading practice is associated with reading proficiency. Teachers were also encouraged to help students reflect on reading milestones (e.g., "I've read a chapter book."). A typical ISA-X seventh-grade student read 40 short books and four or five chapter books in the 50–60 sessions.

Students given the opportunity to choose what they read tend to have substantially higher reading comprehension and motivation (Guthrie & Humenick, 2004). In the ISA-X, whenever possible, students were given choices of topics, books, or both. For example, within the "Geography of New York State" unit, students could choose to read about Niagara Falls, New York City, or the Statue of Liberty. In other units, all students might read about one topic but choose different culminating books.

An emphasis on reading as an enjoyable activity was also used to enhance motivation. Professional development encouraged teachers to use language and tone of voice that shared enthusiasm for reading (e.g., "Today we get to read...") and avoid language in which reading was construed as a chore that needed to be "gotten through" or rewarded. Teachers were encouraged to focus discussion on interesting topics, with prompts such as "The four March sisters went to the party sharing only two pairs of gloves. What does that make you think about them?" and ask questions in ways that would engage readers, such as "What challenge of colonial life would you have found most difficult?" not "What were three challenges that the colonists faced?"

Teachers were also encouraged to provide appropriate levels of challenge and support to foster students' sense of competence and ability to solve problems. Work that is too easy or too challenging does not foster a sense of accomplishment. Professional development provided extensive time on factors that made reading challenging, especially making decisions about whether text was too challenging for a student, and ways to scaffold students and reduce support over time. And as we described earlier, instruction emphasized strategies that would make students independent problem solvers and promoted students' reflection and awareness of the extent to which they have become successful problem solvers and readers.

Concluding Thoughts

Clearly, a great deal remains to be learned before we know how best to intervene with middle school students who require more intensive services, which may be provided through an RTI model. In the study discussed in this chapter, the students who received intervention had already been identified to receive special education services. The rather dramatic growth which at least some of the students experienced suggests that a responsive approach to intervention should be a major feature of RTI. Indeed, the rate of student progress raises the question of whether some (perhaps many) of these students would not have evolved into "disabled" readers if responsive intervention had been implemented earlier in their educational careers.

It is important to note that the teachers in this project learned to provide a different kind of intervention than they had previously provided to struggling readers. We suspect that the changes in teachers' practices, combined with the opportunity to do extensive reading in appropriately challenging and thematically related texts, led to the strong gains that were observed. We also hypothesize that aligning the intervention with content area instruction contributed to its success.

The professional development offered to teachers was an integral part of the intervention approach. The teachers' comments suggested that they benefited from a multifaceted approach to professional development. Teachers suggested that video demonstrations were critical, as they learned to adopt new practices. They also relied on a detailed teacher handbook, which elaborated on the ideas presented in the professional development. Teachers read the handbook to reinforce the workshop content and continually referred to it as they planned lessons or discussion. Ongoing professional development allowed the research staff to revisit and clarify topics that were challenging for teachers.

Much as students needed individually tailored and responsive intervention, teachers needed professional development that was responsive to their individual needs. In this project, coaching was used to address individual teachers' needs. We found it useful to have audio and video recordings as sources of information about teachers' strengths and needs. Portions of these recordings could then be used to help teachers reflect on how students were responding to different instructional activities. As teachers, like students, became aware of the effects of different strategies, they could choose to use or abandon them.

NOTE

The research reported here was supported by grant #R324A07223 from the Institute for Education Sciences, U.S. Department of Education. The authors would also like to acknowledge the generous support for this research provided by the teachers, administrators, and students involved.

REFERENCES

Almasi, J.F. (1991). Helping students deal effectively with comprehension failure. *Literacy: Issues and Practices, 8,* 59–66.

Almasi, J.F., & Garas-York, K. (2009). Comprehension and discussion of text. In S.E. Israel & G.G. Duffy (Eds.), *Handbook of research on reading comprehension* (pp. 470–493). New York: Routledge.

Clymer, T. (1963). The utility of phonic generalizations in the primary grades. *The Reading Teacher, 16*(4), 252–258.

Cunningham, A.E., & Stanovich, K.E. (1998). What reading does for the mind. *American Educator, 22*(1/2), 8–15.

Fountas, I.C., & Pinnell, G.S. (2007). *Fountas and Pinnell Benchmark Assessment System 2: Grades 3–8, levels L–Z.* Portsmouth, NH: Heinemann.

Gelzheiser, L.M. (2005). Maximizing student progress in one-to-one programs: Contributions of texts, volunteer experience, and student characteristics. *Exceptionality, 13*(4), 229–243. doi:10.1207/s15327035ex1304_4

Gelzheiser, L.M., Scanlon, D.M., & D'Angelo, C. (2001, April). *The effects of community volunteers and poor readers engaging in interactive reading of thematically-related texts.* Paper presented at the annual meeting of the American Educational Research Association, Seattle, WA.

Gelzheiser, L.M., Scanlon, D.M., Hallgren-Flynn, L., & Vellutino, F.R. (2008). *Extending the Interactive Strategies Approach to older struggling readers.* Poster presented at the Institute of Education Sciences Principle Investigators conference, Washington, DC.

Guthrie, J.T., & Humenick, N.M. (2004). Motivating students to read: Evidence for classroom practices that increase reading motivation and achievement. In P. McCardle & V. Chhabra (Eds.), *The voice of evidence in reading research* (pp. 329–354). Baltimore: Paul H. Brookes.

Hirsch, E.D., Jr. (2006). Building knowledge: The case for bringing content into the language arts block and for a knowledge-rich curriculum core for all children. *American Educator, 30*(1), 8–29.

Klingner, J.K., & Vaughn, S. (1999). Promoting reading comprehension, content learning, and English acquisition through collaborative strategic reading (CSR). *The Reading Teacher, 52*(7), 738–747.

Meyer, B.J.F. (1984). Text dimensions and cognitive processing. In H. Mandl, N. Stein, & T. Trabasso (Eds.), *Learning and understanding texts* (pp. 3–47). Hillsdale, NJ: Erlbaum.

Neuman, S.B. (2006). The knowledge gap: Implications for early education. In D.K. Dickinson & S.B. Neuman (Eds.), *Handbook of early literacy research* (Vol. 2, pp. 29–40). New York: Guilford.

Palincsar, A.S., & Brown, A.L. (1986). Reciprocal teaching of comprehension-fostering and comprehension-monitoring activities. *Cognition & Instruction, 1,* 117–175.

Perfetti, C.A., Landi, N., & Oakhill, J. (2005). The acquisition of reading comprehension skill. In M.J. Snowling & C. Hulme (Eds.), *The science of reading: A handbook* (pp. 227–247). Malden, MA: Blackwell.

Ryan, R.M., & Deci, E.L. (2000). Self-determination theory and the facilitation of intrinsic motivation, social development, and well-being. *American Psychologist, 55*(1), 68–78. doi:10.1037/0003-066X.55.1.68

Scammacca, N., Roberts, G., Vaughn, S., Edmonds, M., Wexler, J., Reutebuch, C.K., et al. (2007). *Interventions for adolescent struggling readers: A meta-analysis with implications for practice.* Portsmouth, NH: RMC Research Corporation, Center on Instruction.

Scanlon, D.M., Anderson, K.L., & Sweeney, J.M. (2010). *Early intervention for reading difficulties: The Interactive Strategies Approach.* New York: Guilford.

Scanlon, D.M., Gelzheiser, L.M., Vellutino, F.R., Schatschneider, C., & Sweeney, J.M. (2008). Reducing the incidence of early reading difficulties: Professional development for classroom teachers versus direct interventions for children. *Learning and Individual Differences, 18*(3), 346–359. doi:10.1016/j.lindif.2008.05.002

Scanlon, D.M., Vellutino, F.R., Small, S.G., Fanuele, D.P., & Sweeney, J.M. (2005). Severe reading difficulties: Can they be prevented? A comparison of prevention and intervention approaches. *Exceptionality, 13*(4), 209–227. doi:10.1207/s15327035ex1304_3

Share, D.L. (1995). Phonological recoding and self-teaching: *Sine qua non* of reading acquisition. *Cognition, 55*(2), 151–218. doi:10.1016/0010-0277(94)00645-2

Stahl, S.A., Kuhn, M.R., & Pickle, J.M. (1999). An educational model of assessment and targeted instruction for children with reading problems. In D.H. Evensen & P.B. Mosenthal (Eds.), *Advances in reading/language research: Vol. 6. Reconsidering the role of the reading clinic in a new age of literacy* (pp. 249–272). Greenwich, CT: JAI.

Vellutino, F.R., & Scanlon, D.M. (2002). The Interactive Strategies approach to reading intervention. *Contemporary Educational Psychology, 27*(4), 573–635. doi:10.1016/S0361-476X(02)00002-4

Vellutino, F.R., Scanlon, D.M., Sipay, E.R., Small, S.G., Pratt, A., Chen, R., et al. (1996). Cognitive profiles of difficult-to-remediate and readily remediated poor readers: Early intervention as a vehicle for distinguishing between cognitive and experiential deficits as basic causes of specific reading disability. *Journal of Educational Psychology, 88*(4), 601–638. doi:10.1037/0022-0663.88.4.601

Williams, J.P. (2005). Instruction in reading comprehension for primary-grade students: A focus on text structure. *Journal of Special Education, 39*(1), 6–18. doi:10.1177/00224669050390010201

New Roles for Educational Leaders: Starting and Sustaining a Systemic Approach to RTI

Karen A. Costello

East Lyme Public Schools, Connecticut

Marjorie Y. Lipson

University of Vermont

Barbara Marinak

Penn State Harrisburg

Mary F. Zolman

Arlington Public Schools, Virginia

It is clear that RTI is being adopted slowly in some places and quickly in others. It is also clear that there is wide variation in how RTI practices are being implemented. It is extremely important for literacy professionals to be involved in RTI efforts from the very beginning, because the initiative starts in general education. The majority of students identified as learning disabled are experiencing difficulties with language and literacy.

Getting started with RTI can be difficult for schools and districts, especially if leadership for the initiative is not clear. One of the difficulties is that the responsibility for RTI initiatives may be located in many different places. In our experience, directors of special education, curriculum coordinators and supervisors, school psychologists, building administrators, literacy/reading coaches, and even classroom teachers have sometimes been charged with designing and implementing an RTI plan. However, the promise of RTI can be realized only if there is genuine collaboration among knowledgeable and expert professionals.

As a result, school and district administrators have a special responsibility to be knowledgeable and involved.

Identifying the Collaborators and Creating a Team

In this book, there are descriptions of several diverse approaches to RTI. Although a number of variations are possible, none will be successful if schools do not bring the full force of professional expertise to bear on the problems. Unfortunately, some districts have tried to simplify RTI by using a brief and limited assessment, focusing exclusively on one aspect of literacy (i.e., accuracy or fluency), or reducing the instructional response to a standard protocol based only on the results from a screening measure. Often these decisions have been made without input from literacy professionals or classroom teachers who are certainly concerned about efficiency and worried about spending too much time testing. On the other hand, teachers and specialists know that literacy is not unidimensional and there is an array of patterns underlying students' difficulties (Valencia & Buly, 2004). Truly effective instruction relies on effective teachers who make decisions about instruction on the basis of excellent assessment information coupled with their knowledge about literacy and individual students. Our most vulnerable students need the most expert instruction and support that we have available. This may not be the easiest or quickest approach, but it is usually required.

Providing the most expert instruction and support possible demands a level of collegiality and collaboration that many schools have not realized until now. Among those who should be involved in planning from the beginning are (a) classroom teachers, because that is where RTI begins; (b) reading specialists and coaches, because they (should) have the most refined knowledge of literacy development and reading difficulties; (c) special educators, because they often have acquired knowledge about how to intensify or individualize instruction for struggling students; and (d) building administrators, because it is impossible to realize the promise of RTI without committed and creative leadership. Building and district leaders must find the fiscal and human resources necessary to provide time to collaborate, engage in data-based conversations, and help individuals acquire new skills and strategies through professional development. Others who should be involved from the start are speech and language professionals, because they can support students who are very young and struggling with literacy and whose problems may be linked to language difficulties and parents who must understand and support new ways of helping their children.

Each school and district needs an RTI committee composed of individuals with expertise in each of these areas. Initially, this committee or team should be responsible for conducting a formal or informal school- or district-level needs assessment that includes an evaluation of how well prepared they are to take steps toward change. An RTI committee would be charged with looking at the school as a whole to decide what systems are already in place, what needs to be developed, and how existing systems will be used by all professionals. This committee may also find it helpful to provide an overview of possible actions. For schools that are initiating RTI implementation, we provide a set of steps to follow (see Figure 10.1). These steps can help districts restart the process if it appears that initial efforts are floundering.

Perhaps the most common problem facing schools and districts is that interest in RTI is not universally shared. Sometimes the special educators want to get started because they have received a mandate to move toward different means of identifying students for special education services, so they draw on resources known to them in their work and focus on procedures for finding eligible students. In other cases, the curriculum director for literacy may start working with general educators because he or she is concerned about the number of students who are struggling and is interested in preventing early reading problems. In most cases, these professionals are likely to be working almost in isolation—one focusing on identification and one on prevention—using different assessments and instructional programs. In Virginia, the state department of education reinforces the need for collaborative partnerships: "Because RTI represents a framework for the delivery of instruction and affects the entire program, consensus must be reached on [RTI's] purpose and use" (Commonwealth of Virginia Department of Education, 2007, p. 38). We cannot emphasize enough how important it is to develop collaborative partnerships as early as possible. This may slow down the process but it will improve the outcomes. Special education supervisors and teachers need to be engaged from the beginning, because they are charged with ensuring equitable and accessible instruction and assessment for students with disabilities (see Chapter 1 for a description of measurement issues) in ways that are often subject to difficult regulatory mandates. At the same time, it is vital for an RTI team to have a literacy leader who is more likely to be in a position to focus on prevention or instructional issues. This person could be a building administrator (e.g., principal,

Figure 10.1. Steps for Getting Started With RTI

1. Identify a collaborative leadership team
   a. Membership should be broadly representative (i.e., district- and school-level administrators; principals; coordinators and experts in curriculum, instruction, and assessment; special education administrators and leaders; Title I or other literacy experts)
   b. From the outset, this leadership team should cross boundaries between general education and special education.
   c. Members can and should be added once there is a consensus about moving forward (e.g., representative teacher leaders, parent advocates)
2. Engage in self-assessment
   a. Display and analyze data to determine strengths and areas for growth
   b. Determine the need for change
      i. Evaluate student performance
      ii. Examine classroom literacy instruction/program
      iii. Consider what interventions are presently available
      iv. Identify what roles and responsibilities are required and determine present levels of expertise and commitment
   c. Consider RTI from a systemic perspective
   d. Develop vision for the expected outcomes
      i. Study RTI requirements (the law)
      ii. Become acquainted with the range of options and approaches
      iii. Establish goals
   e. Build collaborative partnerships (if needed)
3. Develop an action plan for RTI implementation
   a. Consider what existing initiatives and opportunities can and should be incorporated into any systemic plan for action
   b. Describe the approach to RTI to be used in your school/district
   c. Identify and address concerns and barriers for implementation
   d. Identify what will be required in terms of resources, professional development, materials, assessment tools, infrastructure, and technology (include time for planning and collaborating)
   e. Identify which outcomes will be used to measure effectiveness
   f. Establish a timeline for implementation
4. Make the following decisions
   a. Decide who will be involved in shaping interventions and in making decisions about students' response to instruction
   b. Identify the assessment system/components and create a set of guidelines for decision making that includes a focus on both prevention and identification
   c. Determine what professional development will be required for classroom teachers, literacy specialists, and special educators
   d. Establish benchmarks for monitoring students' progress
   e. Decide how data will be collected, displayed, and discussed
   f. Establish procedures for making decisions about students' movement from one level of support to another
5. Other [Given your context....]

Note: Adapted from Shores, C., & Chester, K. (2009). *Using RTI for School Improvement.* Thousand Oaks, CA: Corwin.
Successful Approaches to RTI: Collaborative Practices for Improving K–12 Literacy edited by Marjorie Y. Lipson and Karen K. Wixson. Copyright 2010 International Reading Association. May be copied for classroom use.

assistant principal), reading specialist, or classroom teacher. Regardless of the job title, this individual should bring an expertise in best practices and knowledge of coaching to the process. Familiarity and comfort with coaching allows the literacy leader to support the growth of a team charged with building and sustaining a dynamic intervention system for all struggling readers.

To nurture collaboration within what will undoubtedly be a diverse group of individuals, it is helpful for the literacy leader to think about coaching and collaboration as broadly as possible. Teachers are not the only individuals who might benefit from coaching, nor are those who are called "coaches" the only people who may effectively support change. Members of the team, as well as anyone working on behalf of struggling learners, are more effective when they are open to new learning. Encouraging distributed leadership and diverse learning opportunities makes a difference for everyone concerned and should help keep people focused as they engage in substantive new roles and responsibilities. Important insights can be gained from a variety of sources, such as team members, peers, or colleagues in the building and professionals in other buildings or districts. Learning can also take place in team meetings, classrooms, intervention sessions, professional learning communities, and professional conferences. Research, professional books, white papers, and teacher's editions can be a powerful form of professional development.

Taking Stock

It is important to emphasize that schools and districts do not have to start over with entirely new procedures and processes to develop their approach to RTI. Instead they should start by considering what has already been accomplished over the past several years to improve student performance. RTI does not have to be another "new thing." Schools and teachers should think about how existing initiatives and materials can be used in a more coherent and interrelated way to improve instruction for all students and ensure that the systems are in place to reduce the number of students struggling with literacy.

Any one of the following innovations can advance RTI goals: formative assessment (Council of Chief State School Officers [CCSSO], 2008), backward design (Wiggins & McTighe, 2005), or critical friends groups (Bambino, 2002). Schools that have begun to use learning communities (sometimes called professional learning communities or teacher learning communities) are in a particularly powerful position to effect change, because these approaches have an impressive research base to support school change (see DuFour & Eaker, 1998, and McLaughlin & Talbert, 2006). In their recent review, Vescio, Ross, and Adams (2008) conclude, "The collective results of these studies suggest that well-developed professional learning communities have positive impact on both teaching practice and student achievement." DuFour (2004) outlines three big ideas about professional learning communities that make this approach especially well suited to supporting school efforts to implement RTI:

1. Ensure that students learn.
2. Establish a culture of collaboration.
3. Focus on results.

The professional development and whole-school focus of innovations like professional learning communities are extremely helpful in promoting healthy and powerful school communities. Of course, collaboration can occur without formal organizational structures. If you are in a district that has yet to launch any of these initiatives, you can still work with your colleagues informally. In fact, one of the hallmarks of successful schools is the presence of at least one literacy leader— someone who engages his or her colleagues in discussions about instruction/ assessment practices and supports problem solving to improve student achievement (Lipson, Mosenthal, Mekkelsen, & Russ, 2004). The simple act of stopping a colleague in the hall to ask for advice can begin to establish the climate for change.

It is easy for schools to approach each new initiative as a distinct requirement. A comprehensive description of a district's ongoing efforts and activities, including how they might help create a systemic approach, is a good first step. In addition, every improvement that teachers, administrators, and other school-based professionals have made to create effective learning communities can form the basis for success with new initiatives.

Consider Leadership

Leadership at all levels is required if schools are to realize, not squander, the promise and potential of RTI. Not all administrators need the same understanding or engagement, but all must be committed to a system of responsive instruction and intervention. In this book, most attention is focused at the school and classroom level. At these levels, the importance of building administrators, especially principals or their proxies, cannot be overemphasized. As Crockett and Gillespie (2007) note,

Principals have a key role in fostering consensus within school teams, and the success of RTI in an individual school will start with their understanding, and belief, in the need for change and their leadership during the process of change. The Principal is also a major force...in demonstrating a commitment to creative problem solving. (p. 2)

Throughout this book, all of the authors have emphasized the importance of collaboration. This is an initiative that is too big for any one person to do. Scholars and practitioners in the area of leadership often emphasize the importance of relational factors, and in this case they are essential—what McAndrew (2005) calls "peoplework" (p. 1), as opposed to paperwork. Certainly, a leader focused only on regulations and mandates is unlikely to help others move forward in this challenging endeavor. In their study of change and sustainability, Heath and Heath (2007) suggest that six types of action can lead to success, which we have adapted to the specific context of RTI:

1. *Have a vision*—A vision is a bridge from the present to the future. Create and communicate a powerful but simple vision for RTI. Find common interests and build trust by asking stakeholders for their input. Avoid decision paralysis. After sharing the vision, guard the ways in which it is communicated. Listen to how the vision is being discussed and interpreted by the stakeholders.

2. *Be unexpected*—Take actions that are unexpected. RTI can become dehumanizing by overemphasizing data and underemphasizing the educators working on behalf of students. Personalize communication about struggling readers by holding face-to-face discussions. Reserve e-mail for scheduling. During discussions, pose questions that encourage information sharing. Actively listen before offering suggestions or making a decision.

3. *Be concrete*—Advocate for RTI. Leaders need to be perceived as working consciously and consistently on behalf of struggling students. Take actions that are concrete and directly observable by the (other) staff. For example, teach core or intervention lessons to learn about the needs of your struggling readers. Offer to demonstrate a technique or method you suggest. Learn the strengths and needs of your struggling readers by observing them across the content areas. Be able to speak to their performance in all classrooms. Be consistent in your support and ensure that

you follow up. Schedule the days and times when you will observe or ask for feedback on a student or group of students.

4. *Be credible*—Promote situational interest and commitment to students by honoring all data at the RTI table. Carefully analyze how and why interventions are working or not working. Articulate the attributes of instruction that cause students to gain in proficiency (e.g., careful collaboration between the core classroom teacher's and the specialists' analyses of writing samples to inform reading instruction). Effectiveness can be replicated only if it is understood and defined. Articulate sound reasoning when an intervention is recommended or when modifications are necessary.

5. *Encourage emotions*—Feelings inspire people to act. Approaching RTI from an analytical perspective only can hinder our ability to feel. Emotional discussions encourage RTI team members to view struggling readers as humans (vs. numbers on pivot tables or trend lines). Consider, for example, the assessment wall advocated by Dorn and Henderson in Chapter 4. Be sure to link the efforts of teachers and interventionists to the gains made by students. Attribute growth to the specific actions of the team working on the students' behalf.

6. *Share stories*—Invite discussions that bring a wide range of data to the RTI table. Encourage team members to bring artifacts from the literacy lives of students (e.g., journal excerpts, library choices, writing samples). Model and encourage discussion about students' work. Discuss how the artifacts can inform both core classroom instruction and intervention.

These six types of action make evident that it is not only the school principal who might provide leadership. As important as building administrators are, teacher leaders are essential to a positive outcome for RTI. Hilton (2007) states, "Teachers who [are] viewed as leaders by other teachers play an important role in providing resources and encouragement to other teachers, and therefore facilitate the implementation and continuation of changes within a school" (n.p.). Both classroom teachers and reading specialists need to find ways to influence their colleagues and work productively toward change for students. Sometimes teachers and specialists feel as though they do not have the power or authority to tell others what to do. That is probably true—and even those that have such authority rarely feel that telling others what to do results in positive change. What we can do, however, is look for ways to have positive interactions with colleagues, ask questions that lead faculty to think about students more carefully, and celebrate growth when we see it in students. We discuss the role of coaching later in this chapter.

Consider Literacy

Our interest in this book has been to provide guidance to professionals who want to improve students' literacy development. The International Reading Association (IRA) has been providing leadership in this area since the earliest days of RTI legislation and has recognized the need for a broad-based approach from the very beginning. We recommend using the IRA's set of guiding principles as an organizing document (see IRA, 2010). Using these principles to guide and focus your initial self-assessment ensures that you attend to critical issues right from the beginning. We have provided a self-assessment framework for this purpose as Figure 10.2.

Assessing Systemwide Readiness. The purpose of RTI is to provide the best possible education for all students in the general educator's classroom, provide students with a variety of educational opportunities aimed at advancing their learning and understanding, and provide increasingly expert support and instruction when students struggle. To save time and ensure that various initiatives work in concert, district personnel should meet regularly to agree on goals and summarize (or perhaps consolidate) existing efforts and activities.

A number of existing resources can be used to gather appropriate information. Many states have materials on their websites that can support initial self-assessments, but not all of these websites are equally useful for literacy professionals. When you examine your state's website, be alert for evidence that there is engagement across offices or departments: English language arts, special education, and English-language learners (ELLs). Some states provide information that is generated exclusively by school psychologists or special educators, and many do not support appropriate collaboration across professional boundaries.

Other states have productive materials that reflect cross-disciplinary collaboration. The Wisconsin Department of Public Instruction, for example, has a set of three simple but powerful concepts around which RTI should be organized: (1) high-quality instructional practice, (2) continuous review of student progress (multiple measures), and (3) collaboration. Using just these three concepts, Wisconsin has created a very helpful developmental self-assessment

Figure 10.2. Response to Intervention Principles: A Self-Assessment Framework

Directions: Read International Reading Association's position statement on RTI and the guiding principles it details. Discuss these principles as they relate to your school.

IRA's Guiding Principles						
Guiding Principle	How Are We Doing?				School-Based Evidence	Implications or Action Steps
	This is an area for growth	We are beginning	We are making progress	This is a strength		
I. Instruction—RTI is first and foremost intended to prevent problems by optimizing initial language and literacy instruction.						
II. Responsive Teaching and Differentiation—The RTI process emphasizes increasingly differentiated and intensified instruction or intervention in language and literacy.						
III. Assessment—An RTI approach demands assessment that can inform language and literacy instruction meaningfully.						
IV. Collaboration—RTI requires a dynamic, positive, and productive collaboration among professionals with relevant expertise in language and literacy. Success also depends on strong and respectful partnerships among professionals, parents, and students.						
V. Systemic and Comprehensive Approaches—RTI must be part of a comprehensive, systemic approach to language and literacy assessment and instruction that supports all preK–12 students and teachers.						
VI. Expertise—All students have the right to receive instruction from well-prepared teachers who keep up to date and supplemental instruction from professionals specifically prepared to teach language and literacy.						

Successful Approaches to RTI: Collaborative Practices for Improving K–12 Literacy edited by Marjorie Y. Lipson and Karen K. Wixson. Copyright 2010 International Reading Association. May be copied for classroom use.

(see Wisconsin Department of Public Instruction, n.d.). Similarly, Connecticut describes four major attributes of a successful RTI approach: (1) effectiveness of core curricula, instruction, and multitiered interventions, (2) universal common assessment and progress monitoring, (3) collaborative strategic decision making using data, and (4) leadership and culture/climate for student improvement. Connecticut has taken a very proactive stance about RTI, such that effective in summer 2009, districts are no longer allowed to use IQ-achievement discrepancy formulas solely for identifying students with specific learning disabilities.

What is important about both Connecticut and Wisconsin is that they have provided flexibility for individual districts and schools to make decisions about the particular RTI models and approaches they use. In addition, they encourage local variation in the types of assessments and materials. The U.S. government purposely provided few details for development and implementation of RTI procedures, stating specifically that states and districts should have the flexibility to establish models that reflect their communities' unique situations.

A systemic approach to RTI requires attention to the infrastructure of the school as well as the specific literacy practices. Virginia's department of education suggests that leadership teams should engage in self-assessment by asking the following questions:

- Are core programs meeting the needs of 80% of the students?
- Does the school operate from an "all children can learn" philosophy?
- Is there a willingness to allow data to guide decision making?
- Is there true collaboration between special education and general education?
- Is the formation of student progress-monitoring teams (or the transformation of a current school-based "study" team into one) practical and desirable at both division and school levels?
- Is there an adequate system, including technology, to support data collection and analysis that provides timely feedback to teachers?
- What is the availability of supplemental programs and the capacity to match those programs to the needs identified in the screening and progress-monitoring practices?
- Is there flexible staffing that can be achieved to accommodate the delivery of Tier 2 and Tier 3 interventions?

Taking action must begin with a clear sense of the demands of your particular setting, but you should also imagine that you can be proactive. Local and state IRA organizations can be especially helpful to literacy professionals. For example, the New England Reading Association developed a program evaluation sheet entitled Checklist for Assessing an English Language Arts Curriculum and Program (K–12) that is available at www.eastlymeschools .org/uploaded/documents%2FDistrict%2FCurriculum/Evaluation_English_ Language_Arts.pdf.

More recently, the Wisconsin State Reading Association (2008) has taken a leadership role in its state and created a useful rubric for evaluating literacy intervention programs.

Focusing on High-Quality Core Instruction. The inescapable conclusion from decades of research is that good teaching matters. A significant number of students are less likely to need special education services when they receive appropriately targeted and responsive instruction (Scanlon, Gelzheiser, Vellutino, Schatschneider, & Sweeney, 2008). We know from years of research that students learn best in a classroom environment in which they feel safe and learn through sharing, conversing, watching others model, and having a teacher who is knowledgeable about both child development and content expectations. We also know that, in many cases, existing practices that pull students out of this environment on a regular basis have not yielded long-term benefits.

Given these conclusions, a close examination of the classroom environment and the extent to which it offers appropriately differentiated instruction is essential to moving forward with RTI. Very few educators would argue with these conclusions. However, there is a concern about who decides what good first instruction looks like. This is, of course, highly dependent on the outcomes that have been established by state and local communities. In this book the authors have described a number of effective, research-based interventions, each of which is compatible with the types of good first instruction that lays the foundation for success for all students.

During the "taking stock" phase of RTI, discussion is easier if the RTI leadership team is genuinely representative and collaborative. District administrators and building leaders might consider holding conversations about core reading instruction using a "Tier 1 without tears" coaching approach (Marinak & Mazzoni, 2007a). Because every age presents its own RTI challenges and concerns, it is important to respect this developmental uniqueness by inviting conversation at each grade level before presenting data or suggesting methods. With the stakeholders (e.g., classroom teachers, special education teachers, ELL teachers, reading specialists, building administrators) present, posing the following five questions can inform RTI in important ways:

1. *What are the strengths and areas for growth of the current English language arts program?* Any discussion involving core instruction should begin by inviting classroom teachers to discuss their language arts programs. This sharing should include specific information such as instructional practices, time allocations, group size, and group membership. Questions should include considerations of how important outcomes are being supported. Remember that this is about what is best for the students first, not what is best for the staff.

2. *Are all students receiving appropriate instruction designed to improve their literacy development and achievement?* A comprehensive and balanced classroom program must be multifaceted and attentive to the literacy development of all students. This means that it must address the needs of the most precocious as well as the most struggling students. Although different configurations of instruction may be used at various times for diverse purposes, the classroom teacher needs to plan and provide intentional instructional opportunities for each student every day.

3. *Is daily small-group, differentiated instruction, delivered by the classroom teacher, part of the core instructional program?* If the answer to this question is "no," perhaps Tier 1 instruction is not as robust as it could be. In other words, it might be premature to refer students to Tier 2 or coaching, and conversation around this question may uncover the need for a revision in schedules or for professional development to help teachers manage differentiated, small-group instruction. In either case, opening up this important dialogue can invite RTI teams to be creative in their hunt for instructional minutes or collaborative professional development.

4. *Is there consistency within and across grade levels in how language arts time is allocated across the content domains?* Inconsistency is often seen within or across grade levels in how classroom teachers allocate minutes with the language arts block. Until this question is posed and discussed, RTI teams are sometimes unaware of the variance in instructional priorities. These discussions may lead professionals to determine that instructional needs are different at K–2 and 3–8, which may be appropriate. Capturing

time is only the first step, but it is often a prerequisite to more substantive conversation about the nature of instruction itself.

5. *Has the classroom teacher received professional development in research-based methods to prevent difficulties before they arise and refine their use as soon as they have evidence that students are struggling in reading?* In order to be successful, an RTI system must provide for regular discussion of students' progress within the core program. If RTI teams rely entirely on mandated screening or progress-monitoring data checkpoints, they run the risk of waiting to identify students that the classroom teacher noticed weeks or months before. In addition, without professional development in differentiated methods and the ongoing support of a responsive team, classroom teachers may be reluctant to begin intervening within the core program. This is one of the reasons that some use a four-tier approach, with the Tier 2 intervention occurring within the classroom (see Chapter 4). Recall that research-based instruction is only a meaningful description if it is effective for specific students in specific contexts. Classroom teachers need to be part of regular discussions about their students with RTI team members. Together they can work toward highly effective differentiated instruction that supports classroom teachers in addressing the needs of struggling students within the classroom.

In addition to making sure that all regular classrooms are rich in learning opportunities for students, it also is essential that we prevent the premature identification of students with the label "specific learning disability" by layering additional support and expertise in those classrooms. When a student continues to struggle despite the best efforts of the classroom teacher, a diverse group of professionals should convene to review strategies used and determine the next course of action. Intervention is developed in response to questions like the following:

- What is the problem?
- What are the student's strengths?
- What type of instruction is successful with the student?
- What should be done within the classroom? What should be done with a literacy specialist?
- How long should this instruction/intervention be used before we expect to see improvement?

- What assessment tools should we use to monitor progress?

Looking Closely at a Continuum of Interventions. RTI calls for students to receive additional (supplemental) intervention when they are not responding to good first instruction. It is common for schools and districts to use a three- or four-tier model to describe the increasing intensity that students experience, with Tier 2 and Tier 3 involving smaller groups and greater intensity. This iteration is not required, however, and we suggest that you consider several approaches and orientations before you settle on a process that works for you. Dorn and Henderson (see Chapter 4), for example, use a layering approach with four layers or "tiers." The advantage of this approach is that it suggests that the first intervention(s) should be provided in the general education or content classroom, although it may be supported by other professionals than the classroom teacher.

We also recommend that you think carefully about the idea of intensity. Simply providing more instruction in a smaller group may not be the best possible response for a student. Indeed, in some cases, providing even more of a failing tactic can cause harm (Wanzek & Vaughn, 2008). Creating opportunities for a "differentiated double dose of instruction" (Marinak & Mazzoni, 2007b, p. 3) may involve more refined or targeted instruction and may require adaptations in response to students' cultural or linguistic backgrounds. Tailoring instruction or intervention to students' individual needs may involve new thinking on the part of many professionals. In the past, the typical standard for intervention was simply defined as "30 minutes with the reading specialist." What that might exactly entail was never really identified. Until instruction/ intervention is clearly described, it will be difficult to think about how it could be altered to improve students' chances of success. One of the major difficulties with a standard protocol approach is that it assumes that failure to respond is a function of the student's abilities or motivation, rather than a function of the mismatch of instruction to the student's needs.

The continuum of interventions that we advocate includes several iterations, or adaptations, during each tier. This is not a series of hoops to move through but a problem-solving enterprise. Successive tries in the classroom and during subsequent interventions may be necessary for some students. These may involve very small changes, such as increasing the amount of time a student spends in small-group instruction, or much larger changes, such as changing the way that some students work in small groups (and the amount and type of support they receive).

When taking stock of your present provisions for individual differences, a few key questions might prove helpful:

- How many specialists are available to provide intervention?
- What does customization and intensification look like for each successive tier?
- Are intervention designs documented so that they can be used with other students who have similar difficulties? This is important both for individual students (to track their interventions) and for future professional use.
- Are the interventions complementary to Tier 1 instruction?
- What provisions have been made to limit interventions and keep scheduling flexible?
  - How do we monitor progress?
  - How do we schedule teacher and specialist time?

In our experience, teachers welcome the chance to talk about their concerns, but they typically have not considered a different way of working. The idea is to prevent students from failure that may lead to a designation of learning disability and accelerate their progress if they have slipped behind. This is a more ambitious goal than we have typically set for ourselves, but the examples in this book suggest that it is attainable.

Making Decisions

An effective RTI system requires considerable decision making (see Figure 10.1). Recall that decisions should be made based on the particular constellation of strengths and areas of need for your situation. Some schools and districts, for example, must pay particular attention to providing culturally or linguistically responsive interventions (see Chapter 6 and Chapter 7). Similarly, middle and secondary schools must find solutions and models suited to their unique needs and organizational systems (see Chapter 8).

If your school or district has already engaged in significant curriculum design, professional development, and conversation about student data, then you will be able to move relatively quickly into creating a system of data management and progress monitoring. If not, there will be a period of significant planning and decision making. Decisions about organization and collaboration are among the most critical. How will data teams work? How will existing schedules be adapted to permit collaboration, teaming, and additional intervention time? What should be strengthened in core literacy instruction? What types of interventions will support the major outcomes that you have for your district?

It is important to recognize that, for many schools and districts, RTI implementation requires significant change in structures, resource allocation, roles and responsibilities, and professional interactions. Such change is complex and requires commitment and creative thinking on the part of well-intentioned professionals (Fullan, 1997). It is useful to consider lessons learned from school change research and take into account the factors that are characteristic of successful schools (see Lipson et al., 2004; Mosenthal, Lipson, Torncello, Russ, & Mekkelsen, 2004; Taylor, Pearson, Peterson, & Rodriguez, 2003, 2005). Lipson and her colleagues (2004) conducted research on schools that were unusually successful in supporting students' literacy achievement. They studied schools from all socioeconomic situations and identified four factors that distinguished successful schools from less successful ones:

1. *Expertise exercised responsibly with a complex classroom*—Success is a function of teachers' commitment, knowledge, and expertise across the grades. Although teachers in successful schools had quite a lot of autonomy to make decisions about their teaching in relation to their students' needs, this autonomy was exercised responsibly (i.e., within a larger vision of shared outcomes across the grades).

2. *Responsive school community*—Success was a function of teachers' shared vision and mutual response. Coherent and collaborative structures were in place, appropriate to the particular larger school context.

3. *Opportunities to read within a complex program*—Successful literacy programs provided for extensive opportunities to read and write. Regardless of the type of program adopted, all of the successful programs provided balanced instruction across the major areas of literacy.

4. *School commitment and stability*—All of the successful schools revealed a history of long-term commitment to literacy improvement, and there was stable leadership.

Given the promise of RTI—to improve instructional outcomes for all students—schools should work hard to create the conditions for success as they make the more fine-grained decisions required by the endeavor. Treating this simply as a series of discrete decisions about assessment, programs, and so forth, will not yield the type of systemic change that is possible.

Decisions About Instruction

Remarkably little attention is directed toward instruction in many RTI initiatives. One of the purposes of this book is to detail these instructional issues. As teachers and administrators reflect on their contexts and make decisions, they may benefit from frameworks that will help them establish standards of practice for various aspects of RTI. Gehsmann (2008), for example, worked with the staff of a large, unified school to establish standards of practice for classroom literacy instruction, assessment, and intervention. Using a three-tiered plan, she described standards of practice for various developmental levels (see Figure 10.3).

Making decisions about the nature of instruction and intervention is critical to the success of RTI. Although it is possible to impose RTI on schools, and has been done regularly over the past several years, the likelihood that struggling students will improve their achievement under such circumstances is small. Real change that is sustained over time takes shared commitment and vision among the various groups involved. Whenever possible, decisions should involve all professional participants, although this is not always possible.

As school districts develop an array of intervention programs, what Dorn and Henderson in Chapter 4 call a "portfolio of interventions," they should consider a few key concepts. First, consider the difference between the concepts of remediation and intervention. Remediation suggests that the student is lacking or needs to be "fixed." In the not too distant past, if a student was referred for remedial services, it became, so to speak, a "lifelong sentence." Still today, too many of the students in remedial classrooms in grade 4 are the same students who were identified in kindergarten. On the other hand, interventions as part of RTI should be considered focused and relatively short term. Progress monitoring should be frequent, and the program design should be followed. When it is clear that students are not benefiting, adaptations should be made to the instruction or intervention (see earlier discussion in this chapter). The intent is

Figure 10.3. Standards of Practice for Developmental Reading Interventions

Tier 1 Interventions

Classroom-based interventions are determined by a collaborative team, individual teachers, partnership teams, or coaches. These interventions must be well documented, and progress must be assessed regularly (every 5–10 lessons) and formally (every 6–8 weeks).

Tier 2 Interventions

Student Profile (entry criteria)	Intervention	What the Interventionist Does*	What the Classroom Teacher Does*	Assessment Measures (for entrance and exit)
Emergent Reader:	Type of Intervention: Frequency: Time: Grouping: Who: Training: Materials/resources:			1. 2. 3. 4.
Beginning Reader:	Type of Intervention: Frequency: Time: Grouping: Who: Training: Materials/resources:			1. 2. 3. 4.
Transitional Reader:	Type of Intervention: Frequency: Time: Grouping: Who: Training: Materials/resources:			1. 2. 3. 4.

Note. These frameworks were developed for each of grades K–3. The descriptions of the students and the interventions vary. In addition, there is a menu of interventions and, for each, a description of the student profile that is matched to that particular intervention (e.g. Group: Phonological Awareness/Word Study; Group: Read-Aloud Preview/Review). *Provide a description of the nature of intervention instruction.

to provide intervention to support a student who is beginning to struggle or to accelerate the student who is behind.

Some schools have taken "intervention" to mean "commercial product." Although commercially developed materials can provide some helpful resources, only teacher expertise dramatically affects students' long-term success. To support teachers and specialists, we suggest working collaboratively to create and document interventions and match them to diverse profiles of students (see Valencia & Buly, 2004).

One of the authors in this chapter has recently encouraged reading specialists in one building to work together to describe the types of interventions they use in response to specific types of student strengths and weaknesses. Using the format in Figure 10.4 leads to additional questions that can be taken to the collaborative teams such as the following (see Batsche et al., 2005):

- What is the problem? Teacher(s) provide evidence that supports these decisions (e.g., assessments, student work).

- How do we know that it is a problem? What successive efforts have already occurred?

- What types of instruction and intervention should take place next? Who will provide it?

- What materials and approaches should be used?

Although decisions about instruction are central to the success of RTI, two other issues absolutely must be addressed during decision making: assessment and professional development.

Decisions About Assessment

Decisions about assessment often define what occurs during instruction. Although this has been true for decades, it has never been more apparent than in some iterations of RTI. It is certainly helpful to employ screening measures that are relatively brief and easy to administer, because the purpose of these assessments is to identify students who may be struggling or at risk of failure. However, screening measures are not generally appropriate for measuring progress, because the concern is whether students are acquiring the full range of literacy skills and dispositions. Initial determinations that a student is struggling

Figure 10.4. Overview of School Intervention Plan(s) for Literacy Within a Response to Intervention (RTI) Framework

To support all students while using an RTI framework, we need to know what instruction has been offered and how it will be altered to further support students who are not responding. RTI envisions a series of instructional variations that involve tailoring instruction to students' specific strengths and needs.

There are likely to be several common profiles of student strengths and needs, and it would be useful to describe the interventions that will be used for those students so that we can determine what it is that students are responding to and alter instruction if that is required. Use the space below to describe the types of plans used for particular constellations of student strengths and areas of need. Research suggests that there will likely be four to six different profiles of students, so we should aim to have an intervention plan description for each common profile at our school.

Of course, these plans do not reduce the need for good responsive teaching based on the teachers' observations of what each student is doing. These plans do, however, provide the basis for professional conversations and problem solving among colleagues.

Intervention Plan for Literacy #1
Student profile:

Area(s) of primary concern (circle all that apply):

- Phonological awareness
- Letter ID
- Decoding
- Sight words

- Vocabulary
- Comprehension
- Fluency
- Motivation

- Writing about reading
- Text level
- Other

Goal(s) of the intervention:

Describe the intervention, including information about the following:

- Duration
- Frequency
- Materials to be used

- Strategies, techniques, approaches, etc.
- Person responsible
- Relationship to classroom instruction

should be followed by further exploration to identify the student's strengths and areas of need.

Many districts have moved to using one brief assessment for both screening and progress monitoring, which almost inevitably leads teachers to focus on the skills and tasks that are present on that particular measure. These brief, timed measures (so-called curriculum-based measures, or CBMs) were meant to be predictors of students' abilities in other aspects of reading, but they have become the goal or target of instruction. This is neither desirable nor sensible. Of course, the older the students are, the less this makes sense (see Chapter 8). As you have seen in this book, it is possible to make very effective use of progress-monitoring checklists that are much more closely aligned with instruction (see Chapter 2 and Chapter 4). This type of progress monitoring guides teachers to look closely at the students they are teaching and helps them refine their instruction based on students' growth.

Many schools and districts have been involved in formative assessment initiatives. Although the underlying principles of Formative Assessment for Students and Teachers, or FAST, are entirely familiar to experienced literacy professionals, the current definition of formative assessment is generally credited to the CCSSO. When conceived as "a process used by teachers and students during instruction that provides feedback to adjust ongoing teaching and learning to improve students' achievement of intended instructional outcomes" (CCSSO, 2008, p. 3), it is entirely consistent with RTI, especially because it emphasizes the importance of ongoing, classroom-based assessments.

In RTI, assessment decisions involve not only the type of assessment but also its frequency. The earliest guidelines for progress monitoring suggested very frequent testing (in some cases, weekly). This frequent assessment was designed to measure rate of growth, or slope. Although it is important to pay close attention to students' response to literacy instruction and determine whether further instructional modifications are needed, the recommendations for frequent monitoring on artificial tasks have been extremely controversial.

Recently, researchers and special educators have been reconsidering the type and frequency requirements of RTI, because there is little evidence that frequent, brief measures provide any better predictions of student success than less frequent but more comprehensive measures. Jenkins, Graff, and Miglioretti (2009), for example, report that frequent assessment using brief, timed tasks is no more useful in predicting success than assessments conducted two or three times a year (see also Schatschneider, Wagner, & Crawford, 2008). Early recommendations of very frequent monitoring were based on guidelines that required educators to make a decision about whether students were responding to instruction/intervention after as little as five weeks. Although that may be enough time to make some decisions, this would be too little time to establish whether students will be successful in the long run. As Scanlon (in press) notes,

> For many aspects of reading development, children do not grow in a way that can be adequately represented by a straight line. In fact, Paris (2005) makes a cogent argument for the fact that linear growth is only likely for relatively low level skills such as speeded word reading. (n.p.)

Careful observation of students' literacy behaviors is certainly necessary to make good decisions, so one of the most important decisions teachers and districts can make involves the effective collection and use of assessment information.

We recommend balancing efficiency with utility and maintaining a focus on the quality of the information gathered or collected. In particular, we suggest looking for patterns or trends in success. The quality and depth of students' progress is at least as important as the slope of their growth. If students are showing signs of broad-based improvement in performance, the slope on an isolated measure may not be important. To be sure that student success is durable and important, professionals need to examine the progress data across contexts. Educators should examine evidence from both the classroom and the intervention settings to be sure that the impact that appears visible in one place is evident in another.

Recently, for example, one of the authors sat down with a classroom teacher at the beginning of the school year to discuss a specific student who was about to repeat kindergarten. This is a school that uses a wide array of assessments and makes good use of technology for capturing and summarizing the data. As we examined all of the assessment information in the database, we noticed that some of the data seemed at odds with other information. For example, although the student still did not reliably identify all letter names, she knew many sounds. On an assessment of word writing, she met the standard for mid-year kindergarten. We decided to turn our attention to some evidence that was not in the database—journal entries reflecting her developmental spelling abilities. Using these work samples, we got a much more optimistic picture of her knowledge and skill. However, it was also clear that there might be some oral language difficulties that had not been pursued. The speech-language pathologist had tested her the year before on speech articulation but had not examined her overall oral language development. This collaborative conversation resulted in two decisions. First, the classroom teacher would form a small group to make more systematic use of journal writing with this student (and several others who could benefit). Second, she would ask the speech-language pathologist to take a closer look at this student's narrative development and overall oral language.

Making good decisions about assessment can be one of the most critical factors as you participate in RTI discussions. The knowledge and expertise that literacy professionals bring to these discussions, because they are rooted in deep understanding of the domains of reading, writing, and language, are often unique. As the IRA Guidelines on RTI note, "Assessment should reflect the multidimensional nature of language and literacy learning and the diversity among students being assessed" (IRA, 2010, p. 3). Thus, the primary question you should be asking is, What will our assessment system entail—one that genuinely informs our practice while responding to the need for monitoring and systemic decision making? The utility of an assessment is dependent on the extent to which it provides valid information on the essential aspects of language and literacy that can be used to plan appropriate instruction.

Decisions About Professional Development

By themselves, RTI mandates or initiatives will not change much. After a wide review of research, Hawley, Rosenholtz, Goodstein, and Hasselbring (1984) conclude,

> In virtually every instance in which researchers have examined the factors that account for student performance, teachers prove to have a greater impact than program. This is true for average students and exceptional students, for normal classrooms and special classrooms. (p. 3)

In the intervening decades, other researchers have consistently drawn the same conclusions. The promise and potential of RTI rests with professional expertise and commitment. The question to be decided here is, What types of professional development and collaborative partnerships will we use to help all professionals—classroom teachers, reading teachers/specialists, special educators, teachers of ELLs, and speech-language pathologists—improve their practice and develop a sense of shared responsibility for all students?

Because RTI requires such a systemic approach, successful initiatives typically require that teachers, specialists, and even administrators take on new roles and responsibilities. Literacy leaders may find support and direction in the helpful book *Reading Specialists and Literacy Coaches in the Real World* (Vogt & Shearer, 2006). It is unrealistic to expect teachers and specialists to assume new roles and responsibilities without ongoing, embedded professional development. In our experience, the following topics are centrally important and require additional professional development: expanded knowledge and expertise about assessments (e.g., screening, diagnostic, progress monitoring), intervention methods, data management and interpretation, or team building. The case examples in this book highlight many of these issues. Hayas and Klingner in Chapter 7 describe how classroom teachers and specialists, who had been accustomed to working in isolation, needed to collaborate with colleagues to coordinate instruction and intervention. This can be challenging work.

Although the structural aspects of RTI require change, literacy professionals should not overlook the extent to which RTI is likely to require teachers to change at least some of the ways that they teach and interact with students. Throughout this book, new ways of teaching have been highlighted. Gelzheiser, Scanlon, and Hallgren-Flynn (see Chapter 9), for example, point out that RTI caused teachers to engage in a different kind of intervention than they had previously provided to struggling readers—In order to learn to teach in a different way, teachers needed several kinds of support.

Of course, professional development comes in many forms. One of the challenges of professional development for teachers is that the acquisition of information is not enough; we want educators to employ that new knowledge and, often, change behaviors. The RTI leadership team, especially building principals, might find it useful to consult the groundbreaking work of Joyce and Showers (1987) when planning and implementing effective professional development. More than 20 years ago, these researchers found that the most effective professional development is that which includes all the necessary information, demonstration, practice, and feedback as well as coaching. Coaching was the variable that resulted in a significant effect size (i.e., measure of the strength of the impact).

Joyce and Showers's (1987) research indicated that fewer than 5% of learners will transfer a new skill into their practice after receiving information, and 5% of learners will transfer a new skill into their practice as a result of learning a theory. Ten percent of learners will transfer a new skill into their practice as a result of learning a theory and demonstration. Twenty percent of learners will transfer a new skill into their practice as a result of theory, demonstration, and practice. Twenty-five percent of learners will transfer a new skill into their practice as a result of theory, demonstration, practice, and feedback. However, when provided with school-based coaching in addition to theory, demonstration, practice, and feedback, 90% of learners will transfer a new skill into their practice. These findings have been replicated numerous times in a variety of disciplines, leading Lieberman (1995) to argue that professional development must include "authentic opportunities to learn from and with colleagues inside the school" (p. 591).

Therefore, to maximize the transfer of new RTI skills into practice, intervention coaching must be provided in conjunction with theory, demonstration, practice, and feedback. Classroom teachers, reading specialists, and members of the RTI team need to know why and how to implement new skills. But more important, they need to be coached during what will surely be a dynamic process.

Because coaching is critical to the planning and implementation of RTI, it is helpful to consider coaching more closely. Although IRA's new proposed standards for reading professionals highlight the skills required for effective coaching (see www.reading.org/General/CurrentResearch/Standards/ProfessionalStandards .aspx), many reading specialists and other specialist professionals are not well prepared to facilitate and coach colleagues. As your RTI leadership team is making decisions, you may want to decide exactly how everyone involved will interact with professional development. Toll (2006) says it is important to ask,

> "Coaching for what?" Literacy coaching has swept into existence so quickly that many literacy coaches find themselves in their positions without ever thinking about what they are coaching for. I see three purposes for literacy coaching: teacher remediation, program implementation, and teacher growth. (p. 11)

A coaching role within RTI may entail all of these and more. Literacy leaders may find Toll's (2006) text, *The Literacy Coach's Desk Reference: Processes and Perspectives for Effective Coaching,* useful as well as Dozier's (2006) *Responsive Literacy Coaching: Tools for Creating and Sustaining Purposeful Change.*

Indeed, in the context of the types of collaborative communities envisioned for RTI, coaching takes on a somewhat different meaning. In particular, the literacy professionals may be coaching colleagues and administrators in how to participate in broader learning communities. Even if you do not have a coach, you can participate in preparing for a new and more challenging endeavor. This perspective on coaching implies active engagement and could take the form of receiving assistance, reading, talking with others, planning for a lesson, rehearsing for instruction, or reflecting on the functioning of a professional learning community. Those responsible for RTI should be disposed to learn—always open to new ideas and suggestions. By embracing this comprehensive perspective of coaching, literacy leaders will come to view RTI as an ever-present opportunity for professional development in which all stakeholders contribute to and are motivated by the ongoing conversations that results in effective literacy instruction for all students.

Concluding Thoughts

In order for RTI to realize its promise and potential, literacy professionals need to be actively involved. First and foremost, literacy professionals have the responsibility to exercise their expertise to improve literacy achievement for all students. The IRA (2010) has drafted new *Standards for Reading Professionals*. These standards highlight the belief that "all children are entitled to receive instruction that is effectively adapted to meet their particular needs regardless of the factors that lead to those needs" (n.p.).

At the same time, it could be argued that active engagement beyond the classroom is a necessary expectation for effective literacy professionals. Truly effective practice requires not only expertise but also collaboration and advocacy. The IRA's (2010) standards make it very clear that both classroom teachers and reading specialists must take responsibility for school change. Throughout the standards there is language related to collaboration in the service of systemic change. Several examples follow:

> 6.3.3 (Reading specialists): Collaborate with other professionals to create systemic change by analyzing a school's literacy program, identifying strengths and needs, and using results to build a professional development program. (n.p.)
>
> 6.4.2 (Classroom teachers): Advocate with various groups (e.g. administrators, school boards, local, state, and federal policymaking bodies) for needed organizational and instructional changes [to promote effective literacy instruction for Reading Specialists]. (n.p.)
>
> 6.4.3 (Reading specialists): Promote effective communication and collaboration among all stakeholders, including parents, teachers, administrators, policymakers, and community members. (n.p.)

The promise and potential of RTI is that improved collaboration, systemic change, and data-driven conversations can reduce and eliminate disjointed programs across general, remedial, and special education; focus on prevention and reduce unnecessary student failure; provide more effective instruction for all students; and reduce the number of diverse students in special education. When RTI works well, students' needs are addressed as soon as they are noted. We hope that this book provides you with information about effective, evidence-based practices that can be embraced in your own school contexts. We also hope that it provides you with information and frameworks for getting involved with your colleagues so that the promise of RTI can be realized.

NOTE

Authors are listed in alphabetical order to signify the collaborative nature of this effort.

REFERENCES

Bambino, D. (2002). Critical friends. *Educational Leadership, 59*(6), 25–27.

Batsche, G.M., Elliott, J., Graden, J.L., Grimes, J., Kovaleski, J.F., Prasse, D., et al. (2005). *Response to Intervention: Policy considerations and implementation.* Alexandria, VA: National Association of State Directors of Special Education.

Commonwealth of Virginia Department of Education. (2007). *Responsive instruction: Refining our work of teaching all children. Virginia's "Response to Intervention" initiative: A guide for school divisions.* Richmond, VA: Author.

Council of Chief State School Officers. (2008). *Attributes of effective formative assessment.* Washington, DC: Author. Available at www.ccsso.org/publications/details.cfm?PublicationID=362

Crockett, J.B., & Gillespie, D.N. (2007). Getting ready for RTI: A principal's guide to Response to Intervention. *ERS Spectrum, 25*(4), 1–9.

Dozier, C. (2006). *Responsive literacy coaching: Tools for creating and sustaining purposeful change.* Portland, ME: Stenhouse.

DuFour, R. (2004). What is a "professional learning community"? *Educational Leadership, 61*(8), 6–11.

DuFour, R., & Eaker, R. (1998). *Professional learning communities at work: Best practices for enhancing student achievement.* Bloomington, IN: National Educational Service; Alexandria, VA: Association of Supervision and Curriculum Development.

Fullan, M.G. (1997). The complexity of the change process. In M. Fullan (Ed.), *The challenge of school change: A collection of articles* (pp. 33–56). Arlington Heights, IL: Skylight.

Gehsmann, K.M. (2008). Response to Intervention: What is it and how do schools and districts prepare for it? *Michigan Reading Journal, 40*(3), 22–31.

Hawley, W.D., Rosenholtz, S., Goodstein, H.J., & Hasselbring, T. (1984). Good schools: What research says about improving student achievement. *Peabody Journal of Education, 61*(4), iii–vi, 1–178.

Heath, C., & Heath, D. (2007). *Made to stick: Why some ideas survive and others die.* New York: Random House.

Hilton, A. (2007). *Response to Intervention: Changing how we do business.* Sacramento: Association of California School Administrators. Retrieved November 15, 2009, from www.acsa.org/FunctionalMenu Categories/AboutACSA/Councils/Student ServicesSpecialEducation/RtI.aspx

International Reading Association. (2010). *Response to Intervention: Guiding Principles for Educators* (Position statement). Newark, DE: Author. Retrieved March 22, 2010, from www.reading.org/libraries/resources/RTI_brochure_web.sflb.ashx

International Reading Association. (2010, Fall). *Standards for reading professionals.* Newark, DE: Author.

Jenkins, J.R., Graff, J.J., & Miglioretti, D.L. (2009). Estimating reading growth using intermittent CBM progress monitoring. *Exceptional Children, 75*(2), 151–163.

Joyce, B.R., & Showers, B. (1987). Low cost arrangement for peer coaching. *Journal of Staff Development, 8*(1), 22–24.

Lieberman, A. (1995). Practices that support teacher development. *Phi Delta Kappan, 76*(8), 591–596.

Lipson, M.Y., Mosenthal, J.H., Mekkelsen, J., & Russ, B. (2004). Building knowledge and fashioning success one school at a time. *The Reading Teacher, 57*(6), 534–542. doi:10.1598/RT.57.6.3

Marinak, B., & Mazzoni, S. (2007a). Coaching RtI: Tier 1 without tears. *The Literacy Professional, 17*(3), 3–4.

Marinak, B., & Mazzoni, S. (2007b). Coaching RtI: Tier 2: A differentiated double dose. *The Literacy Professional, 18*(1), 3–4.

McAndrew, D.A. (2005). *Literacy leadership: Six strategies for peoplework.* Newark, DE: International Reading Association.

McLaughlin, M.W., & Talbert, J.E. (2006). *Building school-based teacher learning communities: Professional strategies to improve student achievement.* New York: Teachers College Press.

Mosenthal, J.H., Lipson, M.Y., Torncello, S., Russ, B., & Mekkelsen, J. (2004). Contexts and practices of six schools successful in obtaining reading achievement. *The Elementary School Journal, 104*(5), 343–368. doi:10.1086/499757

Scanlon, D.M. (in press). Response to Intervention as an assessment approach. In R. Allington & A. McGill-Franzen (Eds.), *Handbook of research in reading disabilities research.* New York: Routledge.

Scanlon, D.M., Gelzheiser, L.M., Vellutino, F.R., Schatschneider, C., & Sweeney, J.M. (2008). Reducing the incidence of early reading difficulties: Professional development for classroom teachers versus direct interventions for children. *Learning and Individual Differences,* 18(3), 346–359. doi:10.1016/j.lindif.2008.05.002

Schatschneider, C., Wagner, R.K., & Crawford, E.C. (2008). The importance of measuring growth in Response to Intervention models: Testing a core assumption. *Learning and Individual Differences, 18*(3), 308–315. doi:10.1016/j.lindif.2008.04.005

Taylor, B.M., Pearson, P.D., Peterson, D.S., & Rodriguez, M.C. (2003). Reading growth in high-poverty classrooms: The influence of teacher practices that encourage cognitive engagement in literacy learning. *The Elementary School Journal, 104*(1), 3–28. doi:10.1086/499740

Taylor, B.M., Pearson, P.D., Peterson, D.S., & Rodriguez, M.C. (2005). The CIERA school change framework: An evidence-based approach to professional development and school reading improvement. *Reading Research Quarterly, 40*(1), 40–69. doi:10.1598/RRQ.40.1.3

Toll, C.A. (2006). *The literacy coach's desk reference: Processes and perspectives for effective coaching.* Urbana, IL: National Council of Teachers of English.

Valencia, S.W., & Buly, M.R. (2004). Behind test scores: What struggling readers *really* need. *The Reading Teacher, 57*(6), 520–531.

Vescio, V., Ross, D., & Adams, A. (2008). A review of research on the impact of professional learning communities on teaching practice and student learning. *Teaching and Teacher Education, 24*(1), 80–91. doi:10.1016/j.tate.2007.01.004

Vogt, M., & Shearer, B.A. (2006). *Reading specialists and literacy coaches in the real world* (2nd ed.). Boston: Allyn & Bacon.

Wanzek, J., & Vaughn, S. (2008). Response to varying amounts of time in reading intervention for students with low response to intervention. *Journal of Learning Disabilities, 41*(2), 126–142. doi:10.1177/0022219407313426

Wiggins, G.P., & McTighe, J. (2005). *Understanding by design* (2nd ed.). Alexandria, VA: Association for Supervision and Curriculum Development.

Wisconsin Department of Public Instruction. (n.d.). *Wisconsin Response to Intervention.*

Retrieved March 15, 2009, from dpi.wi.gov/rti/

Wisconsin State Reading Association. (2008). *Intervention rubric for literacy in the early years.* Randolph, WI: WSRA Early Intervention Committee. Retrieved February 18, 2009, from www.wsra.org/committees/Early%20Literacy/rubric.pdf

Note. Page numbers followed by *f* or *t* indicate figures or tables, respectively.

Geisler, D., 149
Gelzheiser, L.M., 9, 23, 64, 98, 212, 226, 242
Genesee, F., 145, 150, 177
Gersten, R., 145
Geva, E., 145, 150
Gilbertson, D., 7
Gillespie, D.N., 236
Gindis, B., 101
Goldenberg, C., 93, 99, 145
Gómez-Bellengé, F.X., 99
González, N., 145
Good, R.H., 9, 25
Goodman, Y.M., 190
Goodstein, H.J., 254
Gouleta, E., 143
Graesser, A.C., 179
Graff, J.J., 7, 252
Graham, S., 99
Greenfield, D.B., 148
Greenleaf, C., 186
Greenleaf, C.L., 173, 176
Gresham, F.M., 3, 4, 90
Griffin, P., 99
Grigg, W., 188
Guskey, T.R., 110
Guthrie, J.T., 185, 227

H

Haager, D., 137, 152, 154, 156
Hallgren-Flynn, L., 212, 255
Hamayan, E., 145
Hargrove, R., 111
Harris, K.R., 99, 106
Harrison, L., 99
Hart, B., 91
Hasselbring, T., 254
Hawley, W.D., 110, 254
Heath, C., 237
Heath, D., 237
Heath, S.B., 137
Heller, R., 176
Hemphill, L., 21
Henderson, S.C., 106, 107, 108
Hickman, P., 6
Hiebert, E.H., 99, 148
Hill, P.W., 93

Hilton, A., 238
Hinchman, K., 173
Hintze, J.M., 9
Hirsch, E.D., Jr., 224
Hock, M.F., 188
Hodges, R.E., 106
Høien, T., 7
Hoover, J.J., 164
Hopewell, S., 149
Hosp, J.L., 90
Houge, T.T., 184
Hughes, C., 9
Hughes, M.T., 99
Humenick, N.M., 227
Hurwitz, L., 186
Hyde, A.A., 110

I

International Reading Association, 12, 13, 15, 91, 132, 239
Invernizzi, M., 26, 67, 99, 144t
IRA Commission on RTI, 182
Irvin, J.L., 174, 197
Israel, S.E., 181
Iversen, S.J., 7
Ivey, G., 174, 190

J

James, K.V., 99
Jenkins, J.R., 7, 10, 252
Jiménez, R.T., 145, 150
Jimerson, S.R., 3
Jitendra, A.K., 191
Johannessen, L.R., 185
Johnson, D.D., 180
Johnson, E., 28
Johnston, P.H., 4, 5, 92, 94, 98, 178
Jones, T., 92
Journal of Learning Disabilities, 6
Journal of Reading Recovery, 95f
Joyce, B.R., 111, 255
Juel, C., 26, 67, 99, 144t

K

Kame'enui, E.J., 177

Note. Page numbers followed by *f* or *t* indicate figures or tables, respectively.

C

CBMs. *See* Curriculum-based measures

CFGs. *See* Comprehension focus groups

charts: assessment wall, 108–110; comprehension-monitoring list, 224, 225*f*; language and learning posters, 184; "Words We (I) Know," 55–56

Checklist for Assessing an English Language Arts Curriculum and Program (K–12), 242

CIM. *See* Comprehensive intervention model

classroom talk, interactive, 180

classroom teachers: Standards for Reading Professionals, 257. *See also* Teachers

classroom texts, 178–179

classrooms: content, 175–187; dimensions that support reading development, 187; English language arts, 184–185; interfacing support services with, 37; Intervention Pyramid for, 199, 200*f*; literacy instruction for ELLs in, 145–153; mathematics, 185; program consistency, 81–83; science, 183–184; social studies, 185–186; Tier 1 schedules, 96–97, 97*f*

CLC. *See* Content literacy curriculum

coaches, 235

coaching, 255, 256–257; skills required for, 256; Tier 1 without tears approach, 243

codes for lesson objectives, 73, 79*f*–80*f*

collaboration, 194; cross-disciplinary, 239; Steps for Getting Started With RTI, 233, 234*f*; Guiding Principles, 12, 14; intervention team meetings, 128–129; at Mountain Creek Elementary, 169; self-assessment framework for, 239, 240*f*; Standards for Reading Professionals, 257

collaborative, data-based decision making, 203–204

collaborative teams: Steps for Getting Started With RTI, 233, 234*f*; questions to take to, 250

collaborative writing, 152

collaborators, 232–235

Commission on RTI, 1; Guiding Principles, 1, 6, 12–15, 16, 239

commitment, school, 248

committees, 233

communication with parents, 71–72

community: connections to, 147*t*, 153; responsive school community, 247

comprehension: active, 215, 217*f*–218*f*; codes for lesson objectives, 73, 79*f*; focus on, 181–182; fostering, 221; as goal, 58; high standards for coherence for, 223–224; "Mixed Up? Fix Up!" strategies for, 224, 225*f*; monitoring list, 224, 225*f*; reading comprehension, 146*t*, 149–150; Teacher Observation Checklist, 215, 217*f*–218*f*; as student goal, 215; text comprehension, 73, 79*f*

comprehension focus groups, 104–105; content unit of study, 106; goals of intervention, 106; interventions, 104–106; phases of intervention, 105; in portfolio of interventions, 127–128; reading unit, 106; strategy unit of study, 105–106; sustained writing unit, 106

comprehension strategy instruction, 181–182

comprehensive approach, 196–197; Guiding Principles, 12, 14–15

comprehensive assessment system, 122–124

comprehensive core literacy instruction, 186–187

Comprehensive Intervention Model, xiii, 98–100, 121–122; assessment, 106–108; assessment system, 122–124; institute, 110; layered approach, 94–95, 95*f*; portfolio of K–6 interventions, 100–113; principles of intervention, 100; professional development in, 110–112; small-group interventions, 99; supporting research, 98–100; as systemic and comprehensive, 93–94; Washington School for Comprehensive Literacy case, 121–133

concept-oriented reading instruction, 185, 186

conceptual vocabulary, 179–180

conferences, 127–128

Connecticut, 241

content: classroom life dimensions that support reading development in, 187; core instruction in, 175–187; Enhanced Content Instruction, 197; enhancement routines, 180; as important for students with disabilities, 222–223

content literacy curriculum, 197

content workshop, 96–97, 97f

conventions of print, 39–40

core content instruction: differentiating instruction within, 182–186; tools for, 183

core instruction, 175–182; in content classrooms, 175–187; high-quality, 242–245

core literacy instruction, comprehensive, 186–187

CORI. *See* Concept-oriented reading instruction

credibility, 238

critical friends groups, 235

critical reading, 186

cross-language connections, 146t, 150–151

culturally and linguistically diverse students, 139

culturally and linguistically responsive and appropriate assessment and instruction, 137–138

culturally responsive teachers, 138

culturally responsive teaching, 170–171

culture, 137

curriculum: Checklist for Assessing an English Language Arts Curriculum and Program (K–12), 242; content literacy curriculum, 197

curriculum-based measures, 6, 10, 252

D

Daily Kindergarten Small-Group Lesson sheet, 74f, 78f

data-based decision making, collaborative, 203–204

data-collection form, 122, 123f

decision making, 246–257; collaborative,

data-based, 203–204; Steps for Getting Started With RTI, 233, 234f; problem-solving approach to, 167–171

decoding: codes for lesson objectives, 73, 79f; development of strategies for, 46–47; Daily Kindergarten Small-Group Lesson sheet, 73, 75f

definition maps, 180

developmental reading interventions: standards of practice for, 248, 249f

diagnostic assessments, 189

DIBELS, 9, 25

dictation, 149

differentiation: in core content instruction, 182–186; in English language arts classroom, 184–185; Guiding Principles, 12, 13; helpful questions for assessing, 246; in mathematics classroom, 185; in science classroom, 183; self-assessment framework for, 239, 240f; small-group differentiated instruction, 243; in social studies classroom, 185–186

difficulty levels, 224–226

disability, 20; learning disabled students, 1, 20. *See also* Students with disabilities

"(dis)ability," xi

discussions, guided, 183

diversity: culturally and linguistically diverse students, 139; student profiles of adolescent literacy development, 191, 192f; texts of different difficulty levels and genres, 224–226

documents: assessment wall for progress monitoring, 108–110; Checklist for Assessing an English Language Arts Curriculum and Program (K–12), 242; codes for lesson objectives, 73, 79f–80f; comprehension-monitoring list, 224, 225f; data collection form, 122, 123f; directions for using the Daily Kindergarten Small-Group Lesson sheet, 73, 78f; Steps for Getting Started With RTI, 233, 234f; group snapshot for phonological skills, 42, 43f; Daily Kindergarten Small-Group Lesson sheet, 73, 74f–77f; literacy intervention planning sheet, 129–131, 130f; record form for strategic word learning, 52, 53f; Teacher Observation Checklist, 215, 216f–219f; word-identification strategy list, 48–50, 49f

dual-emphasis reader profiles, 213

E

early intervention, 96

early literacy collaborators, 32

educational leaders, 231–259

ELA. *See* English language arts

ELCs. *See* Early literacy collaborators

elementary classrooms: K–3 interventions, 96; K–6 interventions, 100–113; RTI in second grade and beyond, 31; Tier 1 classroom schedule, 96–97, 97f

ELLs. *See* English-language learners

Embedded Strategy Instruction, 197

emergent language, 101–102, 127–128

emergent readers: standards of practice for reading interventions for, 248, 249f

encoding strategies: codes for lesson objectives, 73, 80f; development of, 46–47

encouragement, 238

engagement, 178; opportunities for, 35–36; recommendations for, 178

English as a Second Language, 134, 154

English as a Second Language specialists, 143, 145

English language arts classrooms, 212; Checklist for Assessing an English Language Arts Curriculum and Program (K–12), 242; differentiation in, 184–185

English language arts programs, 243

English language development test, 140

English-language learners, 2, 134, 135–136; assessment of, 139; classroom literacy instruction for, 145–153; important questions about, 143, 144t; Mountain Creek Elementary case, 163–172; outstanding teachers of, 137; response to intervention for, 134–162, 163–172;

secondary-school, 177; subtypes of, 134–135; Tier 2 and Tier 3 interventions for, 153–156; word-work activities for teaching literacy to, 148–149

Enhanced Content Instruction, 197

Enrichment Rectangle, 199, 201f

Environmental Scale for Assessing Implementation Levels, 111

ESAILS. *See* Environmental Scale for Assessing Implementation Levels

ESL. *See* English as a Second Language

Everyday Mathematics, 170

evidence-based interventions, 101

exercises, frontloaded, 185

expectations, 237; "Beat the Odds" schools, 36; high, 36–37

expertise, 247; Guiding Principles, 12, 15; teachers as experts, 92–96

F

FAST. *See* Formative Assessment for Students and Teachers, 252

first grade, 29–30

fluency: reading, 146t, 148; Teacher Observation Checklist, 215, 217f

focus groups: comprehension focus group interventions, 104–106; in portfolio of interventions, 127–128

formative assessment, 108, 189; definition of, 252; Formative Assessment for Students and Teachers, 252; formative assessment, 235

Formative Assessment for Students and Teachers, 252

forms: data collection form, 122, 123f; for strategic word learning, 52, 53f; Teacher Observation Checklist, 215, 216f–219f. *See also* Documents

G

genres, 224–226

graphic organizers, 149, 183

group snapshots, 42, 43f

group work, 243

guided discussions, 183

guided reading, 156

Guided Reading Plus, 101, 102–103, 132; in portfolio of interventions, 127–128; writing components, 103

guided writing, 151

Guiding Principles, 1, 6, 12–15, 16, 239

H

Hajdusiewicz, Babs Bell, 54

Hayas, Alysia, 163

high-frequency words, 52–56; codes for lesson objectives, 73, 79f, 80f; Daily Kindergarten Small-Group Lesson sheet, 73, 77f; practicing, 62; as student goal, 215

high schools, 199–204; challenging elements of, 199–201; secondary school literacy, 173–210; student assistance period, 203–204

Hillert, Margaret, 54

historiography, 185

history, 90

home connections, 147t, 153

I

IDEIA. See Individuals With Disabilities Education Improvement Act

IDEL, 144t

IEPs. See Individualized Education Programs

implementation: Steps for Getting Started With RTI, 233, 234f

independence: approaches to teaching for, 219; as critical for students with disabilities, 215–222

independent writing, 152

Individualized Education Programs, 68, 154, 196–197, 213

individualized interventions, intensive: guidelines for, 188

Individuals With Disabilities Education Act, 1

Individuals With Disabilities Education Improvement Act, 1, 21–22, 88, 164

innovations, 235–236

Institute of Education Sciences: What Works Clearinghouse website, 21

instruction: appropriate, 4, 243; classroom literacy instruction for ELLs, 145–153; comprehension strategy instruction, 181–182; comprehensive core literacy instruction, 186–187; concept-oriented reading instruction, 185, 186; in content classrooms, 175–187; core, 175–182, 182–186, 242–245; culturally and linguistically responsive and appropriate, 137–138; decisions about, 248–250; differentiated, 243, 246; differentiating, 182–186; Embedded Strategy Instruction, 197; Enhanced Content Instruction, 197; goals of, 58–60, 59t; Guiding Principles, 12–13; high-quality, 242–245; Intensive Basic Skill Instruction, 197; Intensive Strategy Instruction, 197; ISA-based, 58–62; ISA principles, 33–38; language arts, 58–60, 59t, 243–244; multitiered, 166–167; practices to help improve reading comprehension, 149–150; quality of, 139; responsive, 214–216; self-assessment framework for, 239, 240f; small-group differentiated instruction, 243; small-group interventions in kindergarten, 60–61, 61–62; for students who need support beyond content classroom, 188–193; Tier 1, 2–3, 30, 94–95, 95f, 98, 138, 156–157, 166, 176; Tier 1 without tears coaching, 243; Tier 2, 2–3, 4, 28, 32, 94–95, 95f, 98, 138, 154, 157, 166, 182; Tier 3, 29–30, 32, 94–95, 95f, 98, 138, 154, 158, 166, 188; Tier 4, 94–95, 95f; time allocation for, 243–244; universal first best, 166

instructional goals, 38–58

intensity, 245

Intensive Basic Skill Instruction, 197

intensive intervention: in middle school, 211–230; for struggling students, 191–193

Intensive Strategy Instruction, 197

interactive classroom talk, 180

interactive strategies: to prevent reading difficulties, 20–65; writing intervention, 103

Interactive Strategies Approach, xii–xiii, 4, 5, 22–25, 94, 212; instruction based on, 58–62; instructional goals, 38–58; instructional principles, 33–38; professional development based on, 31–33; professional development program content, 33; Roosevelt Elementary School case study, 66–87

Interactive Strategies Approach-Extended, 212; intensive middle school intervention with, 211–230; key components of, 214–228; premises of, 214–228; rationale for, 214–228; thematic units, 226

interactive writing, 152

International Reading Association, 133, 239; Commission on RTI, 1, xi; Guiding Principles, 1, 6, 12–15, 16, 239; Standards for Reading Professionals, 256, 257

intervention(s): administration, 199, 200*f*; assisted writing, 103–104; as class, 213; comprehension focus group interventions, 104–106; comprehensive intervention model, xiii, 88–120, 121–133; continuum of, 245–246; development of, 244–245; developmental reading interventions, 248, 249*f*; dynamic, 94–95, 95*f*; early, 96; effectiveness of, 100; emergent language and, 101–102; for English-language learners, 153–156; evidence-based, 101; Guided Reading Plus, 102–103; guidelines for intensive, individualized interventions, 188; interactive writing, 103; K–3 interventions, 96; K–6 interventions, 100–113; layers of, 94–95, 95*f*; literacy intervention planning sheet, 129–131, 130*f*; moving students in and out of, 70–71; multistep system, 93; portfolio of interventions, 127–131, 248; pyramid model for, 199, 200*f*; schedule for, 68–70; school, 199, 200*f*;

selection of students for, 67–68; small-group interventions, 99; standards of practice for, 248, 249*f*; team, 199, 200*f*; Therapeutic Intervention, 197; Tier 2, 153–156; Tier 3, 153–156; time frame for, 68–70; writing process, 104

Intervention Pyramid, 199, 200*f*

intervention team meetings, 128–129

ISA. *See* Interactive Strategies Approach

ISA-X. *See* Interactive Strategies Approach-Extended

J

James Madison High School, 203–204

K

kindergarten: K–3 interventions, 96; K–6 interventions, 100–113; response to intervention in, 26–29; small-group intervention lessons in, 60–61, 61–62; Daily Small-Group Lesson sheet, 73, 74*f*–77*f*

kindergarten literacy night, 72, 86

L

language: cross-language connections, 146*t*, 150–151; emergent, 101–102, 127–128; integrating, 176–178; multidimensional nature of, 141–144; oral, 56–57, 136, 145–147, 146*t*; second-language acquisition, 135–136; as student goal, 215; suggestions for integrating, 177; Tier 1 classroom schedule, 96–97, 97*f*

language and learning posters, 184

language arts instruction: components of, 58–60, 59*t*; time allocation for, 243–244

leaders, educational, 231–259

leadership, 236–239

leadership teams: collaborative, 233, 234*f*; Steps for Getting Started With RTI, 233, 234*f*; questions for self-assessment, 241–242

learning: to be learning disabled, 91; literacy, 91–92; professional teams, 111–113; strategic word learning, 48–52;

Vygotskian perspective on, 34–35; word learning, 47–56, 215; word-learning emphasis reader profiles, 213

learning disabled students, 1, 20, 90, 91, 154

lessons: codes for objectives, 73, 79*f*–80*f*; intervention minilessons, 213; Daily Kindergarten Small-Group Lesson sheet, 73, 74*f*–77*f*, 78*f*; small-group interventions in kindergarten, 60–61, 61–62

letter names, 73, 79*f*

letter–sound association, 44–45

letter sounds, 221–222; codes for lesson objectives, 73, 79*f*

letters: codes for lesson objectives, 73, 79*f*, 80*f*; identification of, 42–44; Daily Kindergarten Small-Group Lesson sheet, 73, 75*f*

literacy, 239–246; adolescent development profiles, 191, 192*f*; domains of, 145, 146*t*–147*t*; factors contributing to difficulties with, 91–92; school commitment to, 248; school intervention plan(s) for, 250, 251*f*; secondary school, 173–210; word-work activities for teaching, 148–149

literacy coaching, 256

literacy defense, 96–98

literacy groups, 127–128

literacy instruction: appropriate, 243; classroom, 145–153; comprehensive core literacy instruction, 186–187; for ELLs, 145–153

literacy intervention: emergent language and, 101–102; rubric for evaluating programs, 242. *See also* Intervention

literacy intervention planning sheet, 129–131, 130*f*

literacy learning: difficulties with, 91–92; as struggle, 91–92

literacy process: integrating, 176–178; suggestions for integrating, 177

literacy programs, 96

literature circles, 150

little books, 83–84

M

math workshop: Tier 1 classroom schedule, 96–97, 97*f*

mathematics classrooms, 185

meaning-emphasis reader profiles, 213

meetings, 128–129

middle school(s), 198–199; context of, 212–214; intensive intervention for, 211–230

"Mixed Up? Fix Up!" strategies, 224, 225*f*

monitoring progress, 131–132; assessment wall for, 108–110; formative assessment for, 108; goals, 142–143; important questions about, 143, 144*t*; role in RTI framework, 142–143

motivation to read and write: as goal, 39, 215; importance of, 227–228; Teacher Observation Checklist, 215, 216*f*

Mountain Creek Elementary, 163–165; assessments, 169–170; case study, 163–172; collaboration, 169; culturally responsive teaching, 170–171; problem-solving approach, 167–171; professional development, 171; professional learning communities, 165–166; response to intervention, 171; RTI model, 163–164, 166–167, 169

N

narratives, personal, 153

National Assessment of Educational Progress, 188

needs, student, 83–86

New England Reading Association: Checklist for Assessing an English Language Arts Curriculum and Program (K–12), 242

O

observations: Teacher Checklist, 215, 216*f*–219*f*

oracy, 127–128

oral language, 145–147; development of,

for, 247; rereading, 60; small-group intervention lessons in kindergarten, 60, 61; standards of practice for developmental interventions, 248, 249*f*

reading aloud: codes for lesson objectives, 73, 79*f*; Daily Kindergarten Small-Group Lesson sheet, 73, 74*f*; scaffolding, 180

reading apprenticeship, 186

reading comprehension, 146*t*, 149–150; codes for lesson objectives, 73, 79*f*; instructional practices to help improve, 149–150; modeling, 149; during text discussions, 149–150

reading fluency, 146*t*, 148

Reading Recovery, 4, 5, 91–92, 94, 99, 101, 111; intervention team meetings, 128; in portfolio of interventions, 127–128

reading specialists: Standards for Reading Professionals, 257

reading texts: of different difficulty levels and genres, 224–226. *See also* Books; Texts

reading workshop: Tier 1 classroom schedule, 96–97, 97*f*

Ready Readers, 61

record forms: for strategic word learning, 52, 53*f*. *See also* Documents; Forms

rereading: Daily Kindergarten Small-Group Lesson sheet, 73, 74*f*; small-group intervention lessons in kindergarten, 60

research: CIM-supporting, 98–100; professional development in research-based methods, 244; about RTI, 6–12

research projects, 153

response to intervention, xi; for adolescents, 211–230; appearance of, 2–6; assessment wall method, 124–127; central concepts, 239–241; Commission on RTI, xi; concepts central for success, 239–241; cornerstone of, 138–139; elementary classroom framework for, 96–97, 97*f*; emergence of, 21–22; for English-language learners, 134–162, 163–172; factors that distinguish successful schools, 247–248; features

for ELLs, 136–139; in first grade, 29–30; foundation for, 137–138; Steps for Getting Started With RTI, 233, 234*f*; goals covered by, 89; Guiding Principles, 12–15, 16; important positive consequences of, 138–139; innovations that can advance, 235–236; integration into team-based middle schools, 198–199; and Interactive Strategies Approach, 22–25; in kindergarten, 26–29; major attributes of successful approach, 241; making the most of, 1–19; model of, 25–31; Mountain Creek Elementary case, 163–172; purpose of, 239; schoolwide and comprehensive, 196–197; in second grade and beyond, 31; for secondary school literacy, 173–210; self-assessment framework for, 239, 240*f*; systemic and comprehensive approach to, 93–94; systemic approach to, 231–259; systemic issues, 193–204; systems approach to, 92–93; tiered approach to, 3, 94–96; types of action that lead to success, 237–238; what research tells us, 6–12

responsive school community, 247

responsive teaching: as critical for students with disabilities, 214–216; Guiding Principles, 12, 13; self-assessment framework for, 239, 240*f*

retelling, 150

reviews, structured, 183

role-play, 185

Roosevelt Elementary School, 66; ISA case study, 66–87

RR. *See* Reading Recovery

RTI. *See* Response to intervention

RTI committee, 233

RTI system, 25

S

SAP. *See* student assistance period

scaffolding, 35

scaffolding read-aloud, 180

scaffolding retellings, 150

scenarios, 185

scheduling: for intervention, 68–70; reorganizing time, 201–202; Tier 1 classroom schedule, 96–97, 97f

school interventions: Intervention Pyramid, 199, 200f; plan(s) for literacy, 250, 251f

schools, 139; commitment from, 248; in Enrichment Rectangle, 199, 201f; factors that distinguish successful schools, 247–248; responsive community, 247; stability of, 248

schoolwide approach, 196–197

science classrooms, 183–184

screening, universal, 26, 107–108

screening team, 71–73

second grade, 31

second-language acquisition, 135–136

secondary school literacy: high schools, 199–204; response to intervention for, 173–210; systemic issues, 193–204; underlying principles and structures, 193–197

See My Pets: two renditions of, 54, 55f

self-assessment: framework for, 239, 240f; Steps for Getting Started With RTI, 233, 234f; questions for, 241–242

self-teaching mechanisms, 220

semantic maps, 180

sensitivity in text: group snapshot for, 42, 43f

sequential bilinguals, 135

shared reading: codes for lesson objectives, 73, 79f; Daily Kindergarten Small-Group Lesson sheet, 73, 74f; Tier 1 classroom schedule, 96–97, 97f

sharing stories, 238

Short Books, 54

sight vocabulary: development of, 47–56; word-work activities for teaching literacy to ELLs, 149

simultaneous bilinguals, 135

skill instruction, 197

small-group interventions, 99; differentiated instruction, 243; kindergarten lessons, 60–61, 61–62; Daily Kindergarten Small-Group Lesson sheet, 73, 74f–77f, 78f

social studies classrooms, 185–186

sound blending: codes for lesson objectives, 73, 79f; group snapshot for, 42, 43f

sound counting/segmentation: group snapshot for, 42, 43f

sound sorting: codes for lesson objectives, 73, 79f; group snapshot for, 42, 43f

sounds: codes for lesson objectives, 73, 79f, 80f; Daily Kindergarten Small-Group Lesson sheet, 73, 75f

space: reorganizing, 202

Spanish, 134

Spanish-speakers, 143, 144t

specialty teachers, 104

spelling: Tier 1 classroom schedule, 96–97, 97f

Standards for Reading Professionals, 256, 257

standards of practice: for coherence for comprehension, 223–224; for developmental reading interventions, 248, 249f

starting and sustaining a systemic approach to RTI, 231–259; Steps for Getting Started With RTI, 233, 234f

Steps for Getting Started With RTI, 233, 234f

storytelling, 238

strategic word learning, 48–52; record form for, 52, 53f; Teacher Observation Checklist, 215, 216f

strategy instruction: Embedded Strategy Instruction, 197; Intensive Strategy Instruction, 197; purpose of, 219–220

strategy-promoting texts, 84

strategy unit of study, 105–106; subunits, 105–106; units of study, 105

structured reviews, 183

struggling students, 188–193; identifying, 188–191; intensive intervention for, 191–193; questions that might guide investigation of, 189–190; reading texts of different difficulty levels and genres for, 224–226; tools for identifying, 190